Travels with My Donkey

By the same author

FRENCH REVOLUTIONS
DO NOT PASS GO

Travels with My Donkey

One Man and His Ass on a
Pilgrimage to Santiago

Tim Moore

St. Martin's Press ⋈ New York

www.stmartins.com

Library of Congress Cataloging-in-Publication Data

Moore, Tim, 1964–
    Travels with my donkey: one man and his ass on a pilgrimage to Santiago / Tim Moore.—1st U.S. ed.
        p. cm.
    ISBN 0-312-32082-5
    EAN 978-0312-32082-9
    1. Spain, Northern—Description and travel. 2. Christian pilgrims and pilgrimages—Spain—Santiago de Compostela. 3. Moore, Tim, 1964—Travel—Spain, Northern. 4. Santiago de Compostela (Spain) I. Title.

DP285.M66 2005
263'.0424611—dc22   2004051389

First published in Great Britain under the title *Spanish Steps* by Jonathan Cape Random House

First U.S. Edition: February 2005

10 9 8 7 6 5 4 3 2 1

To Shinto

Acknowledgements

Thanks to: Jon Bryant, John Perring, Hanno and Marie-Christine, the Donkey Sanctuary, the Confraternity of St James, the Weed Science Society, Jessamy, Per, Brigitta, Simon, St John of Bedford, Jon Bjornsson, and Birna, Snáðó, Spons and Olbus Hispanicus. Also to most of my fellow pilgrims, and nearly all the people of northern Spain.

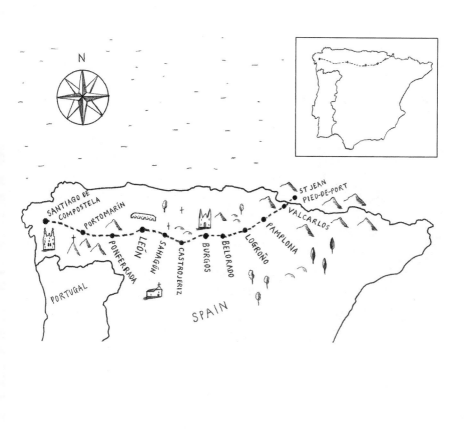

Prologue

○

I was on a small boat in Norway when I first heard about
it. 'Now I am going to do the Camino de Santiago,' said
Per, and for a heady moment seemed primed to leap to his
deck-shoed feet and perform a vigorously sensual one-man
tango up and down the galley. When this moment had ended
– and with Per being a bald and precise teacher of languages
I couldn't say it was a long one – he explained that the camino
was a path or way in Spain, or in true accuracy across Spain,
a path or way with a most particular historic and religious
tradition, a . . . a . . .

'A pilgrimage?'

Just so, said Per. A pilgrimitch. In the next summer. He
looked through the porthole beside my shoulder and nodded
distantly at the bobbing horizon.

It was the sort of revelation that made me glad we were putter-
ing up a sunny fjord beneath a merry deckful of day-tripping
divorcees, rather than alone together on a vast and wild ocean.
The pilgrims I'd mumbled about in hymns and seen in Monty
Python films wore pus-crusted hoods and hair shirts. They
crawled across continents on bare and bleeding knees, fuelled
by turnips and raw zeal towards that distant shrine where
divine deliverance awaited those who pressed their blistered
lips to the shrivelled gall-bladder of St Pancras.

I stole a surreptitious look at Per and saw him cowled in a filthy felt cloak, chanting Latin and smacking himself in the teeth with a stout plank. Eyes ablaze with fundamentalist fervour; clawed hands ready to force some sarky heathen's face through a porthole of slightly inadequate diameter. Perhaps I heard the first echoing organ chord of John Bunyan's 'To Be a Pilgrim', a school-assembly regular of wrathful, Old Testament righteousness, whose indefatigable protagonist fought with lions and giants and then, as the fearsome Judgement Day descant kicked mightily in, saw off the last wave of hobgoblins and foul fiends to inherit eternal life.

This was first-degree Christianity, ill at ease in the third millennium. On the ferry home I pondered that these days, in England at least, even its mildest churchgoing variant was no more than an eccentric if harmless hobby, as might be poodle clipping or my father's enduring love for the Red Army Marching Band's rendition of 'It's a Long Way To Tipperary'. Say 'pilgrim' in a questioning tone and people might mutter about the *Mayflower* fathers, or possibly a Gothic-scripted supermarket cheddar. But footsore fanatics? Not now, not in Europe. We've been there, done that and worn the hair shirt. Per might as well have told me he was giving up teaching to retrain as a cooper. Yet he had spilt his seed on my stony soil – I'm going to have a word with him about that when we next meet – and there it lay awaiting germination.

My wife Birna and I travelled, settled, bought a house. One Christmas a card from Per dropped on the doormat – he had met a new woman, been promoted to head of languages, and what he had learnt and felt while treading the hallowed path to Santiago had been the catalyst to it all. I thought, Well, good for him. Here was a man whose life had been a bit of a mess, and a nice long walk in Spain had helped him clear his head and sort things out. My life, pleasingly, was not a mess. But then we had a child, and then children, and suddenly it sort of was.

Pushing forty, or rather being pulled brutally towards it, I had felt the usual twinges of angst; not quite a what-does-it-all-mean existential crisis, perhaps, but the vague sense that my soul-ometer might benefit from a little recalibration. I'd find myself sitting on a Tube train with a Boots carrier bag on my lap, wondering how 'Ideas for Life' had triumphed as the under-logo corporate slogan, rather than 'Just a Bloody Chemist'. The Power of Dreams, Engineered with Passion, Because You're Worth It: all these preposterously overblown mission statements suddenly seemed the anthem of a consumerist society disappearing up its own two-for-one arse. But then what were my Ideas for Life? Why was personal growth just something I read about in medico–sexual junk emails?

Responsibility for three young humans sharpened concerns over the poverty of my spiritual bequest, and the mirror wasn't shy in emphasising that I really ought to get my immaterial affairs in order for the next generation. With empathy furrowing my brow I read an interview in which Bob Geldof described the improbable tipping point that had caused him to reappraise his own life values: his innard-withering dismay on hearing a daughter tell two visiting classmates not to put their cup in that rack of the dishwasher, as her dad was very particular about how it should be stacked. 'Was that really all I'd taught my children?' he asked himself in anguish. 'How to stack the fucking dishwasher?'

For this unkempt firebrand is describing a discipline in which I give quarter to no man, and outside that warm, white door it only gets worse. Has Bob browbeaten his family into ensuring that every Bic in the jar by the phone is correctly placed nib down? Does he press-gang and dispatch a junior litter patrol into the foot wells after a long journey? Are the perishable contents of his fridge arranged in order of sell-by date from the top shelf to— Oh, make it stop.

The medieval pilgrims did what they did because they *believed*. As a cop-out cynic, what did I believe in? I couldn't even start the relevant sentence without finding myself sniggering through a Celine Dion chorus. Despite the fact that we had named our eldest son Christian Holy (well, in Icelandic), my exposure to the Scriptures has been limited to the Lord's Prayer and *The Omen*. My solitary religious pursuit was at best metaphorical, the scrupulous quest for precision regarding the time within my house and the meteorological conditions without. I don't mean to boast, but I apparently do mean to reveal myself as a career dullard: even my oven clock is synchronised to Ceefax Mean Time, and I have the outside temperature projected on to my bedroom ceiling in insomnia-sized red numerals.

Sixty-one per cent of Americans agree with the statement 'Life is meaningful only because God exists'; in Britain, you'd only match that figure by sticking 'alcoholic fermentation' in there instead. Empirical knowledge, understanding the world through observable fact and experiment, might have killed off traditional religious belief as a mass phenomenon in twenty-first-century Europe. But without pledging myself to Hare Krishna or L. Ron Hubbard, it might be nice to imbue life with a little more . . . *depth*.

Per's seed was beginning to crack and swell, but it took two newspaper features to force that frail stem up through the crust of shrugging inertia to unfurl majestically before a new dawn. The first was a poll in *USA Today*, which listed Santiago at number six in its top ten 'great places to rejuvenate your soul'. I can't remember where I read the second, but let its topic and salient revelation never be forgotten: prominent amongst the world's cheapest holidays was walking the camino, the pilgrim road across north-west Spain.

I found myself tentatively introducing Santiago into conversation, testing the holy water, and discovered a popularity in excess of all expectation. People would say, 'Oh, I know someone who did that.' Usually it was their yoga teacher, but not always. A bloke who painted my parents' house had walked the camino to get over a divorce, encountering en route the young French girl who was now his wife. I learnt that a friend of ours, Nicky Chambers, had cycled to Santiago six summers before with an unconventional fellow thrice her years, in search of something spiritual; serenaded by a choir as she slept in a pilgrims' dormitory above a church, she had found it. 'A died-and-gone-to-heaven experience,' was the conclusion when I quizzed her on the phone, and despite the explosion of derisive merriment which thereafter assailed my left ear I found myself impressed.

If a common theme was emerging to these crusades, then it was the search for something beyond the typical tourist routine, an antidote to the vacuous consumerism of contemporary travel. A trip to the moral high ground – I hear the view's excellent from up there. 'Pilgrimage', even more so than 'sabbatical' and 'retreat', added an instant gloss of worthy righteousness to what on the face of it was just a very long holiday. Plus, three years on from the monstrous bike ride round France that represented my last proper workout, I was at the stage of my athletic career where triumph meant successfully returning the big Le Creuset to that shelf above the fridge–freezer. A physical service was long overdue, and this one came with a spiritual overhaul thrown in.

A structured rationale was taking shape in my mind's eye, and I liked what I saw. A trip purged of the empty decadence that characterised most foreign trips, yet still demanded alcoholic indulgence in the name of historical authenticity. A holiday that wasn't a holiday, even though it involved going to Spain. A journey of transcendental discovery that was also a stiff but sensible aerobic challenge, and whose inherent asceticism had the happy side benefit of economy. A medieval tale retold for our times, but at 1350 prices.

One

I t's 500 miles from St Jean Pied-de-Port on the French side
of the Pyrenees to Santiago de Compostela near the north-
western coast of Spanish Galicia. From the dawn of the last
millennium until its final quarter, countless millions walked
this route as the final leg of an epic hike from their own dusty
thresholds, partly to stretch their legs in one of Europe's most
scenically appealing regions, and partly for remission of accumulated sins and a consequently more benign afterlife. Their
goal was the cathedral in which were housed the crumbly
mortal remains of Santiago, the patron saint of Spain: St James,
as I learnt while watching the first British contestant win top
prize on *Who Wants to Be a Millionaire*?

The fourth apostle recruited by Jesus, James was hardly an
obvious choice for a thousand-year personality cult: so volubly
stroppy his fellow fishermen nicknamed him and his similarly
ill-tempered brother John 'sons of thunder', so petulantly arro-
gant he demanded to be placed at the Son of God's right-hand
side in paradise. When he was dispatched westwards by his
doomed master on an evangelical mission, these attributes
helped ensure that by the time James wound up on the left-
hand tip of the Roman Empire, in north-west Spain, he had
somehow managed to attract just seven disciples. That mouth
clearly did him no favours after his return to the Holy Land:
in AD 44 he became the first of the apostles to experience the

afterlife, beheaded on the orders of Herod Agrippa.

Still, a martyr is a martyr, and after being sneaked out of Jerusalem, James's body was taken by sea to Galicia, terminus of his inefficient prophetic crusade. If I reveal that this voyage was made in an unmanned vessel hewn from solid marble, you will begin to understand that we are now on a voyage of our own: a journey beyond the shores of Factland, now gingerly skirting the Cape of Myth, now steaming gaily through the Straits of Arrant Cobblers. (Precisely where this figurative journey of ours set sail is a matter beyond sensitive debate, though for contextual ends I'll point out the lack of even biblical back-up for James's previous visit to Spain.)

Washed up on the beach – a beach littered with the scallop shells that came to symbolise Santiago – Jim's hefty aquatic hearse is met by a divinely forewarned army of disciples, perhaps all seven of them. His body is promptly absorbed into a large stone slab, before being carted away by oxen for interment on a hillside significant only for its peculiar remoteness: an ox-whacking 25 miles from the shore.

Despite the many arresting features of its history, Jim's final resting place is quickly lost, and lost so completely that it takes 750 years to find it. By then the Romans have given way to Visigoths, who in turn are handing over the Hispanic reins to the Moors, rushing up from North Africa with Europe-alarming haste: by the early eighth century, Spain finds itself almost completely under Muslim control. I say almost, for in their impatience to get at the French they overlook a few Christian huddles hunkered down in the northern mountains. One might draw parallels with Asterix's home village in Gaul, neglectfully unconquered by the surrounding Romans. And if one did, one would be more right than one supposed.

The embattled Christian guerrillas begin fighting back, assisted by Charlemagne, Holy Roman Emperor in waiting, who crosses the Pyrenees to harry the Moors. Yet it's still proving difficult to form a front line across northern Spain, a bridgehead for the Christian Reconquest to start pushing the heathens back to Africa. If only there was something or someone to rally around, a figurehead to unify not only the various anti-Muslim factions in Spain, but focus righteous, fund-raising wrath across the Christian world. If only we could find some— What's that, old hermit type? You saw stars twinkling over a cave on a hillside? You went in there and dug up these bones? Here, Bishop Teodomiro, check this skelly out. Really? Well, that's a result. What about these other two? Fair enough. Hey, everyone: we've just found Santiago! And, like, a couple of other stiffs who are probably his disciples or something.

In a slightly random, *Life of Brian* way, it was all in place. *Campus stellae*, field of stars: Santiago de Compostela. The body of St James, a proper apostle, was one of the most prized relics in Christendom – two of them, in fact, because along with the humble Santiago Peregrino, Pilgrim Jim, the pilgrim's pilgrim, we now had the parallel promotion of Santiago Matamoros, James the Moor-slayer. Riding out of the sky astride his white charger, Big Bad Jim was regularly spotted dispatching the heathen foe in splendid profusion: no fewer than 60,000 kills to his name at the (probably fictitious) Battle of Clavijo in 852. A mascot for the cuddly Christians who sought to love their neighbours, and an insatiable psychopath for those who'd sooner decapitate them.

It was this broad fan base, tempted from their homes by a praise-one-get-one-free pilgrimage, that made Santiago de Compostela one of the Christian world's must-sees. The local king, Alfonso, built a church and monastery on the site, around which a city began to grow up. The first authenticated pilgrims arrived in the late ninth century, and by the mid-tenth the Camino de Santiago was already an institution. At its twelfth-century peak, with anti-Moor Christian fundamentalism rampant and the crusades in full flow, it has been estimated that between 250,000 and 1,000,000 pilgrims were arriving in Santiago every year; even more in a Holy Year, when Jim's feast day, 25 July, fell on a Sunday. (By papal decree, pilgrims arriving in a Holy Year received total remission, a plenary indulgence, for all previous badnesses committed. Notch up the pilgrimage hat-trick – Santiago, Rome, Jerusalem – and you could build up a credit balance, Sin Miles redeemable against the perpetration of future wrongness.)

At a time when there were fewer than 65 million Europeans, with an average life expectancy of perhaps thirty-five, the demographic implications are arresting: by one calculation (yes – it's mine) between a fifth and a third of the medieval populace would at some time have paid personal homage to St James. As the Council of Europe noted when declaring the camino its first Cultural Route, 'the Compostela pilgrimage is considered the biggest mass movement of the Middle Ages'.

Google-based curiosity was hardening into something like intent, and this new level of preparation was soundtracked by the weighty thump of footnoted product of academic industry on doormat. An early casualty of the reading was my *Monty Python* image of pilgrims as a brainwashed corpus of robotic, masochistic zealots: though that Get Out of Hell Free card was clearly top of the Santiago bill, it was difficult to generalise about the pilgrims' motivations. The sick – the horribly, medievally sick – were lured by the hope of miraculous cure. So too the troubled: Thomas Becket himself recommended the pilgrimage to a woman who feared herself possessed by Satan. The curious came for education and adventure – Chaucer's Wife of Bath, no sombre devotee, visited twice in the late 1300s (accurately fictional, as lone women of good repute were a pilgrimage rarity). The naughty came to plunder this invitingly vulnerable tourist army, by violence or deception; and if they were caught, they might come again, as criminals given the option of walking to Santiago in lieu of a less appealing punishment. (Actually, they'd have been strung up and left to rot by the road – on the medieval rap sheet only those guilty of less straightforward crimes would have been spared the noose, such as the Surrey adulteress who in 1325 was given the choice of visiting Santiago or 'being beaten with rods six times around various churches'.)

Some were sent by their village to seek heavenly relief from famine or pestilence, and some by indolent lords and masters on a sort of pilgrimage-by-proxy. Your pain, my gain: by papal edict, the sin-remission was granted to whoever's name decorated what was by now known as the compostela, the commemorative certificate granted at journey's end. At Santiago, the good, the bad and the ugly came together.

And they came from the furthest-flung corners of the known world, or at least the well-known world. God-fearing, foolhardy pilgrims set off for Santiago not just from France, Italy, Britain and Germany but Greece, Poland and Hungary. One of the earliest pilgrim accounts tells of a Viking's trip to Compostela in 970; an Armenian hermit recorded his visit in 983. As their paths converged and their numbers grew, so recognised routes were first trodden bare, then developed. The main route from northern Europe wound through western France and nipped over the Pyrenees just past the town of St Jean Pied-de-Port; gradually joined by other paths from the Mediterranean side, it proceeded ever westwards as the Camino Frances, the French Way, largely following roads laid down by the Romans.

Dropping coins on inn table and collection plate, all pilgrims left a thin trail of gold behind them, and some laid down a fat seam of it. Driven by piety and PR, medieval notables from St Francis of Assisi to El Cid walked to Santiago and most made conspicuous donations. Particularly the procession of monarchs, who arrived in such profusion that the Camino Frances became also known as the Camino Real, the Royal Way. Prince Sigurd of Norway, Louis IX of France, Ferdinand and Isabella of Spain: all keen to display their credo credentials, perhaps keener still to promote the fight against the forces of anti-Catholicism. (Our own Edward I copped out by sending a proxy, and Henry II, having sworn to the Pope that he'd pay personal homage to St James, later quietly switched to the less onerous Canterbury option.) If local entrepreneurship provided the inns and taverns that catered for a pilgrim's physical needs, then the spiritual infrastructure, the gilded, jewelled shrines that sustained their faith along the way, was built by the wealth of kings and their noble henchmen. So too the network of fortified monasteries and churches that offered a haven from the Moors, and the castles dispatching the soldiery that provided protection in its more proactive form.

In 997 Moorish raiders turned Santiago over and nicked its hallowed bells: they were put to contemptuous use as olive-oil containers in the southern city of Cordoba until the Christians nicked them back 240 years later. Yet by the twelfth century the northern road to Compostela – the Way of St James, the Camino Real, the Camino de Santiago – was largely secure from heathen attack, and prospered not just as a holy procession but as a trade route. The grain and wool merchants of Navarre and Castille were now able to export their produce in confidence: wealth begat wealth, and in gratitude they too funded the cathedrals.

With the Moorish menace receding over the southern horizon, the hard-nosed religio-political rationale that had underpinned every cobble along the camino was now itself eroded. More and more would-be pilgrims were opting for a sort of no-win, no-fee approach: they would beseech St James from the comfort of their own homes, and if the leprosy cleared up, or it started raining, then it was off to Santiago in cheerful gratitude. With the urgent zeal diluted, penitential piety degenerated into tourist loutism: scuffles began breaking out at the Santiago altar, sometimes over queue-jumping at the apostle's tomb, sometimes on crude racial lines, sometimes so bloody that more than once the cathedral had to close for re-consecration. Papal intervention was required to clamp down on stalls flogging 'spurious' scallop shells and other dubious souvenirs in the cathedral square. Professional beggars and quack doctors were beginning to ply their ignoble trade along the route in growing numbers; Louis XIV forbade his subjects from walking to Santiago because of the number of pick-pockets, false priests and harlots. 'Go a pilgrim, return a whore,' declared an arresting adage. The golden age was at an end.

*   *   *

11

For the first time Christian Europeans began to think the unthinkable, and even to write the unwritable. 'There is not one haire nor one bone of Saint James in Spayne in Compostell,' carped sixteenth-century British traveller Andrew Borde – and that was while he was on his way there as a pilgrim. The Reformation, and the resultant establishment of Protestantism across much of northern Europe, turned the pilgrim tap down from a multinational flood to a steady stream of Frenchmen and Italians. The religious scepticism fostered by science and the philosophical Enlightenment in the eighteenth century reduced the stream to a trickle; the infrastructure of Church-run pilgrim sanctuaries, the *refugios* and *hospitals* where walkers found succour in all its forms, collapsed in 1835 after the Spanish state seized and sold almost all property and land from the major religious orders.

Hidden in 1588 lest Sir Francis Drake follow up his routing of the Armada with a relic-pillaging raid, the bones of Santiago were lost once more. A trio of skeletons turned up under the cathedral floorboards in 1884, but even when the Pope hastily confirmed them as those of Jim and his two disciples, no one was really listening. The sacred way that had for long centuries resounded to the shuffle and thump of holy footsteps fell quiet, and much was gradually reclaimed by nature: by the 1950s, anyone intending to follow the route needed a tent, a compass and a machete. An American who walked from St Jean to Santiago in 1982 found herself regularly stumbling about in dark and forested circles, untroubled by human company save the occasional old soldier fulfilling a wartime vow to some heavenly saviour.

Anywhere else but Spain the whole business might perhaps have been forgotten altogether, and with some relief, as the shaming embodiment of religious extremism and intolerance. But because the Spanish still pelt each other with tomatoes in God's name, and christen their boys Santiago and their girls Camino, it wasn't. Built by King Ferdinand and Queen Isabella, the Hostal de Los Reyes Católicos in Santiago's cathedral square might have been converted from the grandest of all pilgrim hospitals to a ponced-up hotel favoured by Julio Iglesias, but by obscure decree the management still fulfilled an ancient obligation. Turn up at its regal reception in your filthy road-clothes with a compostela in your hand, and its management would serve you a complimentary meal, in fact three of them, every day for three days. Whatever they say about free lunches, I could taste them already.

Two

If the Confraternity of St James suggested some sinister Masonic sect, then its Pilgrim Workshop had the ring of enforced labour in an airless peat-fired foundry. Almost a disappointment, then, to walk into a South London church hall one Saturday morning in early March and find it filled not with hooded moaning and the laboured wheeze of heavy bellows, but quilted gilets and Styrofoam cups of Nescafé.

A few shrewd-eyed, wild-haired academic types, two pairs of doughty bluestockings, a couple of note-scribbling loners and plenty of apple-cheeked, fol-de-ree fleece fanatics: this was the Continental arm of the Ramblers Association. Looking around and finding myself very possibly the youngest delegate, I contemplated the enduring truth that this pilgrimage was a senior pastime. The typical medieval pilgrim wasn't a king or a bishop but a serf, a man who would only have been given permission to set out for Santiago once his master had worked him to the end of his productive life. In those days that would have been about forty-five; we might have raised the retirement bar a little since then but nearly all those around me were still wage slaves granted their belated freedom. On cue, a check-shirted greybeard who'd just walked to Santiago from Canterbury ('Mmm – now *that's* the way to do it,' came an approving mutter) rose to address the hundred-odd pilgrim wannabees.

'Hardness of heart and selfishness,' he said, sweeping the room with eyes abruptly aglow. 'These are your stones; leave them at Santiago.'

Well, that was slightly more like it. It had been proving difficult to square these hearty nodders with the Camino de Santiago's recent spiritual resurgence, a renaissance that saw the number of annual pilgrims soar from 2,500 in 1986 to 154,000 in the 1999 Holy Year. You could certainly imagine them volunteering to rewire a *refugio*, or to paint yellow arrows on walls and tarmac, the arrows that apparently now waymarked the route with almost overbearing efficiency. But not, I'd felt, participating in the sort of business that I'd recently been reading about in accounts of the contemporary pilgrimage experience.

Would the small bearded fellow on my right have confided to a Californian anthropologist that whilst on the road to Santiago he had woken every morning with a painfully vast erection? Would that cardiganed librarian on my left have revealed to the same academic that throughout her pilgrimage the sound of church bells had brought her to shuddering orgasm? It was just possible to imagine the current speaker covering the entire route without eating, as I'd read that a German dentist had four years previously, but only just. And of course it was only a matter of time – seconds, perhaps – before I leapt to my feet and manifested a barefoot, filthy Shirley MacLaine, who would urge us all to make peace with our ancient emotions and live up to mankind's moral obligation to seek joy.

Endeavouring to trace the origins of the camino's rebirth, I'd had to look back to its birth, and that meant going back beyond St James. If I started this quest believing religious faith to be a form of delusional madness, then I'd soon be encountering many other forms. Shirley MacLaine's *The Camino*, loosely billed as an account of her walk from St Jean to Santiago, mentions St James only twice, five pages from the start and five pages from the end. For Shirley, and not only for Shirley, the pilgrimage's roots go deeper: the route is at

least as old as the Celts, a route along – inhale, exhale –
telluric ley lines, a route that lies directly under the Milky
Way and ends not at Santiago, but further west, on the coast
at Finisterre.

Finis terra, end of the earth – as Celtic geographers had
calculated, this jutting promontory formed the left-hand edge
of the known world (it seems unfair to criticise them for overlooking the rather more westward tip of Ireland, though if they
hadn't their Gaelic brethren would have been saved a bit of a
hike). The Celts were big on solar worship, and it's tempting
to regard the camino's undeviating drive to that western-most
cliff as a beeline to the sunset of sunsets. Certainly, some of
the cairns built up from stones left by passing walkers have
been dated to pre-Roman times.

Shirley, most notable of the tens of thousands of Americans
who have arrived in Santiago the hard way since the pilgrimage's renaissance, walked the camino to – and clearly I quote
– understand the destructive fragmentation of our own souls.
'Thus I came to believe that the surface of the earth is the
matter and form through which a higher subtle electromagnetic spiritual energy flows,' begins the second paragraph of
her book; later highlights include 'I decided my stick was male',
'Taureans like to run with ankle weights on' and 'Was life my
gorilla?'. Shirley is accompanied much of the way by an angel
who smells of vanilla, reveals assassinated Swedish Prime
Minister Olof Palme as the reincarnation of Charlemagne, and
describes at length – indeed for well over half the book's 307
pages – her own amoeba-like birth in a tank filled with gold
liquid, at some unknown point in cosmic history, in the now
submerged realm of Lemuria (where the temperature never
falls below 52°F and multicoloured electromagnetic lizards
share the sky with extraterrestrial crystal transporters).

Shirl's is a book so mad it howls at the moon, a book that
with any name on its cover but that of a Hollywood legend
would have had orderlies with soft, placatory smiles knocking on the author's door. Yet *The Camino* has inspired countless pilgrimages, and reaching the last page (a page I'm ashamed

to say now features a large ballpoint bird shrieking 'CUCKOO!' into a speech bubble) I thought I understood why. Just as I'd envy any full-on Christians I'd meet for their appealing belief in an eternal paradise, so, in a less straightforward fashion, I envied Shirley: an understanding of one's destiny in life, enhanced etheric vibrations in the brain, the multidimensional presence of gnomes, fairies and trolls – what's not to like?

New Age mysticism offered answers to those big questions previously taken care of by organised religion: this was the pilgrimage's growth area. At its radical Shirlean fringe were those who believed that coded messages had been left along the camino for us to find and unravel, that the extraordinary number of towns it passed through featuring the Spanish word for 'goose' in their names (um, two) linked it, in some mysterious manner tantalisingly beyond our current comprehension, to a traditional board-based pastime entitled the Game of the Goose.

In the mainstream were those content to ally themselves to the catch-all view I'd read in one introduction, that 'the camino represents the human desire to seek beyond the self, to delve deeper into the soul'. A little mystery, some embedded energy – in any event, there was just something about the camino, its cosmic ambience, its pagan and post-pagan history. You walked it and you walked in the shadow of the past. Surely all those millions of medieval devotees had left behind something more than mere footprints.

These were the people who went to Santiago and embraced the apostle's gilded statue as tradition demanded, then caught the bus on to Finisterre, burnt their clothes on the beach and ran nude into the crashing Atlantic. These, in fact, were my people, and one of them was up before me now, talking of inner transformation, of repaid kindnesses.

'When you get up to the altar and hug St James,' concluded the check-shirt in an air of sermonising drama, 'you're bonding old and new friends into the new you.'

I looked around the room: the new him, the new her, the new them . . . the new me. Was I really ready for this, or the slightly overbearing eye contact that seemed to go with it? 'I guess I'm hoping it will change me,' whispered the little man beside me in a matching voice as we rose for our coffee break. 'I don't know if that's scary or not.' One thing was certain: doing this walk never made anyone less weird.

Blowing steam off my Nescafé I mingled uncertainly with proto-pilgrims motivated by unhappiness, perhaps even a slice of spiritual desperation: people who didn't like themselves, and wanted to do something about it. 'Religion is for those who are scared of hell,' I now remembered reading. 'Spirituality is for those who have been there.' This wasn't just a long hike – somehow, though with a twenty-first-century twist, it remained a transcendental, life-altering experience. 'It's a kind of catharsis for tremendous grief or personal shame,' said someone behind me, and I almost retched with foreboding. 'The real camino only starts after you get back,' announced the veteran of a recent pilgrimage, a woman whose intense features seemed at odds with the mellowness of her words. 'These days I think about why I'm doing something, and the consequences when I've done it.' People were talking about solitude and solidarity, about finding 'a whole new set of things to learn'. Could I handle that? A tall order, certainly, for a brain that's been steadily leaking facts and knowledge since about 1982. Learning curves have become learning cliffs. Three years I've had that Volvo, and I'm still indicating an intention to turn right by squirting foam all over the rear window.

It was a relief to take my seat once more for the technical workshop, to shift from chicken soup for the soul to Deep Heat for the feet. No sooner had we all settled than a red-faced woman leapt from her chair and, with a savage rip of parted Velcro, violently severed her trouser legs at the knee. 'Two pairs in one,' she barked. 'Now, who wants to see my self-inflating mattress?'

For a middle-aged Englishman this was safe ground, home territory, and I wasn't the only one happy to find myself there. Those around me oohed over a rucksack with integral water hood, championed the multifunctional utility of the safety pin, argued keenly over poncho designs. 'Can we talk blisters?' someone piped up, eliciting a hall-wide chorus of pent-up enthusiasm.

In its way, this particular debate proved more unsettling than the transcendental module. Prevention was all well and good – wear synthetic socks, soak your feet in surgical spirit – but oh, how much more rewardingly hard core, more medievally authentic, was the cure. 'Obviously if there's fluid under it you'll just jab that out with a needle and stitch it up,' intoned a weather-beaten three-timer. Obviously? Just? 'But what a lot of people forget is to leave the thread under the skin,' and here he fixed his hard, candid eyes on my saucered counterparts, '*to wick away the badness.*'

Of course, there were so many other ways the camino could ravage the mortal physique. The red cover of the Confraternity's *Pilgrim Guide to the Camino Frances* was ominously laminated against inevitably brutal elements; within I read of temperatures that carelessly roamed the centigrade scale – from 2 degrees to 42, sometimes within a day, in my chosen departure month of April. One man stood to describe a storm so violent he'd had to link arms with four others while they dodged wind-borne farm machinery: 'That was the day after two pilgrims ahead of us had been killed in a blizzard crossing the Pyrenees.' There were still wolves in some of the lonelier forests, and bears had been reintroduced by someone with his heart in the right place and a desire to see mine in the serrated, slavering wrong one. And only the month before, fourteen pilgrims had been throttled in their sleep by hobgoblins.

The discussion turned to packing and minimum human payloads, and as it did the voices around were sharpened with the boastful harshness of competition, perhaps even obsession. 'I take my lead from the original pilgrims,' said a sturdy woman with a face like a toby jug. 'A hat, a coat and a stick.' Here were people seriously debating whether to cut their toothbrushes in half; whether to take just one pair of socks; whether *not to wear any underpants.* 'Did that last year,' blurted a man in army shorts with fearfully misplaced smugness. 'Went

commando. You know: nothing on under these.' Either
Cleanliness didn't fancy the trip, or Godliness just sneaked off
without telling him. As a vague but familiar sense of inadequacy settled upon me, an epiphany presented itself, a sudden
understanding of an important truth about myself as a pilgrim:
buggered if I'm carrying a rucksack.

Ignoring the fact that I would have to join these people, I
didn't see why I was obliged to beat them. Cut your pants in
half and floss with a bootlace and you'd still be shouldering
8 kilos – the bare feasible minimum, yet nonetheless equivalent to piggy backing a set of fat new twins for 500 miles. And
in any case there was something desperately dispiriting about
rucksacks: put one on and the visual perception of your
humourless inanity is boosted by as much as 24 per cent.
People with rucksacks on don't have fun, or if they do it's the
sort that involves a Thermos flask and brass rubbing.

There were about eighty walkers in our group, and, in a
separate huddle on the other side of the hall, perhaps fifteen
cyclists. Panniers, trailers, baskets . . . the weight seemed to
be lifting from my shoulders. I was half out of my seat en
route to their ranks when a whispered comment from the
barrel-chested sobersides three chairs down caught my ear. 'I'm
thinking about taking a mule.'

'Not a mule,' someone I couldn't see replied. 'Terrible
animals in inexperienced hands. Wilful. Everything they say
about them is true. I live near the Army's Mule Pack Transport
Troop in Melton Mowbray, and even they've switched to
ponies.'

I sat back down and listened.

'Not a horse neither. I did it last year and on day two we
saw a woman in tears with this big mare. Couldn't cope with
it.'

'Fussy eaters.'

'Hypochondriacs.'

'If I could find one, I'd take a donkey,' said the anti-mulist.
'They eat anything and they're incredibly resilient.'

A distant but determined smile annexed half my face, and

it was still there when I walked out into the spring wind half an hour later.

In 1878, Robert Louis Stevenson went to the South of France, bought a canvas sleeping bag and set about finding himself a holiday runabout. 'What I required was something cheap and small and hardy,' he wrote in the subsequent journal, 'and all these prerequisites pointed to a donkey.' In my mind, of course, they pointed to a Fiat Panda, but a résumé of Stevenson's adventures with Modestine provided heady inspiration. For 65 francs and a glass of brandy, he had bagged himself a slow but steady beast of burden, and one – as I could not stop reminding myself – with a uniquely authentic pilgrim heritage.

In recent years there has been some theological debate, mostly fought out on bumper stickers in America's more rural states, as to how the Son of God might sort out his transportation during any second coming. A derivative of the 'What Would Jesus Do?' mantra of youth-oriented evangelism, 'What Would Jesus Drive?' has inspired entertaining reinterpretation of the Scriptures. Chiefly to the benefit of Honda: it's well known that Jesus endured three Civic trials, and clearly dissatisfied with these test drives bagged himself something a little bigger – we learn in the Book of Acts that 'the disciples were in one Accord'.

Reluctantly discarding this tempting solution to the mysterious origins of that central initial in Jesus H. Christ, the more pertinent question should surely be: What Did Jesus Ride? And here we have an answer beyond speculation – from foetus to saviour, the Son of God was carried about on the back of a donkey. As I've said before, albeit only in regard to long hair and immortality, if it's good enough for him . . .

'A *donkey*?' blurted my family as one. For a moment it didn't seem they'd ever be able to list all the reasons that made this so entertainingly ludicrous. Almost at random, my seven-year-old daughter Lilja alighted on just one. 'He'll . . . stamp on your toes.' And then she laughed, and laughed, and laughed.

There was to be a lot of this in the weeks ahead, and I soon honed the gently beatific smile that was my response: forgive them, Lord, for they know not why they hoot. Yes, I'd never ridden a donkey on a beach or petted one at a city farm; never even pinned a cardboard tail to one's throat after the jelly and ice cream. There were obvious counterbalances to that momentous unburdening of the rucksack, yet any logistical disadvantages could, with a little imagination, be repackaged as spiritual bolsters. For a lifelong Londoner with mild farmyard phobia, assuming care of a proper, large animal instantly upgraded my camino from big walk to revelatory voyage of self-examination.

So a donkey would be my hairy-coated hair shirt, making the journey a truer test of the will, a trial. The contemporary pilgrim, I'd read, departed with a burden of doubt or distress – in charge of a jackass, I'd saddled myself with a ready-made bundle of both. Maybe even a little bottle of Christian spirit, in an *All Creatures Great and Small* kind of way. And because I'd already proved myself unable to resist pondering the opportunities for labour-saving pilgrimage dishonesty – bicycles, hitch-hiking, public transport – here was a guarantor of moral correctitude. How could I cheat with a donkey? A question I hoped not to be asking Birna on my first night home.

'You don't want to over-prepare,' someone had said at the Confraternity meeting. 'Without surprises it's not a journey of discovery.' Waylaid by donkeys, in thought if not in deed, this was a homily I embraced so tightly that after a month you could read it backwards on my chest. I downloaded a Spanish language course off the Net, but as is often the way with such material found it hacked by some corrupted absurdist. I tried, really I did, to concentrate on 'I am not from Venezuela' and 'Here is the ferry terminal', but it was never going to be easy when 'Eat shit and die' and 'Get the fuck out of here' were on offer. Then I bought a torch, and some safety pins, and – may the Lord have mercy on my soles – a pair of open-toed sandals. I knew there'd be something I wouldn't be able to find when the time came to pack. Why did it have to be the safety pins?

We were into April, I was nowhere near finding myself a

donkey, and the Internet, for once, had failed to unearth a willing ass. But it did add grist to the mill, with a surprisingly large number of contemporary paeans to the donkey as long-distance porter. All were in French, however, and because I don't even know what fetlock or withers mean in English, I was obliged to make use of an online translation service. Being complimentary, this was also magnificently wayward, refer-ring to God as 'Our Mister' and to sundry European towns as 'Population of Fields', 'Queen Bridge' and 'Pony'. Thus I read of the Breton man who had taken his donkey across France 'not as physical exploit, or tourism, but order gait witty'. There was the retired optician whose donkey had been led through Lyons' dark streets by 'girls of small virtue' and – oooh – the Belgian couple who had walked with a pair of donkeys and two young daughters all the way from their home to Santiago. I was also, in more general terms, appraised of the 'Five Advantages of the Luggage Donkey'.

First of these was, of course, that 'one not carry more'. Here, having explained why 56 kilos is not large issue for donkeys, the author rails against the misplaced nostalgic sentimental-ity that, to atone for cruelties past, now aims 'to treat our modern donkeys as living-room toutous'. Advantages two and three emphasised that a donkey does not cost nothing and provides an amicable and confident link with the native popu-lations. The donkey's mischievous nature as a joker who will imagine sometimes the worst stupidities to go interesting was explored in 'Comedy – The Fourth Advantage'. And finally, with my mouse arrow hovering shakily over the 'clear screen' button, I read of the donkey as a small companion, very discreet, very complicit, who will know to share you a beauti-ful love history.

'You can give the donkey a happy ending, but the miserable beginning remains for ever.' Scrolled beneath Eeyore in its promotional material, it's this ethos that has made the Donkey Sanctuary one of Britain's most successful charities. Largely funded by bequests from women old enough to remember doe-eyed long-ears being beaten in field as on beach, it now raises £13 million a year. Its founder, Elisabeth Svendsen, has done her job so well that 3,500 living-room toutous – three quarters of the entire UK donkey population – now browse the sanctuary's 2,500 rolling Devonian acres. Three quarters! Yet still sixty full-time sanctuary inspectors roam the land, looking for donkeys in distress, or really just any donkeys at all. Now there's a job. 'Dr Svendsen? Inspector Forty-six here. Listen, I'm at the Savoy tonight . . . Yes, same story as Claridges, really – loads of people, couple of dogs, no donkeys . . . Actually, no, that's a very good point. I'll check under the bed right away.'

It had recently lodged in the back of my mind, and more regrettably at the front of my mouth, that I was about to do something bad to a donkey. When I'd phoned up the sanctuary to book a place on their Basic Donkey Care training course, why hadn't I lied? I could have claimed to be researching a horsefly-on-the-wall TV docu-soap, or said that my vastly rich and terminally ill grandmother had asked for a report on current levels of deserving poignancy in the donkey community. The woman I spoke to didn't approve at all of my intentions as I outlined them on the phone, and it was hard to blame her. Slave-driving a donkey up and down the Pyrenees and onwards for almost 500 miles, with a backload of stuff I couldn't be arsed to carry myself: precisely the type of persecution they'd been set up to eradicate, and here was some bloke asking them to help make it happen. It was as if I'd gone to Help the Aged for advice on tattooing a confused uncle.

Instead she'd given me the phone number of a husband and wife of their acquaintance who'd recently taken a mule through France. 'Talk to them first, then see if you still think it's a good idea.' Her tone said I certainly would not.

In fact, Rex Johnson and his wife tried their very best to encourage me when I spoke to them – a shame, as I'd have dearly loved to dismiss almost everything they said as defeatist propaganda. 'A bit nervous, was Sparkle. Bolted a lot. Didn't like forests much – any large trees, really. Or birds.' This revelation caused me to emit a noise which Rex interpreted as implying modest curiosity rather than distraught panic. 'Yes, funny thing. Swans in particular. I think it was the reflection of their wings on the water. I had to sit up with him all night a few times.'

The terrible red tape at the borders, the importance of teaching the animal to drink from a bottle – it was some time before the Johnsons stopped supplementing the burgeoning stock of equine tribulations I'd already built up. I'd anticipated that saddling up in the morning might prove a mild chore, but by their estimate, leaving at 9 a.m. meant getting up in the dark. Every two hours thereafter you had to take everything off again to let him rest, prior to the early night that ensured what my Internet translator had so engagingly described as 'evenings of grass and of water'. As a result the best they'd ever managed in a day was 16 kilometres, and even averaging that, seven days a week, would mean fifty days from St Jean to Santiago – at least ten too many if I wanted to stay ahead of the summer rush of Spanish student–pilgrims the Confraternity had warned me about.

The train of thought that all this set in motion was a one-way express to Sod That, and before it scooped me aboard I quickly phoned back the lady at the sanctuary. 'I've never felt more sure about anything,' I boomed, sweeping aside her scepticism more melodramatically than intended. There was a silence, presumably while she contemplated the alternatives: accept me on the course, or let a clueless novice loose with a donkey in a land not known for its enlightened attitude to animal welfare. 'You're not to ride him,' she said at length, in a scolding tone. 'I promise,' I replied: don't tell Jesus, but an adult's weight comfortably exceeds the maximum humane payload for a donkey. Another pause, ended by a sort of defeated sigh. 'We'll see you on April the 8th.'

So there I was, in a room wallpapered with best-in-show rosettes and a floor space dominated by a four-legged skeleton. Without having yet beheld a living counterpart, I was reminded by the dimensions of this fleshless beast that by being larger than a cat, the donkey fell into that category of animals I was at least slightly scared of.

My fellow training-course delegates were three schoolgirls, their teacher and a family group that included a pair of pre-teenage boys. The schoolgirls were there, I suppose, because of the peculiar hold that equine beasts exert on young females, and the family because they were hoping to adopt a pair of Sidmouth donkeys as living-room toutous – sorry, as cheerful additions to their weekend farm in Hampshire. 'It's no longer clear what donkeys are *for*,' I'd read in a newspaper critique of the sanctuary's success. Well, I was putting that right, I thought, bolstered by the pronouncement on the Donkey Breed Society's website that 'a busy donkey is a happy donkey'. At the time this seemed a pilgrim's charter, but looking from face to kind and earnest face as Judy, our tutor for the day, doled out the information packs, it tolled out in my mind as the slogan beneath which I'd have driven through the sanctuary gates had Dr Goebbels been in charge.

A scent of manure wafted in through the lecture-room windows along with the springtime Devonian sun. Two girls in sanctuary sweatshirts popped their heads round the door to announce they were 'taking the donkeys out into the woods for a bit of a jolly', and I looked in vain for someone to share a ribald smirk with.

We kicked off with a video. The donkey, I learnt, evolved in Africa and first came to Britain with the Romans: jackass beat Jesus to our shores, but – by happy historical coincidence – only just. Being biologically designed to roam arid landscapes in search of food, the modern British-based domestic donkey's chief enemies were over-feeding, lack of exercise and moisture-related fungal conditions. Everyone else scribbled frantically; for once I smiled and folded my arms. (This was perhaps two weeks before the twin discoveries that Galicia's meteorological reputation has earned it the nickname 'the urinal of Spain', and that I would be starting my pilgrimage at the end of the month known colloquially as 'water thousand'.)

'What you're seeing here,' said Judy, as on the screen two

pony-tailed girls chaperoned an unenthusiastic long-ear across what was probably a paddock, 'is a pretty outdated method of leading a donkey. We don't teach that now.' I couldn't begin to see what rendered their approach so shamefully *démodé*, but the prospect of being tutored in state-of-the-art leading techniques was one that quietly excited. I saw myself being fêted by grateful locals as Don Burro del Futuro, the man who brought Castilian donkey handling into the twenty-first century.

I'd smelt the donkeys, and I'd heard them – an extraordinary, painful noise, not so much a hee-haw as someone trying to push-start a seized-up traction-engine. After lunch I finally got to see some. We were led into a small, cobbled courtyard, and there before us stood half a dozen examples of the beast known to the rosy-cheeked and exclusively female Training Centre staff as 'donks'. They'd seemed big enough on the screen. Now, here, around me, they were huge. Huge and stubborn and indomitable.

Judy informed us that Coco, a feisty male dedicated to the detection and ruthless humiliation of 'donkophobic' visitors, had been locked away. This still, however, left my asinine virginity in the hands of one animal who routinely battered visitors about the chest and legs with the business end of a jaw-gripped traffic cone, and another who specialised in the removal of jewellery by dental means.

'Oh, Mimosa's a sweetie,' I heard someone say. And: 'George – he's a terrible tinker.' I'd been told that the dearth of published donkey-handling guides was down to the impossibility of generalising usefully on such individual animals, but this lot seemed almost identical to me: idling about the courtyard with expressions of bleary bemusement, like big-eared ponies with hangovers. These were show donkeys, yet they looked, and indeed felt, as if they'd been stitched together from old doormats. The girl next to me patted one and a great brown dust-cloud rose up into the sun.

One of them shared my name, a fact regrettably divulged only after I had entertained the courtyard with a panicked response to the command 'Shift your bum, Tim, you daft lummox!' He wasn't the only one, in fact: I'd found another in the index of Elisabeth Svendsen's *A Passion For Donkeys* (not a book, I've discovered, you'll want to keep spine out on a prominent shelf). 'Some six years ago,' began the relevant page, 'Timothy was a happy, normal gelding in his early thirties.' A personally memorable introduction to an unforgettable tale of friendship, of jealousy, but above all of almost continuous Timothy-directed mutilation. The final episode was recounted with lurid relish: 'Armed with a carving knife, the gang attacked Timothy, slicing through one ear and then the other . . . He was still blundering desperately around the field, blood flowing down his eyes, when the unsuspecting owner arrived with his evening carrot.'

It was gratifying, therefore, to turn to this more junior namesake and find him fighting fit, fully eared and displaying his Fifth Advantage in the form I believe is known as a 'lazy lob'. As we watched, this already majestic appendage developed further still, inspiring him to engage Mimosa in an activity described by Judy, with the junior delegates in mind, as 'playing wheelbarrows'.

That wasn't strictly speaking good news, but it was as good as it got. Even a small donkey, I was told, could drag a 20-stone man around a field. Wrap the leading rope absent-mindedly round a digit and if the animal bolted you might – and in two reported cases actually would – find yourself thumb-hunting in the hedgerows.

I couldn't begin to master the crucial knot used to attach the donkey to anything: the simple loop Judy held in her fingers was, by some innocuous flick of the wrist, magicked into a multi-whorled, Gordian worm-cast. George bit a hole in my new coat. Asked to indicate Sam's 'withers', I inaugurated another round of jolly guffaws by displaying the anatomical competence of a blindfolded child in a party hat.

All this, of course, was before I'd actually touched one. I'd noticed while watching the video that the more donkeys I saw the bigger they seemed, and as Judy eased me towards Sam's shoulders I felt hopelessly overawed. It wasn't just the size, or even the strength. I'd become accustomed to assuming exec-utive control for all my personal transportation needs: you pressed one foot on a pedal and you got somewhere fast, or both feet on two pedals and got there more slowly. But here the boot was on the other hoof. I was not in charge. Finally, displaying the tactile relish of a man compelled to operate a humming light switch with wet hands, I jabbed a finger into Sam's offside haunch. It yielded and he flinched slightly. I had poked my first donkey.

As new dawns go, few have proved falser. I put the head collar on the wrong way round, was butted indecorously throughout the parade section, and spent so long worrying about how to inspect the back hoofs without having them forcefully applied to my throat that Sam actually fell asleep on his feet. (I'm particularly ashamed to admit it would be over a month before I accepted this as the default stance for a dormant ass.) 'Use your shoulder,' urged Judy. 'Lean into him and he'll let you take his foot up.' Everyone else, even the small boys, had long since dealt with their animals and now inevitably gathered round to watch. I applied my weight to Sam's heated bulk, and gradually, in a procedure that had less in common with veterinary best practice than an attritional arm-wrestling contest, pivoted his knee backwards and brought a foot hoof-side up into my lap. Then I dropped it in disgust and jumped upright. Where once had rung chortles now star-tled silence reigned. 'What?' I said indignantly, challenging the frozen faces around. 'Come on, it was all full of bits of crap and stuff.'

I did in the end manage a quick couple of scrapes, but neither of us enjoyed the experience. 'To them it's just like having their nails cut,' said Judy bracingly as Sam lashed out once again.

'Pulled out, more like,' I muttered.

Sam needed to be appeased, and Judy showed me how to do it. 'In fact, why don't you all give this a try,' she said, happily plunging her hand into a nearby donkey's cavernous ear and rasping the oiled contours of its internal landscape with an extended knuckle. The hearty delight that warmed the crisp air suggested that for everyone else this was a fully mutual pleasure, but as I eased up to my watch-strap in Sam's near-side waxen head tube and watched him dribble and quiver in response I felt dirty, as if coerced into an obscure act of wrongness. Here I was, in the dark corner of a West Country stable-yard, fisting my donk.

I barely slept in my cosy little b.& b. up the road, beset with misgivings of the most fundamental sort: the day had impressed upon me that what I didn't know about donkeys you could write in an enormous empty book entitled *The Donkey*. I'd hoped day two might fill in at least some of the gaps, but in fact it just added in more blank pages. This was Basic Donkey Health Care, and back in the lecture room we were soon in the realm of periopic horn. A labelled line drawing, the sort of thing you might have found in a Haynes manual, betrayed 'withers' as merely a drop in the huge and murky ocean of asinine physiology. Everywhere I looked there were pasterns, croups, crests, polls, coronets. Each hind leg alone incorporated a hock, a gaskin and a stifle. There was even an eel, and not where I expected it.

'The farrier's got a case of laminitis to show you,' said Judy brightly, 'and I'm hoping to find some seedy toe.' The daily health check required smelling a donkey's breath, snipping waxy bits off the inside of his ears, making a 'mental note' of the temperature of each foot and, in the case of a gelding, 'checking round the sheath and cleaning if necessary'. I was introduced to sweet-itch, which if left untreated swiftly transformed any donkey into a four-legged Homer Simpson: bald and yellow. The only remedy – one that aroused the first suspicions that this whole business had been designed as an elaborate joke at my expense – was an all-in-one donkey romper suit fashioned from stout blankets. The other complaints all sounded rather medieval: rain scald, mud fever, quidding and – ow! – sandcrack. 'Bastard strangles' was down as a lymphatic infection, but looked like half a tabloid headline on my pilgrim shame, the other half being 'lovely donkey'. 'If sinusitis becomes really severe,' intoned Judy sombrely, 'then the only effective treatment is facial trepanning.'

Even as I read through the less invasive remedial techniques that evening it was clear I'd never be able to prepare or apply a single one. I'd hardly find Stockholm Tar in the 'At the Farrier's' section of my Berlitz phrase book. And unless anyone told me different, a 'glucose drench' would mean a bottle of Lucozade up the croup.

My concept of the donkey as a low-maintenance beast of burden had already been brutally qualified the moment *A Passion for Donkeys* landed on the doormat. This might have been a book aimed at pre-teenage girls, but though it started with an introduction by Virginia McKenna, it ended with the words, 'See abscesses, castration, lameness, oedema, tetanus.' Now I learnt that donkeys even got sunburn, for cock's sake, which made rather a mockery of their African heritage. And by Christ their guts were fragile. How could the buttercup be a donkey killer? And acorns? 'Yew is also toxic,' I read on the leaflet Judy handed out, 'infected animals usually being found dead.' Most lethal of all was ragwort, an innocuous weed which at various stages of its illustrated life cycle resembled almost everything that grows anywhere.

There was a whole module on worms: ring, tape, lung. I realised I'd gone past caring when I found myself muttering 'pinworm round his anus' to the tune of *'Lipstick on my Collar'*. By the end I was just blankly transcribing overheard words almost at random: scab, zinc, wart, mould, crust, flies, scrotum. On the plus side, I learnt that as I wouldn't be travelling in February or November, there was no need to worry about encysted redworm. Also, only some of the diseases were transmittable to humans. 'Oh, yes,' chirped Judy, aiming a silver-lining smile at me, 'and donkeys can't vomit.'

With her reservoir of grim pestilence finally drained, Judy led us down to the stables. Here, a stooped but jolly farrier was working away at an infected hoof with a vicious blade, energetically carving off bony shards until the weathered concrete was littered with oversized nail clippings. 'I take it you're not planning to adopt a donkey,' he laughed, seeing me flinch. 'God no,' I said. 'Just taking one across Spain.' And with a shocked jerk and a rustic imprecation, he cut his finger.

Time was running out, and Judy could feel my fear. She ferried me down into the courtyard for a private hands-on tutorial in applying a hoof poultice, and without an audience it was all a bit less *Faking It.* She ran through the health-care essentials I was likely to need, and what sort of ailments I'd face given what I was doing and where I was doing it. 'At least you won't have a lot of rain and mud,' she concluded. 'They cause most of the trouble.' In my happy ignorance I managed a smile of relief.

There was a test at the end, two tests in fact. I read the first question – 'Which of the following would tell you that your donkey was healthy?' – and as soon as I saw that this involved a choice between 'limping' and 'bright eyes' I knew I'd pass. But though the certificate I came away with – my droving licence – declared proficiency in every aspect of Basic Donkey Care, even stable management, no one in the room was under any illusions. They'd watched me running away from George and being snouted about the courtyard by Sam. They knew that I was scared of donkeys, and they knew the donkeys knew it too. Even in French, as I discovered three weeks later.

Three

C omfortably more convenient than pilgrimage rivals Rome and Jerusalem, Santiago was always the British holy traveller's preferred destination. Shakespeare included references to 'cockle hats and staffs' in *Hamlet* and Sir Walter Ralegh even composed a rhyming eulogy to the pilgrimage. 'Give me my scallop-shell of quiet, My staff of faith to walk upon . . . My gown of glory, hope's true gage, And thus I'll take my pilgrimage,' he wrote, and though he actually never did, skeletons clad in decayed pilgrim cloaks and clutching scallop shells to their ribs have been uncovered in church crypts throughout the land.

The eleventh-century British vanguard came on pray-and-slay crusades to take on the Moors; later, we helped pioneer pilgro-tourism and so, say I, inaugurated a long tradition of holidaying in Spain (and as souvenirs go, it's tough to top remission of accumulated sins). We stayed loyal to Santiago even as the ever shifting allegiances of medieval Europe threw up new hazards: British pilgrim ships were regularly held to ransom in Spanish ports, and in 1375 six pilgrims from Yorkshire were executed as traitors on their return from Santiago, unaware that they had passed through Castille during a period of alliance with the hated French.

No one is certain how many Brits travelled overland, but good records exist of those who took the pilgrim ferries direct to Spain – William Wey, the most notable British pilgrim chron-icler, sailed from Plymouth to La Coruña ('La Groyne' in his unfortunate translation) in an impressive four days. Even in the fifteenth century, with the pilgrimage's popularity well past its peak, over 3,000 pilgrims were voyaging from Britain every year.

But even when Anglo-French relations sank to their murder-ous worst, there were always those for whom the express sea route was a little lightweight, a little inauthentic. To walk, it was said, was to pray with one's feet. And for those, as I discov-ered between the forbidding covers of *Jacobean Pilgrims from England to St James from the Early Twelfth to the Late Fifteenth Century*, a regularly favoured stopover was at any of the friendly monasteries of southern France, where many – oh, happy, happy words – 'were given or lent an ass for the journey'.

I'd found Hanno after a desperate request to Jan and Nick Flanagan, at whose cycling-based lodging house Pyrenean Pursuits I had been a guest some years before. I needed a donkey, I needed him in or near Spain, and with the summer pilgrim rush I'd been urged to avoid now encroaching, I needed him fast. Hanno, I should perhaps point out, was not a donkey. He was very much a man, indeed a vital, bearded Hagrid of a man who hurled my belongings into the dusted rear of his much-travelled Landcruiser with a single swing of a long arm. The Continental donkey enthusiast was evidently a breed apart from his pigtailed Sidmouth counterpart.

Apprehensive as to how I might recognise my donk vendor when he arrived to meet me at a bedrizzled Carcassonne airport, Hanno had described himself as having 'much disor-der in the hair'. As long as this hadn't seeped into the head below I didn't mind. For two weeks I'd been in constant, if indirect, contact with Mañuel Bazquez, a man tracked down by a Spanish-resident friend of mine, John Perring. The service Mañuel provided seemed ideal for my needs: he hired donkeys to Spanish pilgrims, providing all the medical kit and saddle-bags and so on, and after a month drove all the way to Santiago to pick them up in a horse trailer. A one-way rental, and for only 600 euros all in.

There were a couple of drawbacks. One was that I'd never manage 774 kilometres in a month. Another was that Mañuel didn't have any donkeys.

I'm not sure why it took Mañuel so long – a dozen emails and as many phone calls – to divulge this important fact to John, but his failure to do so didn't augur well for future dealings with the tradesmen of Spain. On day one Mañuel had fourteen donkeys, but by day eight a party of pilgrims had led half of those away. Then on day twelve, without explanation, a solitary jackass browsed Mañuel's yard. 'We've got to make him an offer on that one pronto,' I told John.

'Absolutely right.'

Twelve hours later John phoned me back. 'He's just sold it to a shepherd.'

A day of silence was followed by an email of blurted self-castigation, in which Mañuel confessed that his rental business was no longer an active one; that indeed it was now – put the chisel down, Mr Moore – *two years* since last a bray had been heard in his grounds. 'People who rented his donkeys couldn't cope,' elaborated John that evening as I held the receiver to my limp and sallow features, 'especially when it rained a lot. They just abandoned them by the road.'

I can't say this was a happy time. Mañuel's customers had been Spanish, and so by definition more culturally at ease with donkeys: so at ease that when they weren't weaving toy examples together out of raffia to flog to unsophisticated foreigners, they were lugging real ones up the church tower and heaving them off as a fiesta ice-breaker.

As we rumbled and roared through damp villages, I waited for Hanno to explain in his proficient English why I had nothing to fear. Instead I learnt that people would think I was a *gitano*, or gypsy, and would consequently drive the donkey off their land, to be met by real *gitanos*, or gypsies, who would steal it. I learnt how I'd need to treat the animal for ticks every three weeks, and then in dramatic terms how to effect this by jabbing a stout hypodermic through its breast – an enactment that required him to remove both hands from the steering-wheel whilst overtaking a tractor.

'You are strong?'

Hanno glanced at my T-shirt and what it contained, saving us both the discomfort of a verbal reply. 'But you will be. You must be. In the first days the *donkay* must understand that you are the boss. You will be . . . *physical* to him.'

Walking a donkey on asphalt, as following the camino would regularly require me to, dangerously eroded its hoofs; better to take a compass and just head off cross-country, snipping barbed fences with wire-cutters. I should also be wary of crypto-fascists, two-faced priests and snakes. 'Be very careful, huh?' he warned at the end of almost every sentence, rather superfluously for what had now been upgraded from a culturo–spiritual voyage of discovery to a fatally ill-equipped commando raid by the *Sergeant Bilko's* cavalry.

Tarmac turned to mud and we bumped up, across and then down a mist-wreathed hillside. The sudden violence of our progress seemed to dislodge a rogue nugget of inner defiance: what did he know, anyway? Panoramane, Hanno's one-man ass-for-hire operation, rented donkeys for cosy three- and four-day hikes around the foothills of the French Pyrenees. Long-distance travel was not his business, and nor was anything Spanish. By his own admission he'd never even sold a donkey before.

Despite this stage of the journey causing his considerable head to impact repeatedly against the cab roof, the proximity of home seemed to mellow Hanno. 'But what you are doing, it's a . . . a very *strong* experience.' He kissed the bunched fingertips of his right hand. 'You will find again the, ah, ancient rhythms of life, a *nomade* with another *nomade* at your side.' We rumbled down a muddy hairpin and up to a wooden house in the latter stages of construction; he killed the engine. 'Possessions will have no meaning,' continued Hanno, his glassy gaze on the bedrizzled valley below, perhaps willing me to imagine no religion.

'*Voilà.*' An asinine honk blared out, and there, trotting down through the tussocked greenery, were a dozen damp donks. Big donks: wildly shaggy, almost bison-like in their brunette sturdiness. Feeling like a motorist whose car has broken down in a safari park, I managed a mechanical wave.

'Which one is mine?' I asked, unable to keep a quaver out of my voice.

Hanno scanned the long, dark faces. 'He's not here at this moment. Sometimes you find him, ah . . .' Bleeding? Foaming? Sinking? Hanging? '. . . Hiding.'

'So, um, how do you know?' I enquired as Hanno climbed into the back to pass me the bags out under the gormless scrutiny of his herd, mercifully coralled behind an electric fence.

'Hmm?'

'About, you know, the experience. And its strength.'

Boldly oblivious to the constraints of his surroundings, Hanno depicted incredulity with the very Frenchest of all body gestures. 'But I have done it!'

All we'd established in the first of our two brief calls was that he had a spare donkey, and would sell it to me for 800 euros. The second had covered logistical arrangements.

'But you knew, no? Five year ago I walk from Belgium to Santiago with my family and two donkays.'

It was him! And he wasn't even French! This was quite something. 'Why will I sell you donkay if not for this reason? I don't sell donkays, but this adventure you make, it's special, and so I like to help.'

Following Hanno up into his home I felt as if I was being inducted into a benign secret society. Within lay yet more evidence that the people who did this pilgrimage were clearly not as I was. No television, but a computer monitor with a donkey-themed screen saver. A wood-burning stove and a supper-cooking wife, the welcoming, winsome Marie-Christine, chopping home-grown vegetables at a long, slender table. The more youthful of their two daughters breezed about in a headscarf. Her elder sister, evidently at a more challenging stage of young adulthood, had by mutual request been installed in the guest room. This was an old caravan 100 yards uphill, yet still her parents found themselves within the radius of adolescent loathing: asked to find alternative accommodation with friends for the two days of my visit, she had apparently almost smiled.

We dined by congenial candlelight, Hanno divulging relevant facts as they occurred to him. I'd brought a voice recorder along, and pushed it next to his plate as he listed and described more poisonous plants, and the importance of feeding a donkey – in fact my donkey, wherever he was – a handful of rock-salt every morning, and the need to find shelter if the rain lasted more than two days. He talked of the time a Spanish farmer kidnapped his donkeys in the night and held them for ransom. Had he mentioned the snakes? He had. And the thieves? Well, some of them. *'Oh, c'est pas comme ça,'* tutted Marie-Christine at the end of almost every one of his more lurid stories. But every time she did he raised a bushy eyebrow the short distance to his tangled fringe and smiled knowingly.

Postprandially spread-eagled in an ancient, low-slung armchair with his booted feet steaming against the stove door, Hanno described how the walk to Santiago had changed his life. Seven months it had taken, requiring him to take his two daughters – then six and nine – out of school for a year. Romany meandering by day; maths and French round the evening campfire. Upon return, his inner nomad out of the box and restless, Hanno flogged the family home and moved down here; a portraitist of startling talent, he now earned his crust depicting from photographs the children of Belgium's aristocrats and industrialists. For him this had become a mechanical chore, but by spreading that crust with donkeys he had made himself an improbably toothsome life sandwich. Drawing children gave this irrepressible trend-bucker the freedom to indulge his passion for hosing crap out of a big shed. In another year Hanno and Marie-Christine, this time alone, would be heading off again, circumnavigating the Iberian peninsula with the same two donkeys.

Outside it was black and wet. En route to the caravan Hanno and I were joined by two lumbering, long-haired dogs; mindful of the looming festival of contrived hearty petting, I treated the fatter to a couple of manly slaps. Hanno led me through the slick grass towards the first of the electric fences: 'With care here,' he warned as his torch picked out the first electric fence. 'One time I touch with my head and my mouth is frozen for twelve hour.'

'But I thought these were just run off car batteries. 12 volts?'

'Sometimes, but here is too many fences. I put it on the, ah, real *electricité*.'

'What, 240 volts?'

He recoiled in bafflement. '*Non*, 22,000.'

I looked at him, my mouth pre-frozen.

'But with small watts.'

Once past this appalling forcefield, our menagerie was unsettlingly complemented by half a dozen silhouetted equines. 'They're all *men*,' I said, playing a torch across their undersides as Hanno fumbled for the caravan key. Almost universal advice to source a more placid and willable female ass coloured my voice with a disappointment that he handsomely failed to detect. 'Yes,' he said, gurning lewdly at a wrist-thick parabola of swarthy love muscle. 'We have an expression – *monté comme un âne*.' Hanno inhaled loudly and expressed his comic awe with that burnt-my-fingers shake of the hand. 'You know – mounted as a donkay.'

'Yes, we say something a bit like that.'

'My donkays are all, ah, cut, but they still enjoy to cover the ladies. Eh! Here is your one.'

And so I first beheld my ass. Blinking into Hanno's torch beam he shuffled up through the trees, then idled circumspectly in the background as his fieldmates jostled and stamped and nuzzled steam at my throat. As they were dark so he was mousy; as they were loudly tousled so he was neat and petite. Tiny and tawny. Low-key, reticent: My Little Donkey amongst the rodeo rowdies, Charlie Watts at the back of a stage full of posturing Jaggers.

'Eh, Shinto!'

I'd been thinking about a name for two weeks; on the plane the choices had been distilled to a toss-up between Doug and Judas. But now it was Shinto, and as he perked up his browny-grey ears at its bellowed enunciation, I knew that however inappropriate it seemed to travel a hallowed Catholic trail with a beast named after a polytheistic Oriental religion, I couldn't change it.

Shinto looked me in the eyes, blinked once more, then sauntered off into the night. 'He is the most intelligent of all my donkays, and the least nervous.' An appealing claim, whose relative nature did not at this stage occur to me.

The caravan was pertinently monastic – clean but spartan. Before he left Hanno shone his beam at its plumbed facilities, a few yards downhill in a log cabin of his own design and construction, solar-heated shower and all. (Though as I'd later discover to my nocturnal disadvantage, he'd cut a few corners on the toilet: a plastic dustbin and an adjacent bag of sawdust, a bran tub I'd be stocking with mystery prizes for two days.) The donkeys parted for him, and now I was alone. Alone in a caravan cornered by donkey shit and high voltage, yet if the accounts I'd read of the pilgrim *refugios* were to be believed, this was as good as it would get for the next 774 kilometres.

I listened to the tape I'd made at dinner as mountain rain shot-blasted the thin roof. Even amidst the racket I could detect in Hanno's tone a slight incredulity – he evidently hadn't believed I was quite as useless as I'd insisted I was. 'You don't know the different type of straw, not at all?' 'The chair or bowline knot you can do, of course. No? Really, no?'

The tape clicked off, and as I yanked the paisley curtains together a herd of rustling shadows swished into the trees. Now was not the moment to recall Hanno's tale of the time he'd borrowed a lady donk, a jenny, for breeding purposes: his boys had all had her up against the caravan, and in the process knocked it over. As I pondered this, a mighty, awful bray banged off down the valleys – no more apocalyptic by day than the hearty priming of an ancient hand pump, that night, alone in the caravan, it was the rusted gates of hell being effortfully forced ajar.

Throughout the long hours of darkness I was unsettled visibly – and on one unhappy occasion audibly – by extraneous asinine activity. As dawn fingered in round the curtains I felt like rushing down to the house and shaking Hanno by his huge shoulders: It's all right for you, mate, you build solar showers and train your own donkeys and . . . and . . . and I just can't do this. Because I didn't even have to. You didn't need a donkey to take a Southwest Airlines baggage allowance across Spain. Nineteen kilos on the nose – dump a couple of books, and whatever I'd said before, I could shoulder that. Or I could . . . get on the next plane back to London.

At breakfast the phone ruptured a sombre silence. Marie-Christine handed me the receiver: it was Birna, reporting in fretful distress that the children's scalps were alive with lice, and that the plumber had just found a rat behind the boiler. Someone didn't want me to give up and go home. Our Mister was already working in mysterious ways.

I followed Hanno out into the paddock, and looking around began to feel better. The rain had gone and under a big blue sky I saw what the Pyrenees had that Belgium didn't. Densely medieval forests pitched and rolled, surrendering at distant length to fearsome snow-veined peaks: here were the Himalayan foothills transplanted to Somerset on a perfect morning in the butterfly season. Walking from Italy or central France, a medieval pilgrim would typically bank on getting to Santiago and back in four months; those setting out from Britain or the more distant central European lands might allow a year, over-wintering in Spain before heading home. Either way, spring was the time to set out if you wanted to avoid that chilly short cut to paradise on some snowbound Pyrenean peak. Chaucer noted that no month aroused wanderlust more powerfully than April, and though he was talking about an English April, or rather Aprille, contemplating the panorama I saw what he meant.

At least until that panorama had donkeys in it. Albeit largely in the background, for despite Hanno's beckoning clucks and whistles the bulk of his herd – though happily not Shinto – just gawped blankly at us from a great distance. Here was a man who bred and rented donkeys, who had walked halfway down Europe with donkeys, and still they sometimes ignored him, sometimes slipped his knots and got lost in the night, sometimes bit him. 'They bite? What do you do then?' We were outside the stable now, being jostled by over-familiar quadrupeds.

'Oh, a bite is not so serious. But if he kick you – then you must attack with your hands.' He thrust out a taut fist; I began to explain that this wasn't quite the pilgrim ethos I'd had in mind. Was that really how Jesus prepared for his Palm Sunday ride into Jerusalem? 'Of course! You cannot train a donkay without pain! When he kick, you hit him with power in the stomach.' With disquieting relish he thus punished an imaginary animal. '*Bof!* Always in the stomach. Their pain centre.'

Shinto? Kung fu more like. I pictured a trio of stubbled apostles – perhaps St James himself among them – pinning down a disobedient jackass while their grim-faced messiah systematically worked him over. I remembered my grim encounter with a full edition of Robert Louis Stevenson's donkey journal: 'I must reach the lake before sundown, and to have even a hope of this must instantly maltreat this uncomplaining animal. The sound of my own blows sickened me.' And I found myself recalling how a friend's father had once had a fight – a proper fists-and-feet brawl – with a pony who'd thrown off one of his daughters. Did it really have to be this way?

Shinto's associates wandered away and we were left with a rather circumspect grey animal. By the end of a long night I'd become rather good at blotting out the brooding enormity of what lay ahead, and watched in gone-past-caring nonchalance as Hanno lashed the toughened plastic packsaddle to Shinto's back by means of a fiendish cat's cradle of straps and buckles. 'Ah, this strap here to the behind, have it low so he don't *caca* on it.' He threw me the head collar and watched as I confidently attached it in a new way, a way that pinned Shinto's left ear to his neck. Wordlessly Hanno put this right, and we were off, taking my new donk for a test drove.

My mentor took the reins, lightly holding the five-foot-long red-and-green leading rope in finger and thumb and positioning himself just behind Shinto. 'Eeeeeuuuwwww,' he groaned, like a one-man football crowd bemoaning a near miss. It wasn't a noise I'd anticipated, but before it was even halfway out of his throat Shinto broke into a brisk trot that had us jogging up the forest path behind him.

Five minutes on Hanno handed me the rope, along with a pliable length of willow, and trying to gloss over the momentousness I took my place at Shinto's rear. 'Eeeeeuuuwwww,' I said, or tried to. It would be a lie to say Shinto didn't move, because one of his ears swivelled back. 'Eeeeeuuuwwww!' Nothing. Hanno stood in front, looking at me like a driving instructor watching a new student put the ignition key in his own ear and twist. He took a step back towards us, half a step really, and Shinto immediately jolted into motion.

Hanno never had to say anything twice to Shinto, but with me even that was never enough. Repetition lent his more despairing exhortations the familiarity of a catchphrase. 'It is a problem of *autorité*,' was one. 'So once more – *why* a donkay?' was another. 'You are not so convincing' – his favourite – was typically accompanied with a palsied shake of the wrist that paralleled my attempts at physical chastisement to an incredibly old woman trying to coax ink from a reluctant Bic. 'Don't make my donkay too English,' said Hanno after one such episode. '"Oh, please, Mr Shinto,"' he went on, his voice ascending to a prissily camp facsimile of a flustered public schoolboy from the inter-war years, '"Would you care to advance a little faster?"'

'He's not your donkey now,' I said, letting my willow fall to the soft earth.

At my persistent and desperate behest Shinto eventually moved forward, with the eager brio of a hill start effected in third gear. We toiled up through an empty village, and onwards to an open escarpment girdled majestically by muscular peaks. It was hot. Hanno threw his leather jacket over Shinto's saddle and sparked up a Marlboro. 'There is Spain, there,' he said, jabbing its lit end at the southern horizon. And then we headed back down.

Shinto quickly took stock of this new approach to gradient, and used it to develop momentum. For perhaps five of my steps and ten of his we were in the zone, striding purposefully as one. Then the footpath steepened and in moments he was hurtling crazily down its sun-dappled hairpins; I grabbed the rope in both hands and was pulled helplessly along like a novice waterskier. Hanno's jacket flew from saddle to nettles, but before stopping to retrieve it he distantly crooned out a noise that sounded like his 'Eeeeeuuuwwww' played backwards. Shinto slammed on the anchors and I slid groin first into his rump.

'When you go up,' panted Hanno as he rejoined us, 'you stand behind with your *baton*. But when you go down, you must be ahead, and hold the *baton* in front of his eyes. As a brake?' He snapped a leafy switch from an adjacent birch and handed it to me, not unfriendly but with determination. Nodding wordlessly, I wiped the back of a wrist against my humid brow. Getting Shinto to move had appeared to be the significant problem; now I understood the more fundamental disadvantages of not getting him to stop. If he decided to go, he was gone: unless I mastered that noise or got hold of a stun gun, there was nothing to be done. Shinto stood there, motionless and four-square, like an eighteenth-century livestock portrait. Shakily I raised the branch to his face. He gazed through its resident foliage for a moment, then with a sudden snatch of the jaw broke the stick off about three inches from my fingers and settled into its protracted consumption.

'You have too much *fatalisme*,' said Hanno as he led Shinto up the rutted drive to his German friend Mikkael's house. I said nothing. The almost constant reiteration of my ignorance and incompetence was coagulating doubt into a clot of raw fear, a mass that having filled my stomach was now pressing painfully into the diaphragm. I tried telling myself that this was precisely the sort of feeble unmanliness I'd come to confront, but then if Hanno's assessment of my character really was accurate – which of course it was – then why be a pilgrim? Just as fatalism dictates that nothing a man does can alter his destiny, so a pilgrimage was predicated on the precise opposite. The options for the weeks and months ahead were hardening: philosophical overhaul of the starkest profundity, or stupid, craven, self-fulfilling shambles.

Mikkael was a retired professor with two donkeys and a cottage he rented out in the summer. During our brief stay Shinto damaged all three. As we ate salami and yoghurt on an overwhelmingly panoramic terrace, Shinto contrived a confrontation with his new equine associates that had them all flailing about in a limb-knotted cartoon brawl. Chastised, and with a red-crescent bite on his neck, he then trotted up to the immaculate gardens fronting Mikkael's cottage and lowered his big snout purposefully into a flower-bed.

We could see his jaw working, and I was the nearest. 'Tim, maybe you, ah . . .' said Hanno. And so I, ah, did, quickly finding myself in a ridiculous Mexican stand-off, meeting a gaze that if not quite withering, was unsettlingly implacable. Eating flowers might be fun, but how much more fun to stare out this silly new man. I looked hard into those eyes, round and shiny as freshly shelled conkers, and beheld the very essence of dumb insolence. Then Hanno appeared at my shoulder and he trotted smartly to heel.

Marie-Christine contemplated our belated return from their stilt-propped veranda. I saw her whilst urging a static Shinto towards his field with a nervously jabbed forefinger in the haunch, like an anxious toddler trying to rouse a foully hungover stepfather. So it was that she too came to see me for the feckless nance I so surely was.

'But I'm too English to abuse an animal,' I said in a haughty whine as Marie-Christine poured me out some sort of infusion.

'Maybe you think it is not love, but your relationship will be better if you are strong and take no bullshit,' she replied in mild exasperation. 'Just imagine how it is sometimes with dogs.'

But I have never owned a dog. 'I could tell you how it is sometimes with cats,' I offered, and she shot a quick glance at Hanno. In the name of all that is holy, said the glance, who *is* this baby's arse of a man?

The donkeys came to me again that night, massing snortily around the caravan as I pursued elusive sleep. A huff led to a puff, then to a bray and within a minute the formica walls around me were shaking to the nostrilled trumpets of a frenzied wind section. Was this a warning to safeguard their diminutive colleague? A hearty '*bon voyage*'? Drawing the covers up to my taut features, I began to understand their dreadful orchestra. They were laughing at me.

Four

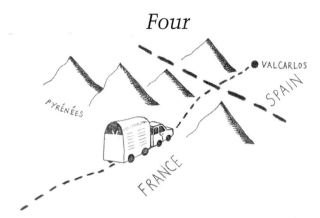

Agricultural peasantry formed over 90 per cent of Europe's medieval population, and theirs was an almost claustrophobically tiny world. The hills girdling a village were its ultimate horizons, broached only for a rare trip to fair or market; a serf would live and die in the same house that had been home to his family for generations. What a thing, then, to step beyond this world, to walk and keep walking, to cross seas and cities, through lonely woodland stalked by wolves and brigands. To stand awed before ecclesiastical structures of unimagined might and splendour, to encounter alien realms of senseless words, bewildering customs, funny food. A leap of faith indeed. Try as I might not to, I could only contextualise the heroic recklessness that sent a pilgrim on his way by picturing Frodo and his hobbit mates setting forth from the Shire.

No wonder that departing pilgrims were blessed by the local cleric and seen off by emotional fellow villagers, who'd typically accompany them for the first few miles. Nor indeed that it was considered poor form for a pilgrim not to have made provision for the future care of any dependants. How did they ever make it, there and back? For obvious reasons of security pilgrims always travelled in convoy, but even then the basics – navigation, shelter, provisions – can't have been any easier to sort out. With a motley crew of road buddies, you'd have

47

had the blind leading the blind, the deaf leading the Welsh, the thieves leading them all into a big hole covered over with branches. All those brave but clueless millions, tramping blithely through foreign field and forest seven hours or more a day.

What they needed was a travel guide, and in 1137 they got one – no less than the world's first. 'Thanking you, sire,' breathed a humbly awed pilgrim as he weighed the *Liber Sancti Jacobi* in his filthy hands. 'Um, now can you read it out for us please?'

Also known as the *Codex Calixtinus* in honour of the Pope to whom it was dedicated, the *LSJ* – or at least its pertinent practical chapters – is widely supposed the work of a French monk, Aimery Picaud. As a good holiday-brochure copywriter, Picaud's aim would have been to maximise interest in his destination by talking up its positives and glossing over any downsides. Regrettably for his readers, but rewardingly for us, Picaud was not a good holiday-brochure copywriter. After the magnificent deceits of a first paragraph in which he confidently decrees the 500-mile, trans-Iberian trek to Santiago as a thirteen-day walk, Picaud allows his quill to scratch and twitch to the darkest whim of xenophobic scaremongering.

Having saluted at onerous length the qualities of his regional brethren – 'handsome, brave . . . vital and giving . . . these are the people of Poitou' – he vaults the Pyrenees with racial malice aforethought. You know what they say about Spanish food: eat beef, pork or even a tiny fish and 'you will no doubt die shortly after'. Most rivers were poisoned, their inviting waters instantly fatal to horses. And then there were the natives. Ferrymen invariably pushed their passengers out midstream; 'having laid their hands upon the spoils of the dead, they wickedly rejoice'. Crossing from France you'd meet the Basques, who 'dress poorly and eat disgustingly, from a single bowl', spoke in a language like 'the barking of dogs', and were 'ugly, corrupt, drunken, savage, impious and uncouth'.

A Basque 'would kill a Frenchman for no more than a coin', perhaps a fate to be preferred to that awaiting any survivor encountering the residents of Navarre: 'Here they not merely rob pilgrims going to St James, but ride them as if they were asses.' Doubts as to the implications of this statement are laid to rest two pages on. 'It is told that the Navarrese affixes a lock to the behind of his mule or horse, so that no one else but he may have access to them. He also kisses lasciviously the vulva of mules.' One imagines St Francis of Assisi, who walked to Santiago in 1214, entering a darkened Navarrese barn with a rueful cough and a raised finger: 'Um . . . Listen, chaps, that isn't quite what I had in mind.' (The translator of my edition of the *LSJ*, a Professor of Medieval Studies at Syracuse, adds in a startling footnote: 'Mutually gratifying erotic liaison between master and his or her pets or domestic animals is widely practiced to our own day.' Put those burning torches down, common-human-decency fans – he died in 1995. 'Cock-a-doodle-don't!' quipped the coroner at an inquest I just made up.)

Too late now to have Shinto measured for a chastity belt.

The night before, sitting round the map with Hanno, I'd been faced with the full scale of my geographical ignorance: mountain ranges were long as well as high, and St Jean Pied-de-Port was right down the other end of the Pyrenees. A good 250 kilometres away, indeed, which at horse trailer speeds warranted setting off at dawn, or rather 9.30 a.m. once the three of us had wrestled a furiously unyielding Shinto into the back. Poor little sod, I thought, watching his ears swivel about in trepidation above the trailer's side walls. Was this sympathy? Well, it was a start.

Marie-Christine and her daughter wept to see their four-legged friend thus dispatched, which didn't do much for my confidence, and may explain why my normally competent map reading badly let us down. So badly that by the time St Jean's stout city walls rose up before us, we'd already contravened EU regulations on the movement of animals. Six hours Shinto had been in the back, seven by the time we'd eaten a very late lunch. Eight when we'd stocked up at a hypermarket with coat brushes, donkey salt and a washing-up-cum-drinking bowl, and a round ten when, having failed to find field or stabling in St Jean, we finally unloaded our – *my* – blinking, sweaty donkey outside a hillside guesthouse in Valcarlos, 10 kilometres up the road on the Spanish side of the border.

Not starting in France comprised a reasonably profound fuck-up, but even as I dusted myself down on the wrong side of this metaphorical first fence I found I didn't care. Yes, yes, so I wouldn't quite be doing the full 774 kilometres. And yes, unless I got really badly lost I'd never now experience the rare thrill of walking a donkey across an international frontier. But these were of little import beside the imminent apocalyptic awfulness.

'So,' said Hanno, tying Shinto's 12-foot 'night rope' to a tree in the corner of the guest house's front garden, a steeply pitched realm rich in mint and thistles and soilable playground equipment. We'd run through all we could think of. Which saddle straps to adjust and attach, and which to leave well alone. A trial run with the packing procedure, looping and lashing panniers and waterproof bags through brass rings and round plastic saddle horns until the two sides hung in balanced harmony. Last-minute supply essentials: a tube of stinking multi-purpose donk-ointment, a kind of stout screwdriver for scraping out Shinto's feet, and Hanno's own chunkily ethnic pullover for conditions I'd forgotten to prepare for. I'd had him do his 'Eeeuuuwwww' into the Dictaphone so I could practise at nights – one way of emptying the bunk above, if nothing else. And again and again and again that sodding knot. He eventually distilled those whorls and twists into terms a drugged Cub Scout could have grasped: the snake comes up through the well, round the tree, and back down the well.

'So,' he repeated. This was it: the hot, hard slap to the face that said I was about to be left alone, in sole charge of a size-able farmyard being, with a trans-Iberian journey of nearly 500 miles – a journey indeed of biblical proportions – ahead of me.

'Just a minute,' I blurted, stalling desperately. 'We haven't talked about the punishment beatings.'

'Beatings?'

'Yes – I mean I'm not going to hit him, but how hard should I if I was going to?'

'No,' said Hanno, with a look bravely purged of despair. 'Not to punish. Just to make some *autorité*. And not in fact hitting.'

He opened the Landcruiser's heavy, battered driver's door and planted a filthy boot on the sill. 'No!' I squeaked. Then, in a slightly better voice: 'The crap. Do I have to pick up his crap? I really don't want to.'

Hanno nodded as kindly as he felt able to. 'By the finish you won't care to hold donkay shit in your fingers. By the finish you will be eating together from this.' He rapped a large knuckle against the washing-up bowl in my hands and jumped into the cab.

'By the finish?' I quavered, my pale face angled up at him.

'You will arrive in Santiago,' he said, but the pause before he said it was rather longer than I'd have preferred. And with that, and a many-pointed U-turn, this lovely big man was gone from my life.

It was all so desperate that I hardly even noticed that the room was 50 euros, a sum that I'd been told would keep a Confraternity hard-noser fed and bedded for a week. And that didn't even bag me a telly, obliging me to make my own fun by impregnating the room with the stench of sweat and crap, a stench supplied for the moment by Shinto's saddle and the thick blanket that protected him from its more chafesome straps.

I bundled both into a wardrobe, then laid all the maps and guidebooks out on the bed. Tomorrow – wince, swallow – was a non-negotiable 22 kilometres, a Grand Old Duke of York job that began with a 2,000-foot climb to the lonely pass of Ibaneta and ended with a swoop to Roncesvalles and its sprawling monastery complex. My test drove with Hanno had suggested I'd experience the starkest difficulties on the more challenging inclines and descents, and on this basis it was a shame that my first task was to get Shinto up the Pyrenees and the second to take him straight back down again. 'A tough stage of great beauty,' was one verdict. Tough indeed: every year at least a couple of pilgrims messed it up fatally, losing their way in the mountain mist and meeting a forsaken, hypothermic end, or over-winding their tickers by pushing too hard on the first day.

The tanks of fatalism were on my lawn; I tried to will them away with mechanical positive thought. This was not a bad idea. Not at all. In fact, there was no way this was not a good idea. Not quite ready to start praying, instead I practised that knot. Interestingly, every time I wrapped the rope round the bedpost and started twisting and threading, the end result deteriorated. First I couldn't find the snake, and then he turned up with a mate. They had a fight up the tree; the tree fell down the well.

After an hour I gave up, but getting to sleep was no easier. My, Spanish people are loud. There were kids still running about at 11.30, which by forthcoming standards qualified as the middle of the night. So relentlessly animated was their parents' corridor banter, and so prolonged, that I feared finding Shinto conversationally relieved of his hind legs. And then he wouldn't be able to walk, and this whole thing would be off, and obviously that would be just awful.

Five

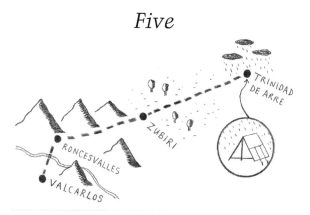

Of the 61,000 pilgrims who completed the camino in 2001, just over a third were non-Spaniards: Americans, Canadians, Germans, French, Brits, Brazilians. Most walked, a fifth did it on bikes; 170 arrived in Santiago astride or beside some sort of equine beast. Almost two-thirds of those who set off gave their faith as Roman Catholic, but fewer than half claimed 'religious motives'; the majority talked of 'cultural' inspiration, though this box could have been ticked by anyone from art historians to those emotionally on the run – jilted lovers, burnt-out executives, white-collar criminals. The tradition of medieval pilgrims sentenced to walk to Santiago in lieu of time behind bars lives on, in a scheme that offers Belgian delinquents the choice between pilgrimage and prison (in 1999, twenty-eight of them opted for the big walk over the big house). An extreme journey, appropriately inspired by extreme circumstances.

Propped up in bed as my fellow guests exchanged decibels, I'd read of big Spaniards bursting into unexplained tears in their sleeping bags, of 'serial pilgrims' who did the camino again and again, of esoteric initiation and abrupt conversions to Catholicism. 'I realised that what I had unleashed within myself while walking could no longer be contained by what had been a stable relationship,' soliloquised an American pilgrim. 'To the shock of all who knew me, I ended my marriage.' All this was hardly helping, and not just because of a donkey-owner's phobic response to the phrase 'stable relationship'.

'Don't come back all funny,' Birna had said, seeing me off at the airport. 'You know: saying grace at dinner and stuff.' I'd laughed then, but who knew what life-messing insights this mobile therapist's couch might extract from me? Even the enduro freaks elevated what I'd thought of as a no-nonsense power walk to 'an odyssey fuelled by pride, guts and stubbornness'.

With saddle and belongings piled up around me and the smell of breakfast coming under the door, I opened a random book in search of final inspiration. 'Their faces registered a combination of joy, tears, disappointment and fatigue,' wrote that aforementioned Californian anthropologist on page one of *Pilgrim Stories*, describing arrival in Santiago in words I could only ever imagine applying to an epic penalty shoot-out or premature ejaculation. In very many more ways than one, I had a long way to go.

'Santiago good!' said the hotelier, slapping me on the back rather too hard as he poured out my third coffee. 'And children happy!' He beckoned me to the window, and we watched the kids who'd been making all the nocturnal racket prancing gleefully around a snout-down, grazing Shinto. What a lovely place for a one-donk sanctuary, I thought: how much better for both of us that he stay right here. But then the owner raised his eyebrows, apologetically moulding the features beneath as he morphed into the reluctant harbinger of bad news. 'Ah . . .' he murmured hesitantly, pointing at the field and then pinching his wrinkled nose. I nodded, drained my coffee and set off outside. It was all over the sandpit. A minute later, as the Internet translation of French donkey hygiene tips had advised, there I was, using two cardboards by way of spoons.

The children gathered to watch as I flicked crap into the nettles with procrastinatory thoroughness. The hotelier had primed them, and I smiled bravely as they fired out the nouns

I would soon become accustomed to hearing muttered around me: *inglés, burro, peregrino*. English, donkey, pilgrim. '¿A Santiago?' enquired a pigtailed ten-year-old, who after my wan nod of confirmation followed up with '¡Que sacrificio!' Fearsomely ominous words, the valediction to a suicide bomber, but uttered in a tone that suggested 'sacrificio' might be Basque for 'twat'.

With an extended internal sigh I laid out saddle and luggage in the dewy grass. Shinto grazed on. He hadn't even acknowledged me yet. How desperate, how ludicrous this all was, like being pushed behind the wheel of a double-decker after half a lesson in a Mini Cooper. Wondering why I had to have an audience on the first morning, I filled the palm of my hand with supermarket rock-salt and lowered it to Shinto's head. 'Look, I know this is the hand that feeds you,' I began, but then he jerked up, snorted half the contents into the grass, then licked the rest from my flesh in three fat-tongued rasps.

Well! The children aahed, and I nearly joined them. And it got better. I saddled and bagged him in ten minutes, and managed to clean out his hoofs, crap flakes and all, almost as if I knew what I was doing. I untied and coiled the night rope and clipped on the dog-chain attachment that fastened the walking lead to his head collar. I couldn't understand it: nothing bad was happening. The *patron* rushed out and gave me a tin of pâté. The children patted Shinto's flanks farewell. There was a pitch-roofed chalet just above us and from each of its open windows waved at least one pair of hands. Returning the gesture to all I launched into a stride and Shinto clattered obediently on to the concrete path. Make way for the ass-meister! Let the pilgrimage commence!

We wound down the curves to the main road: Saturday morning, and almost no traffic. I took my place at Shinto's shoulder – correct positioning for road travel – and with something approaching aplomb off we marched, one man and his donk. With my senses emerging from panic stations to resume their normal duties, I could now appreciate the chilled and dewy morning's development into a fully-fledged azure-heavened

Pyrenean scorcher. Valcarlos was where Charlemagne's rear-guard had been ambushed and slaughtered by Moors (or in fact the first of what's clearly been a long line of Basque guerrillas) in 778, but despite this and the ongoing pilgrim fatalities it was difficult now to imagine it a Valley of Death. Above us on either side soared sheer cliffs and waterfalls, with farms perched impossibly in lofty iridescent pastures. The roadside verge was speckled with yellow alpine poppies. I filled my lungs and stripped down to my T-shirt. Shinto, I thought, looked terrific. The sun glossed and sleeked his mousy coat, his crested mohican of a mane seemed almost lacquered in its upright brilliance. The baggage – red panniers, purple waterproof duffel bags, turquoise tent-bag – lent a vibrant contemporary edge to this warmly nostalgic scene.

An Italian motor home passed with a cheery if alarming toot; Shinto held his ground benignly. And I saw my first pilgrims: three male cyclists, all in late middle years, each sporting a pannier-mounted scallop shell so large and prominent that it might have been crowbarred off the sign outside a red-and-yellow petrol station. The first two waved as they overtook, and the third pedalled by with a gutturally North European cry of *'buen camino'*. We are family, I thought, then sang. I got all my pilgrims with me.

My guidebooks had told me the camino branched off the road after 4 kilometres, and I reached the junction in just under an hour: a speed in generous excess of all professional predictions. How was this happening? If I walked through the nights I could be at Santiago in a week. Perhaps with Hanno out of the picture Shinto was a different beast: less jumpy, more consistent. Perhaps the spiritual adrenalin exuded by pilgrims past was seeping up through his hoofs. Perhaps – a theory that gained weight and credence the more I contemplated it – I was just generally very good.

The path was more authentic than the road. It followed a chuckling brook and meandered through an ancient village, where I tilted my triumphant countenance in greeting at a gold-toothed old man wearing a beret the size of a bin lid. At this settlement's conclusion stood a barn with a yellow arrow daubed on its side, pointing right. I wheeled Shinto as directed, and heading into the densely wooded valley felt myself being forged as the newest link in that 1,000-year pilgrim chain.

If I haven't mentioned Shinto's slight hesitation at a drain cover just outside that village, it's because it didn't seem important at the time. In fact I only appreciated its significance, through a brain clotted with ugly, red ganglions of pure rage, when I passed back over it. Three hours later.

There was a bridge, see. Was it a large bridge? Well, no, it wasn't. This was a little wee feller, six foot of slats spanning that same humble brook. When Shinto stopped with his front feet two inches from the first slat, I imagined he wanted to crap or pee or eat or something. Nothing about this bridge warranted distress, and nothing about his manner expressed it; that long face and those unblinking eyes with their coin-slot pupils remained purged of detectable emotion. For perhaps five minutes I waited for him to fulfil any of the aforementioned physical needs, and for five minutes he stood in mute, empty-headed inactivity.

Things happened rather quickly after that, but there were a lot of these things, and once they all added up I'd been there for almost an hour and a half. I got hold of the rope, advanced to the middle of the bridge and clucked and beckoned. I laid a trail of succulent grasses across the bridge. Hypothesising – correctly but belatedly – that its slatted surface, distantly evocative of a cattle grid, might be to blame, I laid my beach mat and anorak over it. I walked Shinto round in a figure of eight and returned. I gave him a tentative little shove in the back, then a matching tug from the front. To demonstrate its stout resilience I danced upon the bridge, with grace, with purpose, and finally with visceral, plank-stamping abandon, accompanying myself with throat-shredding hoedown shrieks that filled the gorge and bounced away off its wet slate battlements. Moulding that sound into a football-terrace remix of Hanno's galvanising croon I barged repeatedly at Shinto's rear, then staggered to the front and heaved and hauled on the rope until my palms screamed and I was almost horizontal.

My legs gave out before my lungs, and for some time I slumped against the bridge's wooden rail rasping terribleness at the tree-shaded heavens, compound epithets that last made sense in a West London playground during the mid-1970s. It would have helped, somehow, if Shitto here – don't say you didn't see that coming – had in any way or at any point resembled a beast confronting his most elemental terror, rather than, say, being shown a photograph of a bus shelter. The animal before me was not an obvious object for sympathy.

Finally, slick of face and dry of mouth, I sat down on the bridge to wait. Pilgrims would come, I decided, and when they did I'd enlist them to bundle this infuriating animal forcibly across, just as we'd done to get him into the horse trailer. But – and I still don't understand how this happened – they didn't come. Nobody came. At the back of my mind, behind the mighty massed ranks of fury and frustration, piped a tiny voice of forsaken timidity: I began to understand this dark valley's popularity with pilgrim-mugging brigands throughout the camino's medieval pomp.

For nearly an hour I sat there, on a rock already warmed by foliage-filtered sun. Shinto raised his tail and extruded a large bunch of khaki briquettes; after twenty minutes they had hardened brown. Wondering if this was better than watching paint dry, I began to twitch and giggle like Inspector Clouseau's boss, then on some mystery impulse whipped out the Dictaphone, rewound it to the relevant section and held it up behind Shinto's ears. With the loudness turned up to max I hit 'play', and at surprising volume Hanno's 'Eeeeeuuuwwww' rang out. Shinto's ears sprang back and his front legs tonked loudly on to the first plank; if I'd expected this procedure to work, rather than merely unsettle him for purposes of vindictive entertainment, I might have been able to press home the advantage with a well-placed shoulder charge. But I didn't, and in half a second he'd not only whipped his hoofs off the bridge but retreated 20 yards back down the valley path. Even as I rewound for a repeat I knew I'd missed my chance. And then, looking back to the bridge, I noticed that not much further upstream lay another: if I did somehow get him over the first, we might easily end up marooned between the two. Stranded until a helicopter lowered a cargo net down through the tree-tops.

I walked back towards the village, hissing abuse at Shinto and trying not to acknowledge the starkly awful implications of what had just happened. At least here I had the option of returning to the main road and following its bridgeless progress to Roncesvalles, but there would be times when there would be no such option, when the camino ploughed its lonely furrow up hill and down dale and over the bodies of water that generally divided the two. When I went past the old man with the big beret again, he returned my paper-thin smile with a look of lugubrious empathy. Donkeys – can't live with 'em, can't live without 'em. Except that I can, and in fact had for thirty-eight carefree years.

Out of the trees and back on the road it was hot, and we weren't doing 4 kilometres per hour any more. Tim and Shinto's Excellent Adventure had just become their Bogus Journey. For solace I could only remind myself that 20 per cent of the pilgrims who set out from St Jean never make it to Santiago, and that it was better to fuck up in the first mile than the last. A *peloton* of local club cyclists swished past with a volley of spirited hee-haws. More pilgrim pedallers – Dutch, German, American: 'Wow, you going to Santiago with *that?*' A French car passed and pulled over up the road; the elderly husband got out to pee into the pine trees and was still doing so as his wife questioned me through her open window. Where had I bought him, how much had he cost, what did he eat, who would take him off my hands at Santiago, why was I doing this? I answered the first three to the best of my abilities and shrugged over the remainder. '*Eh, mon brave,*' said her husband, slapping Shinto's nearside haunch with an assured familiarity I could only dream of affecting. '*Voilà.*' He leant in through the window and emerged with the knob end of a stout baguette. As Shinto snaffled it up from his open palm I wondered if I should have asked him to wash his hands.

Yellow arrows leading off to the left indicated further opportunities to rejoin the camino proper, but the sound of rushing water below meant I was never tempted. Instead, as the road headed sinuously heavenward, I stayed on the hot tarmac, gradually slotting events into perspective. It was our first day: if I was nervous, so was he. Ten hours in a horse trailer was hardly ideal preparation. And in a way, it was quite sweet – we'd had our first argument. After all, I'm . . . oh Jesus oh no oh buttocking tit-ends I'm being pulled at immense speed into the middle of the road and onwards and upwards and now he's rearing up like a bronco and the rope is burning through my hands and there's luggage all over the asphalt and thank fuck nothing's coming or we'd both now be dead and I've got him back to the side and he's stopped but all the skin has been shredded off the base of my fingers. Oh my great God. Oh God. Oh.

For some time I stood panting in the gravelly roadside weeds, arms extended, palms up, raw flesh pulsing at the sun. Hanno had warned me of the overdeveloped sensitivity of a donkey's peripheral vision, how even a tiny and innocuous rearward swish or flash could trigger a panicked stampede. I turned round and surveyed my shedded load: 50 yards downhill, beyond the ejected bowl and panniers, lay the beach mat. I hadn't even noticed it working loose and falling, but Shinto dramatically had. Yet now this under-brained wazzock stood mildly before me, aware that he was suddenly in a different place but no more than slightly curious as to the apparently reflex response that had brought him there. Donkey see, donkey do.

Hands swaddled in elasticated support bandage, I heaved the luggage over a roadside gate, opened it and elbowed Shinto into the field beyond. I should let him graze and rest for at least two hours at lunch-time, Hanno had said, and though such a break would soon seem tediously unthinkable, on that day it wasn't nearly enough. Only 10 kilometres covered and already I had faced ruthless examination as pilgrim, man and arse.

I constructed and ate salami sandwiches with raw materials acquired in St Jean; I lay down in the cool, high, buttercupped grass; I slept. Shinto was lashed to an oak tree with a clumsily over-engineered knot the size of a bunched fist, and when I woke up he was lying down too. We looked at each other and I held up a bandaged hand in mollification. 'Let's kind of start again,' I said. 'Let's pretend we're just setting out.' And with a roll and a complex levering of legs, Shinto jumped to his feet. His ears sprang forward and his nostrils flared with eager resolve. Let's do it, I thought, then said. Shinto held my gaze, and as I walked purposefully towards him that great flanged cock popped out of its sheath and arched lazily down to his knee.

Whatever the complexities of our personal relationship, that afternoon Shinto and I began to forge a professional understanding. The early pace had evidently been overambitious, and slowing to about 3.5 kilometres per hour he settled into a rhythm. I stood by Shinto's shoulder and talked to him – I'd been told that donkeys thrived on vocal company – and when that earned me an alarmed glance from a cyclo-pilgrim whose approach I hadn't detected, I sang to him.

The trees thinned as we rose, depriving us of shade. Sweat was beginning to blot through to the outside of Shinto's saddle blanket: I filled the washing-up bowl from a roadside culvert, and watched in mild awe as he mechanically siphoned up its contents, 10 litres ingested in half a minute without a single slurp. Two dogs guarding some roadside hovel strained against their chains at Shinto's approach and let forth a furious volley of slavering barks. Raised on a farm alongside two vast canines, Shinto was majestically dismissive of this performance, and when as we passed he angled a bored glance at them they bolted off in silent terror. Dogs were a perennial camino blight – some guides rank pilgrim villages in terms of canine threat – but it was now clear that with Shinto at my side they would cause me no discomfort. Good man, Shints. I think I may have patted his neck.

And his good work was not done for the day. As we neared

the summit I spotted my first fellow pedestrian, a woman of middle years standing by the road, a wits-end expression on her moist red face. Her name was Petronella, she was Dutch, and she'd had enough. Those were tears mingled in with the sweat; her rucksack was too heavy and the gradient too steep. I propped an elbow on the saddle and caressed my stubble in manly rumination. 'Well,' I said, in a cocksure drawl that suggested the next words might be 'little lady', 'I think we might just be able to help you out there.'

Shinto seemed to enjoy the additional company, if not the additional luggage. He laboured audibly up to the pass summit at Ibaneta, then having crested it surrendered himself to gravity for a memorably capricious descent. It was like that circus train in *Dumbo* huffing 'I think I can, I think I can' up hills, and 'I thought I could, I thought I could' as he barrelled down the other side. One moment I was squinting at a plaque marking the proximate last stand of Charlemagne's rear guardsman Roland, and the next my head was being whiplashed back as the body beneath plummeted off down the other side of the Pyrenees. In minutes the incongruous corrugated-iron tin roofs of Roncesvalles were bouncing up and down in my unsteady field of vision, wobblingly soundtracked by a peal from the bells that had for nearly 1,000 years guided fog-bound pilgrims down to sanctuary. The road was suddenly dense with parked cars and amblers – I hadn't bargained on weekending tourists – and somehow, via the equine equivalent of a handbrake stop turn, I brought Shinto to heel with a desperate, shark-fisherman's yank back on the rope. '*Burro!*' piped a child's voice.

We'd dropped Petronella on the descent and when she arrived Shinto and I were fighting our way through the compact zooms of the day-trip paparazzi. Some gasped, some gawped; many more just pointed, their faces split with mirth. In the land of Don Quixote and souvenir raffia quadrupeds I had not anticipated such incredulity. 'It's like he is a celebrity,' said Petronella. Yes, I thought: a fat, nude celebrity.

But Roncesvalles is above such things, and when the tourists started to filter away – it was already gone 6.00 – I found myself beguiled by its age-worn, ecclesiastical majesty. No denying the magnificence of the setting: all that towering churchness counterpointed by those spring-greened lawns called to mind the illustration of Salisbury Cathedral in one of my Ladybird books, a childhood image so rousingly iconic that I had once (but only once) aspired to the priesthood. From the twelfth century this was the camino proper's grandly proportioned front door, offering a physically and spiritually nourishing send-off to pioneering pilgrims, and soon to the millions who followed in their wake. These, remember, were people who'd typically never left the village they'd been born in; walking towards Spain they'd often have stood, grubby jaws sagging, before religious structures of a scale and grandeur almost beyond imagination, structures that radiated divine importance, and now they were staying in one. After a month or more of grimly soiled flop-houses, this was a five-star for free: along with bed and board, they threw in a foot wash and a beard trim. There were doctors and cobblers at Roncesvalles, and rare and succulent fruits served by damsels of fabled virtue and beauty.

None of these facilities came cheap, but as is often the case with internationally sponsored political propaganda, money was no object. Wealthy benefactors queued up to subsidise and donate: as well as underpinning a bulwark against the Moors, this was all sin-deductible. And to foster the cult of Roland – improbably statured martyr to the anti-Moor cause, and so a kind of warm-up act for St Jim – the chapels were full of inspirational relics: his mace and battle horn, along with bits of over thirty saints and the almost obligatory thorn from Jesus's crucifixion crown.

No biblical rationale underpinned the grisly veneration of bleached bones, a practice so distressingly pagan that even the Romans were repulsed, yet it's difficult to understate the role of religious relics in abetting the rise of Christianity. Saints leapfrogged purgatory, and up in heaven they had the ear of God; merely by standing near even their tiniest mortal remainder therefore placed one in direct touch with the divine. This

63

starkly profound leap of faith helped establish many more cities than Santiago: you wouldn't have found Cologne's regional development committee in mourning the day after St Ursula was massacred there along with her 11,000 virgins.

At the second council of Nicaea in 787, the nascent Christian authorities decreed that a church could not be consecrated without its own relic in the crypt. The rapid spread of their religion thereafter encouraged the unsightly dismemberment of existing relics, and the imaginative discovery of new ones. Soon there were two heads of John the Baptist – one as a youth, coughed the authorities, and the other straight off Salome's plate – and the parts to five complete Mary Magdalenes. St James had a body double in Jerusalem, and an octopus-load of limbs bestrewn around Europe.

The gold standard, of course, was anything associated with Jesus himself: fragments of the True Cross were almost ten a groat, and a lot more than 30 pieces of silver turned up in episcopal hands. Regrettably, the existence of anything more valuably corporeal was thwarted by the awkward fact of the Saviour's bodily ascension to paradise. Or so it was first thought. It is impossible not to admire the lateral, out-of-the-box brilliance that inspired the Nappy of Christ, uncritically worshipped throughout Bohemia, or the little statue containing his umbilical cord that still embellishes De Nieuwe Kerk in Amsterdam. And how I'd love to have been there when, with a eureka shriek, some canny monk grasped the crucial implication of the Son of God's Jewish upbringing: of all the shrines in Chartres cathedral, few were more venerated than that of Le Saint Prepuce, home to the Christly foreskin.

Early medieval popes canonised new saints with reckless abandon to meet the burgeoning demand for venerable body parts, but soon even that wasn't enough. A lot of creative thinking went into such extolled marvels as the feather shed from Gabriel's wing in the excitement of the Annunciation; a brazen Canterbury cleric declared the brown pebble in his hand as the leftover clay God chucked out after sculpting Adam. Deft theological gymnastics justified the theft of relics, on the grounds that such potent objects could only be stolen if their saintly owner wished it so. On one level this authorised those tomb-robbing Crusades into the Holy Land; on another, it inspired the Portuguese woman who in 1544 covertly bit off St Francisco Xavier's big toe as she kissed his foot, and the unknown Hungarian who relieved a mummified St Elizabeth of her nipples. Unable to resist the ultimate show-and-tell souvenir, Henry V slipped Le Saint Prepuce in his pocket on the way home from Agincourt. It was subsequently lost – it's tempting to imagine some lady-in-waiting's face light up over the cabinet of curios with an inner cheer of 'Mmmm: Hula Hoops!' – but not to worry: fourteen rival foreskins adorn church crypts around the world.

Housed in gilded, bejewelled shrines, relics were the most sumptuous expression of the Church's phenomenal wealth. Throughout its medieval pomp, the Augustine monastery of Roncesvalles owned land from Scotland to Portugal; it was said that a pilgrim from Germany could walk all the way to Santiago across fields in its possession. The pan-European decline in gullibility heralded by the Renaissance more or less did for the relic industry, and so for an era of dumbfounding ecclesiastical extravagance. In 1630, with the pilgrimage half a millennium past its peak, the monks of Roncesvalles were still welcoming over 25,000 holy travellers a year. Yet when a blizzard tore all the roofs off that winter, they couldn't afford to have them put back on.

Many of today's pilgrimages begin at Roncesvalles, and emotionally mine was one of them. Leading Shinto through the gates and up to the great arched entrance of the Real Colegiata I felt a humbling affinity with the millions who had walked in before, through snow or fog or the hazeless heat of a thousand mountain summers. Before I'd just been on a silly walk, but now here I was at the ministry.

I lashed my steed to a doorside column just inside the main porch, then walked through the adjacent entrance into a cavernous hall. Here was pilgrim reception, where you paid up front for your bed and an evening meal (13 euros all in, I noted with an inner beam) and procured the vital *credencial*, the pilgrim's passport that gave access to the seventy-odd Church- or council-run hostels along the way, the *refugios*, and once stamped at each would procure a compostela – the ecclesiastical certificate awarded to pilgrims at Santiago. The smiling young lady responsible for their dispensation was evidently no Madame Debril, her fearsome (though now deceased) equivalent at St Jean, a woman known to turn away pilgrims on a vindictive whim. 'I see you are with *burro*,' she said, smiling at Shinto's distant hindquarters as she transcribed my dictated details into the concertina-folded document. 'Not many *peregrinos* with *burro*. Now . . . your reason for *pere-grenación*?' She christened my *credencial* with a magnificent Latin-bordered stamp fulsomely decorated with croziers and fleurs-de-lys, then handed me a list with tickable boxes: religious, spiritual, cultural, sporting. 'Can I put more than one?' I asked, my pen hovering between the middle two. 'Pliz of course,' she replied, just as a heavy, moist slap echoed ominously up from the doorway. I peeked over my shoulder to see a tail being lowered, ticked the first box and with a forestalling display of effusive thanks swept up my *credencial* and strode out.

A rarity he might be, but at Roncesvalles Shinto was welcomed like an old friend – a very old friend, with fearful incontinence. 'No, no – *de nada*,' smiled an aged monastic functionary, waving a dismissive hand as I fidgeted unenthusiastically around those steaming devil-pebbles. At his beckoning behest I followed him back through the gates and past a dourly four-square ecclesiastical edifice, which by the number of sandaled red-faces slumped listlessly by its entrance I took to be the *refugio*. At its rear was a field, and beside the field was a patch of uncultivated tussocks. '*Aquí*,' beamed my guide, and I beamed back and thanked him as best I could. The changing of the ropes, the finding of the tree, the knot, the salt, the hoofs, the water: as I blundered and fussed about until my shadow stretched taller than Roland's, I could only hope that all this would soon be routine.

But no amount of practice would ever enable me to cart all my belongings to and from the donkey in one journey, particularly when enhanced by a big fat bag full of Holland. Three trips it took to ferry Shinto's burden to the hallway of the *refugio*. Backpack pilgrims were still arriving and gawped in bemusement as they stepped around my heap of stuff: What's he *got* in there? In fact, what *did* I have in there?

Stout walking boots, tent, can-opener, plastic poncho – packing for a pilgrimage is in many ways like packing for a normal journey, normal at least for people who've never vomited up chunks of raw shame in the changing room at Eastern Mountain Sports (EMS). But in many ways it isn't: what other holiday packing list would include stones?

Pilgrims have always carried at least a few pebbles along with them, for some or all of the journey. Once there was a practical purpose: the cathedral at Santiago is held together with cement made from limestone lugged over the mountains in pilgrims' pockets. Today the burden is more symbolic – you drop off stones at cairns along the way in memory of loved ones, or take them all the way from home to signify the weight of accumulated internal sins. In the throes of another alcoholic addition to my sin-pile, on my last night at home I'd found myself melodramatically inspired.

Assessing one's life in terms of badnesses committed before a tableful of geological shrapnel is an experience I am unlikely to forget – not something I'd be saying had I opened that second bottle of red. In the end, of course, common sense distilled those transgressions into specimen charges. Two quartz pebbles: a couple of hangovers' worth. A slightly larger flint, perhaps somewhere between covetousness and pretending to be Julian Lennon to those Korean exchange students. All three to double up as my three children, whose beachcombed rockery I was currently looting, and a fourth – largest of all, a pitted ovoid of wave-worn house brick – in craven recognition of the fact that I wasn't actually going to carry any of these stones myself. What of it? At least I was doing the walking – more than you can say for all those medieval aristos who bunked off purgatory, with the Church's full blessing, by paying a proxy pilgrim to do the legwork on their behalf. (Having said that, look under all the caravans in the French Pyrenees and you might just find yourself an eroded brick.)

I dragged and kicked my bags through the *refugio* entrance and was instantly dumbstruck. Before me, around me, above me, soared and stretched a cavernous, windowless Romanesque chamber, its gloomily uplit rafters as distant as a cathedral's, the sort of edifice you might expect to find littered with corroded weaponry and the cobwebbed skeletons of dwarfish warriors. And instead there were a hundred barrack-room bunk-beds and the echoing, muttered contemplations of sunburnt ramblers, sharing their wonderment at one of Europe's most compellingly peculiar accommodation experiences. In an only slightly different way, I was as awed as any medieval forebear.

With my mouth charmlessly slackened in wonder I piled half my stuff on one of the last remaining unclaimed bunks – a top one, of course – and heaved all the rest under a huge glass-cased model of the monastery that presided arrestingly over the stairs down to the bathrooms. I'd heard and read almost universally wretched things about *refugio* facilities, and was consequently taken aback to find myself in the changing rooms of a newly completed Scandinavian leisure centre. It was almost a relief when I hit the press-button shower tap and felt my scalp shrivel beneath a mighty and relentless frozen torrent.

This experience, perhaps coupled with the belated onset of malnourished, sunstroked fatigue, seemed to convince parts of my brain that I had died, because the events that immediately followed are imbued with a strangely ethereal quality. I attended the pilgrim mass in the Real Colegiata, but can only recall being vacantly transfixed by some Reynolds Wrapped Madonna above the altar.

'Ssshhh,' hissed a voice beside me, 'you're humming.'

'Sorry,' I hummed.

A minute later an elbow in the kidney jerked me to attention. 'And now you're swaying.'

All rather a shame, as I learnt later that during my trance the presiding padre had rounded things off with a personal blessing to every new pilgrim by nationality. Then it was all out – there must have been over 100 of us – and into the café restaurant for our pilgrim supper, a no-choice three-courser of thin soup, fat stew and yoghurt, doled out by the meaty forearms of a kitchen mama who gave all the men double portions.

It was four to a table, and I shared mine with Petronella, a silver-haired Californian art historian by the name of Thomas and a shy smiler who didn't speak English and so was rather unkindly ignored. Male or female? I can't even remember. This was my debut tête-à-tête with fellow pilgrims, and I didn't want it descending into a stilted exchange of gesture-heavy pleasantries. No matter how funny I felt – and with rather more than my share of our table's complimentary bottle of red inside me it had just got a lot funnier – I was determined to talk pilgrim.

Thomas was here for the ecclesiastical art stuff, and though he claimed to have ticked only the culture box, the fact that he'd been planning this for ten years suggested there was something else he didn't want to tell us. Petronella was more forthcoming. My mountain-top discourse with her had been limited to donkey-loading practicalities, but now she gently outlined the inner journey that had led her here. The usual mid-life doubts – career, family, friendships – had coagulated malignantly into what she called a burn-out and what I suppose we'd call a breakdown. Off sick and in therapy for months, she now wanted to think things through and hopefully come to some conclusions. (How very Dutch of her to work for a wind-turbine manufacturer, and how very Dutch of them to grant paid leave for a lengthy spiritual pilgrimage.) But that clearly wasn't the whole story.

'Did you read this book by Shirley MacLaine?'

'Yes,' I said, in an unconventional tone that discouraged expansion upon this theme, but at least forestalled enquiries into my own motivation. In the state I was in I might have said anything. I might have said 'Eeeeeuuuwwww!'

The food fixed my head just before we were eased out to make way for the tourist diners. At 9.30 it wasn't yet dark, but the near stampede towards the *refugio* reminded me that in half an hour its doors would be locked and its lights extinguished. And so at ten to ten, after a quick jog round the back to verify that Shinto wasn't loose or on fire or anything, there I was on my back staring up at the five distant roof arches in the painterly gloom of those uplighters. At the end of my bed a moon-faced man was having ointment slapped into his lushly hirsute back by a youth I dearly hoped was a relative, and from the bunk below and almost every other echoed the first tentative bunk creaks and sinus snuffles. I half-smothered an epic sigh, largely one of fatigued contentment: it was good to be here with all these people, to rediscover the skill of communal coexistence in a trust-nobody age of social exclusion, to be living how man had lived for all but a tiny fraction of his time on earth. Then the lights clicked off, and after a single cataclysmic sneeze about ten beds down, the first steady snores rumbled into life.

Shirley MacLaine had a dream at Roncesvalles, and so did I. Hers was a kaleidoscopic montage involving every man she had ever known. Mine was a sparser affair involving every donkey salesman I had ever known. Her men described the baggage they had brought into the relationship. Mine kept making me tie knots round the red-hot leg of a wood-burning stove.

Harsh and mocking dreamland laughter segued seamlessly into a real-world phlegmy hack: I slowly opened an eye and beheld the hairy-backed man expectorating into the sleeve of his T-shirt. Almost everyone had left, and those that hadn't were about to, cramming belongings into backpacks. This was no furtive, apologetic rustling; on the sack-stuffing scale of reckless intensity here were elves up against the clock on Christmas Eve. I held my watch up to my face, and as its digits loomed into focus understood that I would be spending the weeks ahead in the company of a great many truly appalling bastards. It was ten to six.

I glowered out into the after-dawn, dragging half-packed panniers behind me, and tramped round to the field, still very sorry to be awake and with my big toes belatedly registering blisters. Shinto saw me before I saw him, and issued the first proper noise I'd heard him make: a stunted, preliminary little honk, more bleat than bray. He did it again as I walked up to him, and this close I was able to rule out the emotion behind the noise as one of welcome or friendship. This was the sound of neat despair. He turned those coin-slot pupils towards me and for once his expression spoke. Cockholes, it said. Not *you* again.

Still, my knot had held fast overnight, the sky was blue and today I'd have back-up. Petronella had been one of the last to wake, and seeing fresh tears well up in her eyes as she contemplated her rucksack I proposed a bargain of mutual benefit: Shinto lugs your stuff, and you help load him up and chase him down and . . . just kind of make me less scared of this colossal being.

Her weeping habit made this a gamble, I accept, but it paid off immediately. With me leading Shinto from the front and Petronella at his rear, progress was arrestingly rapid. She had a pair of metal-tipped walking poles, and every time they tapped or scraped the path Shinto's ears would flick back and off he'd go in a slightly unsettled jog that ate up those first kilometres. Everyone else had long gone by the time we turned away from monastery and mountains and entered a long grove carpeted by the *ronces* – brambles – that I've just realised gave the monastery its name, but soon we were reeling the blister-hobbled stragglers in.

We never caught them, though, because at Burguete, the first village, the camino turned between two houses, rounded a barn and headed merrily across a lazily broad river by means of the Golden Gate of all slatted bridges. Ernest Hemingway had often fished in this river, and if he'd been here, and Petronella had been a man, and so had I, we might have bullied Shinto across. As it was, after a brief but intense pull-me-pull-you session I cut our losses and with surprising equanimity – was the pilgrimage

71

lengthening my fuse already? – led him back to the road. And in fact St Jim was riding shotgun with us, pulling the N135 taut into a corner-cutting short cut, then propelling Shinto up it with a blast of Navarrese wind that flipped that washing-up bowl over his saddle and consequently sparked off another blind panic. I was rather pleased at how I managed to marshal this into a semi-controlled gallop, but when after a breathless half-kilometre I looked behind, there was Petronella trotting laboriously along with her cheeks moistened once more by tears, this time of unbridled merriment.

The pilgrims thus overhauled started catching us up after the camino crossed back over our road at the next town. In common with many settlements along the route, Aurizberri had been founded purely to cater for pilgrims, or in fact in this particular case to offer them refuge from muggers who plagued the Pyrenean foothills. Nearly 800 years on, it was still defined by the camino: iron scallop shells set into railings, terracotta ones on pots, stained-glass ones in the church window.

In the white heat of a brazen sun we set off across the alpine pastures: despite that descent to Roncesvalles it was still over 2,500 feet. A herd of shaggy-footed horses clumped down a hill to challenge Shinto to an over-the-fence stare-out, and won. My nascent blister began to throb. The pilgrims we'd outflanked were now streaming past in twos and threes: lipsticked Frenchwomen mincing along in suede trainers, a trio of hearty German lasses, a tiny bald Englishman dwarfed by his backpack and his wife. All greeted us with an already familiar roster of donkey questions – what does he eat? Where does he sleep? What are you going to do with him in Santiago? – before passing on up the sun-dried ruts with a wave and a *'buen camino'*.

'What *are* you going to do with him in Santiago?' Petronella asked, and I reprised an enormous shrug: I'd cross that bridge when I came to it. Though as Shinto obviously wouldn't, we'd never make it there anyway.

It was really very hot – hot enough for me to put my head under every fountain spout we passed – and having lunched alongside us in a steeply pitched field, Shinto lay down in the shade. That's nice, I thought, and was still thinking so when the time came to leave. 'Let's do it, Shints,' I said, clapping my hands before stooping to raise the saddle with a weary huff. I could understand why Hanno had urged me to unpack and unsaddle Shinto every lunch-time, but as long as the sum of my sloth, fear and incompetence remained greater than or equal to concern for his welfare I wouldn't enjoy the procedure.

He didn't want to do it, of course. He didn't want to do anything. He angled his lazily defiant countenance up at me and then let it fall gently back to the cool meadow grass, grunting in sumptuous repose. It took fifteen minutes of ratcheting foolishness to get that animal to his feet, a success eventually achieved by charging towards him banging that big bowl above my head like a tambourine. If I detailed Petronella's physical response to this spectacle I'd probably have to change her name.

As would typically be the case, the ruminative lunch break put us right at the back of the pack. It wasn't just that we weren't seeing pilgrims – we weren't seeing anyone. At the end of another slightly fly-blown village – most of the camino settlements are strung out along the road, enabling me to say 'ribbon development' for the first time since tenth-grade geography – two boys were idly punting a football at a towering wall of green concrete. I didn't yet know that this was the end flank of a pelota court, or indeed what pelota was, but I did know this: those two boys were the first non-pilgrim, non-motorist humans I'd seen since Roncesvalles. Surely this was taking Sunday too far.

Up an improbably angled ridge of flaking slate, past a 10-foot granite block claiming to record the stride length of Roland, around the desolate remnants of a long-abandoned *refugio*. A sweeping, panoramic glimpse of the green-pined hillocks beneath and around and the vast blue heavens above, then the foliage closed around us and Shinto found something new to scare him to a standstill: dappled shadows on the path. It was interesting, though, to see how quickly he voted these the

73

lesser of two evils, when approached from the rear by the rival evil of that loud man with his bowl. Thus it was that we blundered at some speed through the trees, down a crumbling escarpment and, after eight hours on the road and a further two in the field, up and across the narrow, humpbacked medieval bridge at Zubiri.

It was a splendid little bridge, and not just because Shinto crossed it. A lot of the camino has been rerouted through rebuilt towns and relaid around redrawn fields, but here I knew my feet were in the right place. A reminder of who I was supposed to be following, what I was supposed to be doing, that this wasn't just an overambitious hike. Leading Shinto up its steeply pitched cobbles I accepted that thus far I'd barely paused to consider the pilgrimage's history and legacy. It had been easier, for the sake of both mind and body, to dismantle the 1,000 years behind and the 500 miles ahead into day-to-day logistics, the homespun routine of snorers and lunch-time and laundry.

And so I tied Shinto up to a shrublet that sprang from a wall at the bridge's apex, and got the books out, and found that if I led him down into the river below – hah! – and then walked him three times round the bridge's central pillar – hah! hah! hah! – by ancient tradition he would thenceforth be protected from rabies. The vaccination came at a price, though, because reading on I discovered that for centuries the locals ran a protection racket here, letting through pilgrims who agreed to pay a 'toll', and hurting – or indeed killing – those who didn't. 'Anyone who refuses gets brutally treated,' wrote Dominic Laffi, a priest from Bologna who walked to Santiago in 1670. 'They will break open our heads with their sticks and sometimes get rid of people by making the river their grave.'

Beyond the bridge the path hit the N135, astride which Zubiri splayed endlessly into a pavement-hugging collection of shops and apartment buildings, slathered up to their shuttered windows with trunk-road traffic filth. In the middle of this forlorn main drag lay the *refugio*, a Romanian youth hostel of a construction, with concrete cancer and a forecourt waist-high in weeds where dozens of pilgrims were already hanging up their washed socks. Here I left a rather broiled Petronella, before leading Shinto off in search of a friendly field, a search that within minutes – all right, seventy-five minutes – had a man called Roberto shouting down at me from a second-floor balcony.

Maybe it was all that stuff I'd just read about Zubiri's proud tradition of pilgrim-directed robbery with violence, but I didn't feel entirely happy as Roberto, a small man with the obligatory cig in his teeth, beckoned Shinto and me into a nettled enclosure round the back of a low-rise block. Roberto himself seemed a decent sort, at least until he offered to mind my bags for 10 euros, but what of his unseen neighbours? Or indeed of any itinerant Romany horse thieves of the type Hanno had warned me about? The *refugio* lay at least half a kilometre distant, as I came to appreciate whilst dragging and pushing and shouldering any conceivably thievable luggage (including the saddle, which some German pilgrim had told me was worth more than the donkey) back up the road under a sun that seemed to have forgotten it was gone seven.

This was a two-stage process, though it wasn't until the end of the sweaty, stumbling second that I wondered why I hadn't thought to unload Shinto outside the *refugio*, or indeed to enquire whether he could have been accommodated in that weeded forecourt. But in a way it didn't matter, because – as I gathered from the apologetic faces of the pilgrims who looked up from their blisters as I passed them on the porch steps – there was no longer a bed for me. The scrawled note stuck through the rusted door bars had the same effect on me as a slatted bridge on Shinto. '*Completo*' it read. Like him I tried to make it disappear by staring at it, and when this didn't work, like him I backed away in blank horror.

Rather more interestingly than it may have seemed at the time, finding a single room for a man proved a greater challenge than finding a single field for a donkey. Walking with Shinto, and vocabbed up by my pocket dictionary, I merely had to approach someone and with an appropriately searching expression say, '*Campo?*' (field). Somehow '*Cama?*' (bed) lacked that unequivocal appeal – particularly, I have to say, amongst Zubiri's female population. By the time I found myself a room in a glorified motel, I didn't care that it cost 49 euros. But after I'd finished relocating my belongings, and returned to pick out Shinto's feet, I did care that it was right down the other end of town.

I'd seen my first Spanish cloud just before sunset, and the dripping swish of passing vehicles that dawn brought indicated it now had company. I parted the net curtains with a face like Captain Scott peering at a blizzard-blurred Norwegian flag: the moss-clotted surface of the motel pool was alive with brutal rain. It was good that I'd been able to do my laundry in an ensuite bathroom, but it was bad that I'd draped it on my window sill to dry. I thought of my fellow pilgrims, so trim and neat when they'd set off the morning before. And then I thought of Shinto.

He'd bleated wanly when I'd left him for the last time, and my sleep had once more been punctuated by associated anxiety dreams: donkeys bolting across a busy dual carriageway, or being taunted by youths on mopeds, or just running, running, running, with me in forlorn pursuit. Most memorable – so much so that I had it again the night after – was the one where a dicky-bowed waiter staggered into the dining room of some crusty old hotel and dropped untidily to his knees at the table I was sharing with Hanno, Marie-Christine and – yes – Anjelica Huston. 'You!' he rasped, pointing shakily at me with one hand and with the other tearing open his starched shirt to reveal a torso angrily imprinted with hoof-shaped lesions.

The bar where I'd ingested a rewardingly calorific dinner was now exclusively populated by soldiers; indeed, as I noted carrying my croissant back to the table, the entire building was surrounded by them. There were two right outside the window, sheltered by the canopy, toting enormous automatic weapons with an air of hair-trigger intent. 'Gotta watch their backs,' muttered the stocky young chap as he laid down my coffee. He'd served me the previous night: his father was from the Bronx, and after spending the previous decade there he'd returned to his mother's house in Zubiri. He was really big on Tony Blair, and he was also really big, so rather than distance myself from the whole Iraq business – as I would be required to on an almost daily basis in the weeks ahead – I'd found it easier to nod a lot, particularly once he'd insisted on toasting the special relationship with a complimentary jug of rosé. 'Lotta terrorists round here. The Basque guys – ETA, you know?'

I knew. The preponderance of Zs in the town names was one indication, and the graffiti on the bus shelters was another. On my wet way out to Shinto's field I remembered that ETA regularly blew up foreign tourists. And on my wet way back, with a sorrily fur-flattened ass at my side, I remembered that terrorists, in the West Bank at least, had been known to employ donkeys in suicide-bomb attacks.

As Charlemagne and Roland found out – their mistake was to sack Pamplona – it never pays to rile a Basque. Aimery Picaud, you may recall, was careful to exclude them from that treatise on regional bestiality, and imbued his account of their murderous criminality with a degree of awed respect. For the Basques were a race apart, a people so definitively hard that they were feared as mercenaries throughout the ancient world. When the medieval Church began to promote marine flesh as an ardour-cooling anti-aphrodisiac, fearless, reckless Basques trawled oceans as far afield as Iceland and Newfoundland, and were known as the only Mediterranean people blessed with the psycho–physical wherewithal to catch whales. Halfway through his globe-girdling voyage in 1522, Magellan interacted with island natives in the manner later made famous by Captain Cook; it was a Basque sailor, Juan Sebastian de Elcano, who finally docked back in Spain. They were the first Europeans to import tobacco, and so also to dangle its smouldering, paper-rolled product from the lower lip in a menacing fashion.

If you had cannibals to intimidate or a walrus to punch, you asked a Basque; otherwise, you left them well alone. They liked it that way. How else to explain a language that famously predates the Indo-European family from which most normal tongues are descended, a language whose fossilised complexity foiled even Satan's attempts to master it? Francisco Pizarro, Spanish conqueror of Peru, reported that his Basque sailors were able to communicate with the Incas; an official form of written Basque was only agreed in 1960, and the first Basque dictionary was compiled by an Icelandic farmer. Anyway, I feel oddly keen to stress just what a splendid language it is, and the unique excellence of those who speak it.

It was a mixed morning, but not that mixed. Good: the two black-scarfed ladies who tottered happily out of a bakery to pat and pet and in fact be multiply photographed standing alongside Shinto. Bad: watching their faces as he then hosed the pavement with hot piss. Noting that this was worryingly cloudy. Forgetting to get my *credencial* stamped at the motel. Investing long minutes persuading a fearsome Sybil Fawlty behind the desk of one of the hotels who'd turned me away the night before to do it instead. Checking Shinto's feet and seeing his patch of seedy toe spongily degenerated into something unknown but certainly worse. Discovering, at the ragged height of a clattering downpour, that my £32 poncho was really just two groundsheets formerly held together with poppers.

Zubiri was completely de-pilgrimmed by the time I left at 9.00, and beyond it the camino's sticky undulations were decorated with the streaked imprints of boots struggling for purchase. Shinto engaged four-leg drive and tackled the hills stalwartly, though I can't say he enjoyed the thorny branches weighed down by rain to donkey eye level. Tendrils of mountain mist underpinned a sky of hard, cold lead: if we were wet now, we'd soon get wetter.

The path skirted a titanic and beguilingly hideous factory, identified in my rain-crinkled literature as a magnesite plant (and also, somehow pertinently, as the former site of a leper hospital). From within its smut-streaked corrugations issued the disjointed shouts and clunks of man and machine doing whatever it is you do to produce this mystery compound, before enormous trucks drove it away to do whatever it is you do with it when you have.

Just beyond it was a very long staircase cut downwards into the hill, no doubt a welcome relief for the many pilgrims who had been slipping about on the inclines and descents. But not for Shinto. A portmanteau word is one that blends the meaning of two words in one, such as brunch. I inadvertently coined one after twenty-five loud, wet minutes at the top of that staircase. This word was 'donkunt'.

At least the slippery, stairless detour wasn't too far away, and as we gingerly descended I saw unfamiliar pilgrims loping past, heads down, in the rainy distance. These were the vanguard of those ghastly freaks who had left Roncesvalles before dawn: not yet lunch, and I'd been lapped already. I watched dumbfounded as one hopped past on crutches. An authentically pilgrimish sighting, but not one that made me feel any better.

The farmhouses were few and far between, some unglazed and empty, some window boxed and immaculate. All, though, were splendidly regal structures, with great long balconies and coats of arms above the mighty arches of their oaken doors. It was from one of these that a young female farmer emerged, headscarfed against the elements, with a sack of nitrate under one arm and two loaves of old bread under the other. '*Por burro*,' she said, revealing a single huge tooth before thrusting these at Shinto's sorry, soggy maw. He grabbed one and worried it into bite-sized pieces on the muddy doorstep. I thanked her, then pointed at the weeping sky, and at my steam-faced watch, and shrugged in enquiry. '*Tres días*,' came the reply, accompanied with a dourly girding hand on my ponchoed shoulder. I wished I hadn't asked, or understood.

Despite the most obvious disincentive, there were far more locals around than the day before. I encountered a further two just up the lane, a couple of chaps in red overalls emptying wheelbarrows of concrete slurry into . . . oh. Into a huge, camino-spanning hole. The silt-brown brook frothing through either side of this hole suggested a new, solid, donk-friendly bridge in the making, which had I been here twenty-four hours later I'd certainly have been grateful for.

I knew Shinto looked pathetic, his Neanderthal brow guttering the rain down that great, sad head, mud splashed up to his spindly knees. And I was fairly certain I did too, or if not pathetic then at least poignantly foolish, with those two flapping tarpaulins somehow channelling all the water that fell on my head straight into my boots. The men in red surveyed us through eyes slitted against the elements, and understood; the shorter one hopped up towards a gap in the tangled hedgerow and beckoned me to follow.

I have to say that Shinto acquitted himself rather well in the moments that followed. Keeping up with our red friend meant charging blindly through a battery of thorned gorse-stuff, and across two big fields of chocolate Ready Brek, but we made it. We made it right up to where he'd stopped, his palm pointing down between two low bushes, a quietly satisfied my-work-here-is-done smile on his wet, brown face. Nodding happily at him I eased Shinto towards the bushes. A yank back on the rope suggested he saw it first: here was the same stream, unbridged, no wider than a fully laden donkey but excited by the downpour into an unstable pocket torrent. My hands tensed around the rope – show no fear, never hesitate. Embracing Hanno's mantra meant marching directly into the water; the first stride was just up to the ankle, but the second regrettably cleared the top of my left boot. By perhaps two feet.

I felt the rope tense again – no, not here, you silly sod – and then there was a whoop and a shriek and my little man in red, my Super Mario, was charging towards Shinto's rear, windmilling his arms in an erratic frenzy, like a once-a-season goal scorer.

Well, it worked. Shinto splashed in, crashed through and dashed out, pulling the few remaining dry parts of my body through the brown rapids and out across the field below. I shouted a wayward '*gracias*' over my shoulder and after a brief but messy chase sequence managed to get close enough to Shinto to barge him back through a hedgerow and on to what I hoped was the camino.

'Ah,' said a low, wry voice, whose Teutonic inflection confirmed this hope. I looked around wildly, not that hard a task when you've just endured the mud/foliage variant of being tarred and feathered, and there's a rope in your cold hands with a steaming, slathered donkey at the end of it. Propped up against a sheltering tree was a tall, gaunt man in his late forties, with a greying skinhead which, teamed to a private half-smile, imparted an air of mystical inscrutability. 'I have been following your tracks,' he said, lazily, taking a red-eyed drag on a tiny roll-up. He was wearing shorts and a T-shirt, yet remained curiously unbedraggled. 'Oh,' I countered wittily, just as a violent mechanical whirring cranked up in the middle distance. Whether produced by the magnesite men or the Mario Brothers I'm not sure, but it was one of that family of sounds – the machine-gun flap of a lorry awning in the wind, a jarring metallic rasp, anything you might describe as a thrum – which flicked the big red switch in Shinto's head, a switch that could only be flicked off after a long and ragged pursuit.

By the end of this particular one I found myself at a large village, and because I was now feeling bad in most of the traditional ways I lashed Shinto to a sheltered lamp-post and stumbled under the church's portico. Here I ingested the lumpy gel that had only hours ago been fresh bread, changed my socks, and nodded dully at the pilgrims trudging muddily on up the camino or shuffling into the gloomy *refugio* opposite. It was only after an hour that I realised I'd yet to see the German Dalai Lama pass by. He still hadn't appeared as I resaddled Shinto and set off. In fact I never saw him again, but considering events now I accept that isn't the issue. The issue is whether I saw him at all.

That afternoon Shinto began to experiment with on-the-move grazing, another manifestation of my failure to establish dominance over him. I didn't have the authority to stop it, but then I didn't have the heart either: here he was, loose in a walk-thru all-you-can-eat salad bar, halfway up a hillside lushly carpeted with rain-freshened mint, oregano and thyme – a lot of it even looked good to me. But the corn was the worst. I quickly learnt the importance of bracing myself whenever the camino passed alongside a cultivated field of green-eared shoots; sadly, though, I was soon too damp and knackered actually to do so. The rope tautened, and before I could react Shinto was towing me helplessly through the wet crops, like an unseated jockey with his watch-strap snagged round a stirrup. By the time I'd got to my feet and yelled and bullied him back out on to the path he'd have half an EU grain quota hanging out of his mouth.

Pamplona was leaching out towards me, half-finished suburbs covering the opposite side of a valley, many-laned ring roads forcing the camino into piss-puddled underpasses. Up a hill, around a humming substation, and then – after a slight 'Whither?' moment at a yellow arrow eroded to an indecipherable blob – it was over another Romanesque bridge and into the welcoming porch of Trinidad de Arre, a bijou monastery that has been sheltering pilgrims since the thirteenth century and hardly seemed to have been altered in the interim. Staying here was a smart ruse of mine, or rather of the Confraternity of St James, whose little red book had recommended it as a canny alternative to Pamplona, which lay 5 urban kilometres up the road and where you'd never get a bed. I squeezed Shinto into the porch alongside me and rapped on the big door.

Between us we dripped off a reasonable puddle before it was answered, by a small old man with the fuddled, friendly face of Pinocchio's creator. Defying all environmental and physical indicators, this man almost immediately revealed himself as a horrible wanker. '*Completo, completo,*' he tutted and huffed, thrusting at me a flyer from a presumably proximate commercial alternative named the Hostal Obelix, before applying his minimal weight to the great slab of cleated oak. Suddenly, his was a punchable face. A wet pilgrim with a four-footed Jesusmobile at his side, being brusquely refused shelter at a monastery. A sodding monastery! Maybe I should have shaved again and shoved a pillow up my poncho. He didn't stop shaking his head as he finally eased the door closed: not a scrap of floor for my mattress, not a cloistered corner for my ass. No room at the inn.

It was 5.30: I could press on into the Pamplona rush hour in quest for a bed I'd never find, or cut out the middleman and sink to my haunches crying like a girl right here. I was a bent knee away from plan B when the door creaked painfully open again. The cheery fuddled look had gone, replaced by one of truculent resignation and aimed at the leaking heavens. He set off up the road – I now noticed he had slippers on – and with a surge of expectation we followed. The *refugio* entrance was round the back of the monastery, but we passed it and went up into a crest-topping garden with the turbulent river on one side and a matching bypass on the other. 'Here *burro*,' he said sharply, pointing first at a thistle-circled tree stump, then at me. 'You: Hostal Obelix.' He turned on his ill-chosen heels and minced squelchily away.

Traffic slooshed by; Shinto slowly lowered his head and shut down into idle mode. Your move, poncho boy. A baseball cap appeared above a bush, indicating that there was a footpath by the road, and the face that soon appeared beneath it suggested this was frequented by the sort of people you wouldn't want to leave alone with an unattended donkey. Not for the last time I thought of the *Passion for Donkeys* Timothy, blundering earless around a bloodied field. 'All for one, Shints,' I whispered, and started unpacking the tent.

And it wasn't so bad in the end. Contorting myself into the sleeping bag, damp and sagging canvas inches from my nose, I considered my situation on both micro and macro levels. Yes, I was wet and unwashed, and footsore, and raw palmed, and enfeebled with fatigue, but I was now also stuffed and probably drunk. Furthermore, these latter conditions had been achieved – for almost nothing – in a tapas bar wallpapered with photos of, and I understand regularly patronised by, the great Miguel Indurain, five times Tour de France winner and therefore a personal hero. (The only pronunciation of Indurain I'd been previously familiar with was the one you'd regret if your first name was Singing, so I'm indebted to the splendidly moustachioed proprietor for supplying me with a surprising number of additional syllables, even though I can't quite remember what they were.)

I contemplated the big picture as the white noise of wet traffic lulled me to sleep. Despite the bridge business, and the stairs and mobile grazing and whatever else, I shouldn't lose track of what Shinto had achieved. Only in a dream even more ridiculous than most of the ones he'd been starring in would I have predicted covering 60 kilometres in three days. So it had rained – so what? I had a hair shirt; now it was wet. What was a pilgrimage without adversity to triumph over? Bring on your hobgoblins! Show me the foul fiends! Though . . . though if that's one of them waving a torch about outside, at least let me get my pants on first.

Six

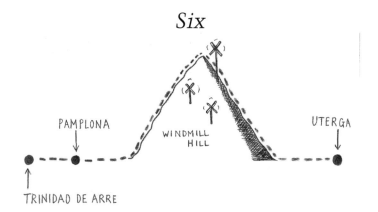

PAMPLONA

WINDMILL
HILL

UTERGA

TRINIDAD DE ARRE

Hell is other people, said Jean-Paul Sartre, clearly a man with little experience of solo camping. But if it was bleak and more than a little lonely for me in that tent, then what fresh terror must every bump in the night have brought upon my displaced medieval forebears, for whom demons were as real as wolves? Most, after all, had been driven here by lurid, vivid fear of a hell that was more than a quasi-philosophical adage clung to by friendless Goths, a hell defined in exact and harrowing terms.

Hellfire, purgatory and Judgement Day were all medieval discoveries; the early Christians hadn't dwelt much on the cost of human naughtiness. But though goodwill to all mankind might have filled the churches, it was fear that kept them full. Theologians gave that fear a face. It was decided that the fires of hell were hotter than those above ground, but emitted no light; St Brigitta conversed with a female soul in torment who spoke of toads growing on her feet and snakes gnawing at her innards and breasts. Precision passed for proof: Lucifer had recruited 266,613,336 angels to the Dark Side for his rebellion, and the Vatican decreed (and still maintains) hell's capacity as 60 billion sinners (including standing).

Of course, if you went to hell you stayed there. The pilgrims were trying to buy time off purgatory, a sort of spiritual anteroom, where searing flames apparently less uncomfortable than those of hell purified the soul. Initially, this grandly proportioned rotisserie was to accommodate all salvageable souls in preparation for Judgement Day – a tough sell for the Church, which in the eleventh century began to promote the idea of a fast-track judgement for those demonstrating piety and devotion via pilgrimage or donation.

These days, the Vatican's line on purgatory is more along the lines of a spiritual Betty Ford, detoxing souls for heaven. Watched over by the graven image of Miguel Indurain, I'd read that the concept of knocking a certain number of days off your time in purgatory for performing a specific good deed, as might be a pilgrimage, had been abolished by the Pope in 1968. A bit of a shame for a blithe heretic like me, but a crushing post-mortem blow for the millions who'd tramped across huge swathes of medieval Europe in good faith. What of the thirteenth-century pilgrim from Toulouse I'd just learnt about, ordered to carry a 24-pound iron weight to Compostela? In particular, what of the tens – probably hundreds – of thousands who'd popped their muddy clogs en route, welcoming death with a frail smile, assured that a backstage pass to paradise, a plenary indulgence, was granted to all whose pilgrimage was thus curtailed?

That may have seemed an appealing option for one of us. A chorus of deafening nasal honks informed me that it was morning, and that Shinto had had enough. When you're in a tent you don't need to look outside to know that it's raining, but I did anyway and it was. Shinto's tree was about 20 yards away, and there he stood, arse to the wind in traditional equine fashion. He heard the zip and turned towards me; it was rarely easy to gauge how he felt from how he looked, but that was a full-on, globe-hating glower. 'Morning,' I called over, only half my head outside. He blinked the rain off his lashes. 'Did you know that St Anthony was the patron saint of donkeys?' I'd read a lot at that bar, and there was no one else to share it with. Shinto looked away; I raised my voice slightly. 'And 23 per cent of Germans believe in the devil.'

Everything I owned – *everything* – was wet, and it would

be three days before it wasn't. Getting dressed under canvas is always a challenge, but when your clothes are soaked they envelop and adhere to the wrong bits of flesh like plastic wrap and, if you're maybe slightly hungover, this results in a wild chaos of wits-end, multi-limbed thrashing. I don't think I've ever taken a tent down from the inside before.

The *refugio* was already closing its doors – at 8 a.m. – and the last couple were chivvied out as I coaxed a monumentally pissed-off Shinto out of the garden gate. There are few conversational ice-breakers more effective than a wet donkey, and we got talking. They were Dutch, she was squat, he was not. Late forties. Matching bushwhacker hats and khaki shorts. I saw these two a lot over the coming days, and developed a real fondness for them. They were always jolly, and winningly forswore the earnest 'honour amongst pilgrims' code that – in the early days at least – forestalled toothsomely malevolent gossip. (Their duologue *'The Snoring Tart of Paris'* will remain with me for some time.) They endearingly fussed over each other's fixtures and fittings as they walked or talked, tightening a pack strap, tying up a bootlace; once, memorably, stopping in the middle of a zebra crossing to tuck each other's vests in.

Here were two professional amateurs: the perfect antidote to the overbearing relentlessness of the power-walking pilgrimators. You'd see them standing at a street corner squinting ineffectually at an upside-down map, or ambling against the pilgrim flow in blithe oblivion. They were of that rare group of fellow pilgrims who felt comfortable proceeding at donkey pace; and in fact conspicuously unique in often dropping below this. ('My problem is I cannot walk and talk,' said the wife, which was a shame because she couldn't stop talking.) In short they were worse than me, and for that alone I loved them.

Pamplona would be Shinto's most significant test to date: a narrow-alleyed city of 200,000, with a worldwide reputation for the drunken goading of farmyard quadrupeds. In two months they'd be running with the bulls, and here was an opportunity for a dry run. In the rain.

It was an ordeal that demanded advance refuelling. Negotiating Shinto up a puddled bus lane through the nascent suburban rush hour I spotted a grocery, and tied him to a drain-pipe outside. When I emerged, with a roll of gardening refuse sacks and a 2-kilo bag of muesli, a crowd of kindly-minded strangers had congregated around Shinto: elderly housecoated shoppers, backpacked schoolkids, a postman. I looked from face to gleeful face; I listened to the sing-song cries of '*Burro!*' The rain was forgotten – people were happy, and it was down to me. And soon they were even happier, watching this flappy-ponchoed fool unload his donkey on to the pavement, and stuff everything into giant plastic bags, and reload him, and dump a huge sack of breakfast cereal into a washing-up bowl. Shinto snuffled the lot, then rounded the performance off by sneezing raisiny oat-phlegm all over the postman's back.

The camino returned to the riverside, meandering towards the city centre past fields and allotments that persisted almost up to the town walls. En route Shinto had a bit of an across-the-fence set-to with a yappy little Shetland pony, which he won after a muesli-powered hoof-stamping snort-off. Then it was over the river, up on to the cobbles and, after a couple of tourist photocalls and a one-sided donk-lore discourse with a cig-wizened umbrella-toter, under a huge, mossy arch and into Old Pamplona.

I'd been advised by Hanno to bypass cities, and actually ordered to by the Donkey Sanctuary. It wasn't hard to see why, but I had vowed to try at least one. And why not the first? Pamplona had the history: founded by the Roman general Pompaelo, it was ruled by the Moors for a century until 799, and thereafter repopulated with Jews and Frenchmen as an ethnic bulwark. Throughout the Middle Ages the city was a vital pilgrim pit stop – unusually, ailing travellers were permitted to stay more than a single night (many, in consequence, pegged out in Pamplona). And flicking through the *Liber Sancti Jacobi* in Miguel Indurain's bar I'd come across the pertinently bracing tale of a pilgrim whose wife, horse and chattels are variously slaughtered and stolen by an evil Pamplonese innkeeper. There! Actually, that isn't the end: the bereaved husband is stoically preparing to continue, the couple's two children on his shoulders, when Santiago himself appears with a donkey. 'Here you go, son,' he says, 'and leave that innkeeper to me.'

I'm not sure if St Jim was smiling on me that day, but everyone else was. They stood in dirty old doorways to beam and point as the camino took the path of most resistance, winding up circuitous alleys barely wide enough for a fully laden donk, let alone the parping procession of delivery trucks we trailed behind us.

Shinto's ears were swivelling about on red alert, eventually settling into a one-forward, one-back set-up for 360-degree surround-sound coverage. I held him on the shortest leash, my knuckles white around the rope, not daring to spare any eye time for the cathedrals, *refugios* or any of the other stately old lovelinesses that I was no doubt passing by. Once I was momentarily distracted by a parked Lamborghini, and before I knew it a bulging pannier had brushed a hefty men-at-work road-hole barrier and sent it crashing to the cobbles. Nothing substantial falls over in a Latin city centre without triggering at least a small domino effect; I was righting an adjacent moped when a volley of squeakily guttural abuse rained down from a mercifully lofty window.

The alleys opened into boulevards, and Shinto's fan club swelled in noise and numbers. '*Burro!*' they shrieked. Or: '*Burrico!*' Or: '*Burriquino!*' As we traversed the central business district, the appealing incongruity of our presence seemed complete. Waiting for a little green man amidst a pavement full of briefcase carriers I was treated to handshakes, back pats and a heartfelt '*buen viaje*'; as I stepped off the kerb I felt part of the most portentous convoy to set foot on a zebra crossing since Paul McCartney left his shoes in the Abbey Road gutter.

Over a couple of technically demanding roundabouts, a slightly erratic passage over a narrow bridge and suddenly we were past the railway tracks and out into what was today a very green belt, Shinto chewing off roadside weeds with happy nonchalance. He'd done it. We'd done it. The two of us, together, as a team. I ruffled his crest, patted his poll, and set him off up the road with a blokeish slap on the dock. If this whole thing was the Steeplechase Triple Crown, we'd just completed the first leg.

It was wet, but we were on a roll and I added to my already impressive catalogue of unseen historico–pilgrimy must-sees by tramping straight by the many Romanesque structures of Cizur Menor. And also past its enticing *refugio*, upon whose garlanded balcony lounged debonaire pilgrims, sipping tall drinks. The priority was getting out of sync with the bed-hogging army of enduro freaks, to which end I'd cunningly plotted to press on to the next *refugio*, over a hill in the tiny and so I hoped easily disregarded village of Uterga.

Initial visual contact with this hill, as Shinto and I lunched amidst the weeds by the perimeter wall of an executive-belt villa, presented the first suggestion that this scheme was not so much cunning, as shit. It was miles away, and it was stoutly colossal. Upon its drizzled brow stood a battery of turbine windmills, which even at this range I could see being storm whipped into a rotational frenzy. (If, as Petronella informed us later, those sixty spinners up there were more than enough for Pamplona's 200,000 residents, then what on earth is wrong with us in Britain, umbrella-shredding gust capital of Europe?) Furthermore, consulting the explanatory index to my Confraternity guide as I tackled a second *chorizo* bap, I learnt that the number in brackets after each *refugio* denoted the number of beds it contained, and that in the case of Uterga this number was two.

These were diverting revelations, so much so that it was well into the second hour of my requisite break before I gathered that something funny was going on in the villa behind me. A suited man in a BMW had parked in front of the villa, scuttled furtively up to the intercom and been buzzed in. He'd scuttled out again a short time later, just as a fat chap with a face like a melted candle arrived in a pick-up truck to repeat the sequence, only this time with measured nonchalance. I peered over the wall and noted that every one of the many large windows was screened with heavy black drapes.

Shinto jerked his head up from the big dandelions and tuned his ears: had that been a giggle? It had indeed, and a moment later the few remaining doubts as to the business being carried on behind those curtains were merrily banished by the appearance through the door of no fewer than four young women, one with a Morticia Addams streak and the rest blindingly bottle blonde. Tittering like playground miscreants they tottered towards us through the grass; I rose uncertainly, not at this stage confident in the finer points of pilgrim/prostitute etiquette. They weren't interested in me, of course, but as I watched them fawn sweetly over Shinto an image of the very vilest impropriety marched unbidden into my mind and would not leave.

'OK, thanks, thank you now,' I blustered, galvanised into action. Get him away this minute, or see that ghastly tableau brought to life in some dank and tramp-lickingly odious Internet dungeon. I pressed through the cocktail dresses and released Shinto from his tree with a twist of the fingers and a manly yank. 'Must press on.'

They looked at me with incomprehension and a spurned sadness, and for a moment I saw four girls drawn away from this short escape to a gentler time, denied a small opportunity to restore their trampled innocence. Then one of them held something out to Shinto. It was a carrot: a buffed and shiny carrot.

Everyone I met afterwards told their own saga of the ascent of what we called Windmill Hill, but is down in the literature and on the maps as Alto del Perdon. Canadian Evelyn, a senior air stewardess with a heart of oak in a bonsai body, had been repeatedly gusted off her feet, pressed face down in the heavy mud for long minutes as she mustered the resources to raise her giant rucksack into that bullying, deafening gale. A little Japanese man softly described how his pack had been torn open, its contents scattered over the hill like the aftermath of a plane crash. Someone said they'd seen that bloke on crutches hopping and sliding up ahead of them. God alone knows how he did it. Perhaps literally so.

The wind, at least, was behind us. But the mud was inevitably beneath, and of an adhesive viscosity I have never previously encountered. You put your left foot in, and your left foot out, but you didn't shake it all about as it was now double the size and treble the weight. Up ahead of me I could see two French couples I'd exchanged '*buen camino*'s with outside the brothel (or in fact '*bon camino*'s – as ever, the French alone stoutly refused to cede any linguistic quarter); every few yards they were stopping to hack clay off their soles with sticks, with stones and eventually with their own weary hands. It was an image consistent with the many I'd constructed some weeks earlier while confronting the chapter in *Pilgrim Stories* entitled 'Pain and Fatigue'.

Watching the French backmarker slide to her derrière with a wind-muted yelp, I thought, Let's hope this whole pilgrimage business is a bit of a slow burner, because so far it isn't perhaps quite what I would have chosen. Slatted bridges notwithstanding I was in this for the long haul, but that haul had never seemed longer.

The hill's lower reaches were flanked by barley, meaning Shinto hardly noticed the unappealing conditions: he'd honed his on-the-hoof grazing technique so perfectly that whenever I looked round there was a sort of thick green Fu Manchu moustache dangling from either side of his lazily masticating jaw. The very few who followed me over later that day reported a path bestrewn with his half-chewed rejects.

But as the path steepened, the paddied grain fields gave way to buffeted heather and gorse, which Shinto never even sniffed. And who could blame him? Maddening as his relentless gluttony, his persistent vegetative state, surely was, I had to respect Shinto's tastes. If we liked to eat it (barley, wheat, love carrots) so did he. And if we didn't – viz. his absolute favourite, a roadside clovery shrub subsequently identified as wild alfalfa – at least it looked like we might, if only in a multi-leaf herb salad or tea-bagged infusion. I was especially delighted at Shinto's dogged refusal to kowtow to farmyard stereotype by eating thistles. In a land so Catholically fertile that asparagus and honeysuckle grow wild by the road, what right-thinking beast would glumly survey the verdant cornucopia around and sigh, 'You know, I could just murder a pincushion'?

With his food supply cut off, my donkey slowed to a mud-hoofed trudge. I turned to exhort him and he gave me a look, which if it said anything said, You think I evolved in Africa for this? On we ploughed – those crest-topping turbines were almost scarily huge, but they didn't seem to be getting any nearer. The French lot had pulled away, and I began to feel just a little uneasy. It was gone 5.00; in the windswept, granite gloom the yellow gorse-buds almost glowed. Shinto lost his footing a couple of times, which was a couple fewer than me. And then, almost bent double by the astonishing rearward blast, I was at the summit, battling with my poncho at the foot of one of the droning rotary giants that poled out endlessly along the hill's spine in either direction. How wittily apposite it could so easily have been: here I was, in Spain, with an equine companion, tilting at wind farms.

There was some sort of contemporary pilgrim monument up here, prematurely weathered wrought-iron figures that quivered and sang in the wind, but even though it featured what looked like a donkey the elements forestalled any photographic dalliance. To think that this monstrously storm-torn brow had for over 500 years been home to a monastery and pilgrim refuge, of which unsurprisingly nothing remains.

It didn't get any less blowy on the scrabbly-pebbled descent, which seemed both unfair and topographically illogical. The wind combed the barley into Van Gogh waves and sent the black plastic asparagus tunnels madly flapping; distantly beyond, the Navarrese landscape settled into a rolling plain, villages huddled in its folds.

Shinto did his best to resist the encouragements of wind and gradient, but in the end we built up a ragged momentum that saw us actually overtake a pilgrim, though as he was on his knees before a pathside statue of the Virgin I thought better of a quick chat. The drizzle got serious, and machine-gunned in the back by horizontal drops we finally broached the underwhelming, unhopeful one-donk town that could only be Uterga.

I'd been concentrating so hard on not thinking about those beds – both of them – that I hadn't troubled to memorise the *refugio*'s location from my Confraternity guide, and if I got that out now there'd be pages all over Iberia. So I did what I later learnt you always do, and continued along the muddy main street looking for signs of pilgrim occupation: filthy boots on a window sill, wet hiking socks on a line. In the climactic conditions this was of course oafishly wrong-headed, so I was almost as happy as I should have been when the head of a young woman appeared through a gingerly opened front door and issued a beckoning jerk.

Soon I'd become accustomed to the warm-hearted weirdness encountered in many camino villages. But you don't forget your first time. The house was old, and had not been made new. Its cavernous, unlit hall was floored with a crazily undulating mosaic of age-burnished pebbles; I was shown into a side room and belatedly grasped that its stall-like wattle-and-daub enclosure was not for dipping sheep but bathing pilgrims. Behind the first door on the upstairs landing was an atmospherically illuminated gilt shrine – more of an altar in proportion – dedicated to *Nostra Señora*. Behind the second was a truckle-bedded dormitory endowed very much more handsomely than the number in the Confraternity's brackets, and now dense with postcard-writing, blister-bursting pilgrims. At its conclusion was another door, which opened into a room dominated by an enormous old brass bed that had evidently hosted the biological beginnings of many an Utergan. This was my room, and my room alone. The price, the young woman gently informed me in broken English considerably more charming than my mallet-shattered Spanish, was 2 euros. Last come, best served.

Shinto did all right for himself, too. I'd been uncomfortably aware that he was only a wet twenty-four hours from the official saturation point, when a donk gets too dank and has to be stabled. And stabled he was, ushered by a couple of young brothers through a pair of ancient, brick-thick wooden doors and into a shed with a big tractor and a mountain of seed potatoes. By way of thanks, Shinto knocked a can of oil over and made a rush for the spud pile. Laboriously restrained and lashed to the tractor, he promptly hosed out a great pool of foamy piss which we watched the densely earthen floor failing to absorb. And do you know what those two boys did? That's right – they ladled it into a wooden pail and tipped the lot down the back of my pants. No. They laughed.

It was all so congenial that even the grubby rituals – the sock washing, the shirt wringing, the boot scraping – failed to dampen my mood. And once they were done, and I'd enjoyed an engagingly daft and rustic shower, it was off over the road to eat at the only option, a jarringly contemporary bar. It was pilgrims only, and eschewing a rather overwhelmingly Brazilian party of dedicated cigar smokers, I sat at the table with the ones I knew. Evelyn was here, and Petronella, and a quiet Danish lady who later described the poignant genesis of her own camino: she'd invited a hundred and twenty people to her fortieth birthday party, and sat sobbing in a big hall with the eleven who turned up. Also three young women from Berlin, who always seemed to be eating bars of Lindt whenever anyone met them, and who we consequently dubbed, rather brilliantly I thought, the German chocolate girls.

It was a jolly evening, though not on the part of the serving staff, whose unswerving determination to counterpoint the definitively cheap and cheerful establishment opposite required them to deny anything other than sandwiches to pilgrims they didn't like the look of (in the case of our table, everyone but Evelyn), and to charge 300 per cent more per bottle of red than any of us had previously been asked to pay. But as this still amounted to three times fuck all, we all got rather drunk. It was our job: so reliably filthy was medieval water, many pilgrims drank only what the *Liber Sancti Jacobi* winningly dubs 'the precious liquor of Bacchus'.

Four days on the road had seemed a month, and already we

were a band of brothers, bound together by shared hardship. There was a long debrief on the lonely toil of Windmill Hill, and a pooling of garnered weather predictions. Somewhere around bottle three we moved on to more profound issues, the sort that separated what we were doing from youth hostelling. Evelyn had first heard of the camino whilst awaiting the results of a tumour biopsy; it turned out benign, but by then a close friend of hers was terminally ill, and all this and a certain now-or-never urgency had sparked off a sort of life-value stock-take. Doing the pilgrimage wasn't an end in itself, more an opportunity to find answers to big questions. And, she divulged with an almost apologetic shrug, somewhere back down the line she was a Catholic.

So were the Berliners, in fact, but they weren't claiming any relevant inspiration: for them this was just a two-week holiday ramble, and pissed off at being pissed on they were already pondering a decamp to the Costa Blanca. Furthermore, they were policewomen – a startling and worrisome revelation. Was it an offence to swear at an animal? To permit grazing within 50 metres of an unlicensed bawdy-house? Almost certainly under obscure EU ordinances that only a German would enforce. And though I hadn't yet been drunk in charge of a road-going jackass, I would be in a minute: someone asked what my donkey was eating in his stable, and because the answer to this was nothing I bolted out into the wind, blushingly unhitched Shinto from his Massey Ferguson and led him through the big doors and over the road to a tree conveniently circled by green straggle.

Poor Shints didn't get much of a meal: with the 10 p.m. curfew looming, very much against the powerful will of his stomach, I had to haul him back inside before creeping upstairs past the shrine, through the snuffling tuts and into my room.

I sat on the bed, initiating a complex and enduring chorus of haunted creaks, and wondered how I felt. My runaway-donkey rope burns were now crudely but effectively calloused, as it seemed were the little-toe blisters. No real surprise there: owing to an accident of birth I would previously have been reluctant to describe as a happy one, my feet are undersealed in a thick layer of friction-resistant tarpaulin. Oh, and I had scabies. Or at least such was the diagnosis until that raw and hairless ovoid on my right upper thigh was traced to the abrasive action of camera in trouser pocket, chafing away with every stride.

But what of the spiritual healing, the personal growth, the evolution of my inner Tim? Whenever pilgrims huddled into reverential discussion of how the Way of St James was inveigling itself into their characters, their personalities, I'd felt left out, guilty almost. I was still just me, only with a donkey. 'You must allow a new person to emerge from within,' one of the Brazilians had announced to the bar at large. Because he then identified these as the words of his countryman Paulo Coelho, whose effortfully esoteric novel *The Pilgrimage* marks him out as a serious rival to Shirley MacLaine as the camino's guffmeister general, I'd dismissed this soulful homily forthwith. ('I had become a tree,' confesses Paulo, quite early on.) But now I reconsidered, and looking down I saw with something approaching horror that Paulo was right. A new person had indeed emerged from within. But I'd have to suck him back inside straight away, because he was wearing socks under his sandals.

Seven

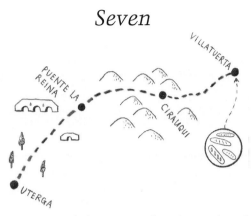

Walking up to 40 kilometres a day, the medieval pilgrims were logistically obliged to get on the road in darkness, but it would be some time before I was able to understand or forgive the pre-dawn stamps, hawks and – yes – whistles of their modern descendants. Those with recent camping experience will understand that even a closed door and earplugs are no match for the decibels generated whilst bullying a 900-tog sleeping bag into its tiny nylon carry-sock. It was like putting a condom on a donkey. I imagine.

I should have predicted that Shinto might be a little fractious after his foodless night, but being blearily off guard I didn't, and as I let him out for a morning graze he bit me. Only a nip on the forearm, perhaps, but probably enough to warrant that reflex yelp of abuse, if not its volume. There were two small girls by the tree I'd tied Shinto to the night before, but instead of running off to look up 'vicious', 'little' or 'sod' in an English/Spanish dictionary, they gambolled over to pet him. Smiling indulgently, I contrasted their easy familiarity with the freak-show hysteria Shinto had roused in Pamplona – much as it pained me to realise, just a fifteen-minute drive away. He's back amongst his own, I thought as I went back up to stuff wet pants into wet bags. A city was no place for such a little donk, and I was glad that he wouldn't have to tackle another for 100 kilometres – 100 clicks in Evelyn's initially irksome but soon infectious shorthand. So much gentler to be here, where the grass was green, the camino quiet, and small girls were always on hand to . . . oh, to jump up on his back and ride him round and round a tree whilst thwacking his loins with big bits of plastic drainpipe. 'Oi!' I shouted out the window, but they didn't stop until a delegation of departing pilgrims chased them off. Later someone saw them throwing a tiny pregnant cat over a wall.

Shinto didn't seem scarred by the experience, which a Brazilian witness controversially suggested he enjoyed, but something had exacted an underfoot toll and it was probably Windmill Hill. That ingrained, spongy silt on Shinto's back hoof was getting worse, or so I gathered from his diligent attempts to knee me in the bollocks as I tried to scrape the mud off it. Certainly he looked rather sorry, still slathered from the stifle down as if he'd just hauled a gun carriage across no man's land. In possible consequence, a line of sympathetic lady pilgrims formed as I saddled him up, all of them proffering hunks of bread. An open-faced young German in pebble-specs addressed me with earnest concern: 'And how is your monkey this morning?'

Beneath more scurrying greyness I set off with Evelyn and Petronella, through almond and walnut orchards, and perhaps once an hour through yet another mysteriously unpeopled ghost town where the barks of unseen dogs echoed harshly off shuttered flanks of wet whitewash. There was no one to see when Shinto besmirched the grassy town square in Obanos, but because he'd targeted the end of a children's slide I thought I ought to shift it. And I would have, probably, had Petronella not rushed to the scene with both hands gloved in plastic bags. Why did she do this? I'm not sure. A donkey made an unlikely babe magnet, and this one was certainly attracting some unlikely babes.

We crossed a main road and it started raining again. Groups of people passed, a couple of Brazilians, the chocolate police-women, the monkey lady. And of course many more we'd never seen before and would never see again, resolutely en route from somewhere I'd passed yesterday to somewhere I'd pass tomorrow.

It was only 7 clicks to Puente la Reina, and singing it to the tune of 'Guantanamera' we got there well before lunch. I thought about going on, but not for long: though my boots were slowly coming round to the idea that they might after all be made for walking, Shinto's right-hand back hoof no longer was. And Puente la Reina was Navarra's pilgrim central, the meeting point of the two great trans-Pyrenean holy routes. Shinto's celebrated unwillingness to cross them meant that I now knew what a 'Puente' was, and I've eaten at Pizza Express often enough to have a pretty good idea that 'Reina' meant queen. And it did, though rather entertainingly no one knows after which queen the long and unavoidably magnificent eleventh-century bridge is named.

In the absence of rival crossings the bridge made the town, and brought the pilgrims. 'To each and every pilgrim is given sixteen ounces of bread and half a pint of wine,' wrote a seventeenth-century *hospitalero* at Puente la Reina's main *refugio*. 'Stew, codfish, eggs and legumes – they are not dismissed until they confess with their mouths full that they have never found such hospitality.' Here was a town with the blood of St James in its veins.

Though not with the doo of a donk on its feet, as Shinto was brusquely refused at the first place I tried, a peripheral motel with a pilgrim hostel in the basement. Evelyn and Petronella checked in there, and as the sun first pierced then dramatically dispersed the clouds I led my animal down to the more agreeable and handsomely refurbished official *refugio*. With Shinto tied up in tall grass down the lane, I paid up, checked in, outmanoeuvred a Brazilian to bag the last bottom bunk and with a happy air of achievement retired to the large garden with a fetid armful of wet cotton and canvas.

As the tent and four days of clothes steamed into a May-coloured sky, I sat with the chocolate policewomen and plumped my jowls with yet another chorizo *boccadillo* (travel through rural Spain and you'll find it's a lot easier to learn how to say 'sandwich' than 'Why are all the restaurants still closed?'). A stork – the first I'd ever seen – flapped lethargically towards a nest wedged in the mouth of a huge old factory chimney. Behind us, bleached and moss-speckled by 500 years of this contrary climate, rose a domed Baroque church tower. I arched my sandalled toes and closed my eyes.

This reverie was as pleasant as it was brief, and it was very pleasant. A distant chorus of pre-siesta juvenile revelry, then an older and slightly more strident shout, a harsher shout, in fact a German shout. 'What's he saying?' I mumbled thickly to an adjacent policewoman. 'Leave him at peace,' she said. A much louder shout, translated instantly and with feeling. 'Leave the donkey at peace.'

My saviour had dispersed the mob when I sandal-flapped breathlessly up to him. 'Boy childrens,' he said, with a gratitude-forestalling shrug. 'You know how is it.' As a tall ginger man in shorts, his ensuing impersonation of a jiggly-limbed donkey teaser was an especial treat. A jeer of unbridled insolence cut the performance short, and we looked for its source: almost every window on the third floor of an institution opposite was open and crowded with contemptuous adolescent faces. Shinto's nostrils flared and contracted, his usual preparation for an epic bray; perhaps sensing this, the youths let forth a spontaneous volley of mocking hee-haws. The German waved a long and freckled finger up at them, and with passion and volume I enquired whether they'd like to come down and find out that bestiality could be a two-way street.

More taunts; louder hee-haws. Gesturing wearily at his tormentors and offering Herr Ginger my effusive thanks, I released Shinto and led him back up to the *refugio*. He'd stay in the garden. Or rather he wouldn't, because as I led him through the gate the elderly *hospitalero* trotted speedily up, shaking head and waving hands. 'No, no, no,' he said. 'No, no, no, no, no.'

In the minimal manoeuvring space this opening gambit allowed, I contorted my recalcitrant features into an approximation of piteous entreaty. 'But please, *por favor*,' I stuttered.

'The bad bambinis at the . . . schoolio.' As he turned away with a shrug, an eavesdropping Frenchwoman called out that it wasn't a school, nor even a young offenders' institute, but a seminary. A college for trainee priests. The sky-directed bellows of incoherent hatred and self-pity that I'd been rather looking forward to died in my throat. I looked back down the lane and at its fundament saw two junior padres idly belabouring a large gas cylinder with lengths of four by two. Another leant against the wall opposite, a coil of sunlit smoke issuing from his cupped hand.

In dumb astonishment I vacantly prepared for departure, stuffing my humid belongings back into the plastic bags. And so much for the codfish and legumes: the *hospitalero* didn't even give me my money back.

The *Polizei* waved me off and in bone-buckling sun I followed the daubed yellow arrows towards Puente la Reina's cool, narrow main street. It was still early, too early to panic. Time even to visit a church, or at least try to. 'Closed,' mumbled a lanky Australian waiting outside the apparently splendid Iglesia de Santiago. Next to him in the shade was a woman half his size with hair down to her ankles; I'd seen them in the Uterga *refugio*, rubbing each other's backs with slightly inappropriate enthusiasm. 'They're always closed.' I hadn't seen the inside of a church since Roncesvalles, but now felt less bad about it.

As the old buildings on either side of the siesta-empty street grew taller, so the shadows darkened. This was the most medieval I'd felt yet, hauling my ass past door after ancient door, beneath crest after regal crest, hoofs echoing off the flagstones. It wasn't hard to imagine the Calle Mayor ringing with the cries of Basque, Navarran and French tradesmen, nor indeed with the clamour of bells, tolled forty times at 10 p.m. each night to guide lost pilgrims to safety, wine and codfish.

Clip-clop, clop-clip. Despite my inner chortles when he'd said it, I was beginning to understand that Hanno was right: however new it felt to me, this was an ancient way of life, lived out for all but a tiny fraction of humankind's time on earth. You walked in search of food, you walked in search of shelter, you slept and you started again. 'When you adapt to this rhythm,' he'd concluded, 'many ancient, dead parts in the head return to life.'

Hoping that these weren't the parts responsible for moon worship or human sacrifice I ambled on, past the shuttered shoe shops and jewellers. For the first time flies began to trouble Shinto, clustering horribly around his tear-ducts, and for the first time I fitted him with Hanno's patent eye protector: a sort of sweatband fringed with long strands of red and green suede. The effect was almost worryingly alluring. When Shinto turned to me I saw in his teasingly shielded eyes the seductive, peek-a-boo enigma of a Sultan-beguiling belly dancer.

I was just wondering if even really dreadful sins would be forgiven at Santiago when it became clear we were no longer alone. From nowhere a great throng of previously unencountered French pilgrims arrived and engulfed us, cooing Gallically over Shinto and patting my back with lunch-dislodging vigour. There were shouts of '*Bravo!*' and '*Courage!*'; three men scuttled in front, retrieved and assembled enormous cameras and walked backwards before us, snapping manically away paparazzi-style. I had no idea why this was happening, but it all seemed most satisfactory.

The climax came as the buildings receded and the road became a bridge, the bridge, the Puente built by Reina or Reine unknown. A cheer, a whoop, then a clap of hands which instantly swelled into a prolonged and rousing round of applause. It was the sort of situation that demanded a cry of 'Speech!', and had my French been up to it, how marvellous to have stopped at the apex of that bridge, at the centre of its third great arch, and turned to address the eager crowd gathered at the town-side bank: 'Friends, this journey of ours is a long one, and a hard one. There will be times ahead when you feel pain, or fear, times when you feel hungry and forsaken. But at times like that I want you to remember that this isn't about you, or you, madame, or you. It's about me – me and my boyfr— my donkey!'

This was almost certainly the best thing that had happened to date, though there was some serious competition up ahead. Borne on a wave of adulation I'd processed across the bridge without plotting my next move. This should have been awful, as Shinto looked as though he might be starting to limp, Puente la Reina had petered out and the next *refugio* was – oh – 17 kilometres off. But it wasn't, because there was a sign by the bridge pointing up a hill, which as promised led me to a cavernous and conspicuously under-pilgrimmed *albergue*.

More accurately an unfinished camping complex, but with tumble-dryers, chips on the menu and football on a great big telly I wasn't about to quibble. Shinto had a nice spot out by the unfilled swimming pool; the two-legged accommodation was in six-bedded dormitories, and scattering belongings on a bottom bunk I noted that four of the remaining five in mine were unclaimed.

In the echoing sports-hall canteen I asked for a glass of rosé with my meal; the grinning chef returned with a brimming dimple-sided British pint pot. So it was that fate, hospitality, comparative economics and an instant capitulation of the will combined to press my lips once more to the naughty cup. A very nice Dutchman dined with me, but drunk on celebrity and otherwise I'm not sure I was very nice back.

All pilgrimages share certain characteristics, features that define them as holy walks. A vow or promise at the journey's beginning; and at its end a ritual prayer for enlightenment, forgiveness or miracle. The traveller should wear a costume or symbol of his mission (shell for Santiago, cross for Rome, palm frond for Jerusalem), and return as an evangelist to tell of his positive experiences. And crucially, the journey must incorporate an element of denial and privation.

Medieval pilgrims often travelled penniless, some because they were, some because of the fear of bandits, but most because by depending on charity they were ascetically purifying both themselves and those who offered it. It was good to walk hungry, as 'the prayers of the starving flew quicker to heaven'. By the same token, it was bang out of order to take short cuts, or to lighten one's burden in any fashion (button it, Shinto). Even if, as was invariably the case, the holy way was deliberately routed to maximise that soul-cleansing pain and fatigue. Valley roads were the devil's work: a true God-fearing zealot went against the grain of the landscape, straight over the hilltops. Certain stages of the camino seemed calculatedly, cruelly attritional. And today, to the fearsome disadvantage of many fellow pilgrims, was one of them.

The foot-dragging afternoon before, it was ridiculous to imagine it ever rained here; the morning after, it was ridiculous to imagine it ever stopped. Thunder woke me, and my solitary room-mate, a Swiss chap who'd arrived at Puente la Reina via the more hard-core Somport route. At one point this had required him to cover 45 kilometres in a day, and though he was young, and Swiss, that had been an ordeal from which he had yet to recover. He hadn't eaten for the last forty-eight hours, he whispered wanly from his bunk, and though it was technically against *albergue/refugio* rules, he'd been given permission to stay for more than one night; in fact until he recovered. If he felt bad, then he looked worse: watching him totter to the loo in his flannel pyjamas I found myself transported to an interwar TB sanatorium.

Yet how much rosier this young fellow suddenly seemed, almost radiant in fact, when during an exchange of pilgrimage bullet points he croaked that it was funny I had a donkey, as he was a muleteer in the Swiss Army. Yes, he really seemed to perk up before my eyes. A minute ago I'd have wanted him propped up on bolsters with his head over a bronchitis kettle and an enamelled kidney dish brimming with bloodied sputum on the bedside table; but now . . . why, what this boy needed now was to get out there in that bracing thunderstorm right away and build up his strength with a spot of light asinine chiropody.

I coaxed a matted and rather thunder-harrowed Shinto across the poolside rubble and up to the *albergue* door. Fleeced and thermalled almost to immobility my Swiss friend laboured out towards us, but the sight and scent of a long-eared demi-mule proved a wondrous tonic. Soon he was down on one knee, the relevant hoof in his lap, carving away horny curlings with an air of fond craftsmanship. His tool – what else – was a Swiss Army knife. 'Oh, I must ask: do you ever use that funny pointy thing to—'

'To take away stones in the foot?' The weariness in his voice suggested that there are only so many questions a Swiss Army muleteer might be asked, and that this was by no means the first time he'd fielded that one. 'No. It is a bad equipment for this. It go back against your fingers and make pain.'

In a couple of minutes the wet grass beneath him was thickly sprinkled with hoof shavings. 'This problem is a bacterium who lives with no air,' he said, squinting critically at his handiwork. 'So you see I cut down this part and make it open to oxygen.' By way of indication he jabbed the blade into the heart of that small blot of seedy-toed thrush. Shinto flinched very slightly; if I'd tried that on him they'd have been identifying me from dental records. 'So – now it is OK for him.' It was the closest I'd yet come to experiencing a miracle. (Though I've just remembered the 10 euros I found outside a bar soon after Roncesvalles. If I haven't mentioned this before, it's probably because when I say 'bar', I mean 'church'.)

Unaware that I was now viewing him at the centre of a pool of gilded light, he stood up, smiled, then seemed to remember he was really very ill. 'Please,' I said, grabbing his clammy hand as he faltered back to the dry warmth. 'Let me . . .' But let me what? This was a pilgrimage, and he was a Swiss invalid: circumstances which precluded expressing gratitude through the traditional offering of cash or alcohol. 'Let me . . . do this.' And I patted him three times on the head.

There were over 200 pilgrim beds in Puente, and the inhabitants of most were shuffling towards me across the bridge. Shortly afterwards our path veered away from the road, then threw itself – rather imprudently I thought – at an enormous hill of red mud. I'd never really walked in the pilgrim pack before, but this wasn't an ideal introduction. Even for a region perennially cursed with biblical weather systems, conditions were candidly extreme: the TV breakfast news had portrayed swollen rivers dammed with bloated livestock, trees wedged under bridge arches and the usual aerial shots of devastated caravan sites. Why is it always caravans? Answer: There is a vengeful God.

Up ahead I could see people scrabbling desperately for purchase and regularly failing to find it; some hauled themselves up the edge of the path by grabbing on to piny bushes, others blundered off-piste through the scrub, where the footholds were surer but the vegetation poncho-piercingly vicious. It was a scene that seasoned inhuman suffering with a dash of comedic *schadenfreude*: *Jackass* reworked by the Spanish Inquisition.

Happily, after a short day and a 100-kilometre service, Shinto seemed to have regained his appetite for the physically monstrous. He powered upwards, losing the occasional hoof-hold but never losing heart, often pulling me behind like a novice skier on a drag-lift. We caught and passed the chocolate *Polizei*, a wincing Petronella, and – this time to a more muted reception – Shinto's French fan club. I passed a cyclist, one of the few two-wheeled hair shirts on the off-road walker's route, staggering up with his clogged and severally panniered machine above his head. (He caught me up later and said one especially demanding section, no longer than 200 metres, had occupied him for over an hour.)

And then the melancholic casualties, heads in muddy hands by the wayside. An elderly chap having his ankle strapped; a small, stout woman I remembered from Roncesvalles, her left leg stretched out on a rock and her face in a rictus of agony. She was from Venezuela, I learnt that evening, a card-carrying Catholic who'd been saving for this trip for ten years. Her knee ligaments had gone; less than a week in and for her the walk was over. She'd come to praise St Jim, and he'd buried her. How can that have felt?

I got stuck in a pilgrim jam behind a dust truck in the first village of the day, and through the dripping curtain of my poncho hood saw the weather forecast showing on a ceiling-mounted telly in an adjacent bar. I stopped to watch: some typically smug tit with a tie the width of his neck was jabbing a thumb at the lightning symbols with a cheesy that's-life shrug. Whatever you're planning tomorrow, his look said, best replan it. Easy for you to say, Señor Cockhole. Your spoilt golf is our Somme hell. But you know what? He was badly, badly wrong. At the risk of alienating any big-weather fans, I might as well tell you now that it barely rained again.

The next settlement was Cirauqui, a perennially strong performer at international vowel festivals and the Basque for 'nest of vipers'. At its lofty conclusion the panorama opened out into a verdant arena of mist-browed eminences: here were the first olive trees I'd encountered, and the first vineyards. And also, arrowing down before me, the first original section of Roman road, a 2,000-year-old stretch of epically conceived crazy paving, neatly capped at the valley bottom by the first of the camino's dozen Roman bridges.

The Way of St James follows the Via Traiana almost all the way to Santiago, a logistical convenience without which the pilgrimage would never have prospered. Two of Rome's greatest emperors – Hadrian and Trajan, after whom the road was named – were born in Spain, and the colonial infrastructure was assembled with an eye on posterity unusually well focused even by Roman standards. Prissily bordered with cypress saplings, this strip of road might have been subject to a rather cack-handed recent makeover, but there was nothing repro about the bridge, bloody but unbowed after two millennia and more of unhelpful weather, and 1,000 years of relentless pilgrim pounding. Even by the most conservative estimates, 10 million medieval Europeans walked over it. And 60,000 a year still do.

The valley did what valleys usually do, and I was soon engaged in another slithery haul up the other side. That first mud mountain had really thinned the pack out, but it was still busier than I was accustomed to. I could see why people grouped together: walking went better with talking, and where conditions and gradient permitted I'd enjoyed enlightening conversations that ran the gamut of contemporary pilgrim motivations. A couple of Viennese medievalists, a quietly charming Chicagoan whose wife had recently passed away, a shiny-eyed young Spaniard in thrall to the goddess Nike. Last year he'd made Santiago in twenty-six days, and this year it would be fewer (this, necessarily, was the briefest discussion).

But at the same time I learnt that despite the comforts of convoy travel – and with the perpetual risk of violent robbery and wolf attack, the medieval pilgrim never walked alone unless he had to – it quickly became a little overbearing. Particularly when your many fellow travellers are largely culled from a socio-cultural stock with unusually robust views on animal welfare; for it was unavoidably the case that the pilgrim/ass combo, embued with such happy, rustic charm on the flat and in the sun, seemed today the bitter distillate of spite, cruelty and despicable human indolence. '*Oh, le pauvre!*' was a regularly encountered backhand reproach. A rearward transatlantic cry asked why I couldn't carry my own stuff. But mostly there were just looks: brow-pleating empathy for him; hard, sour, pinch-faced contempt for me.

At the valley's churned summit a pair of small ladies turned to fix us with imploring intensity. As we drew level, the elder – the much elder – emphasised the point by unattaching her large pack and holding it out to me in straining arms, like a Balkan beggar with a drugged baby. Yeah, yeah, I nodded wearily as I walked on by, you've carried that great big thing up here and I haven't, so you'll go to heaven and I'll spend eternity helping Satan dribble donkey piss on the shrivelled gums of the damned.

I was having lunch under the porch of an empty farmhouse when they passed. The old one was grasping her colleague's arm and limping; her rolled-up trouser leg revealed a thick swaddling of elasticated support plaster. And behind them toiled a bearded young man, his own pack on his back and one of theirs in each hand. Shortly after I set off, the camino crossed a stream by means of a slatted bridge. I suppose the hour-long detour was the least I deserved.

The approach to sizeable Spanish towns, I was learning, tended to incorporate a muddy yomp across some half-finished commuter suburb of ambitious proportion, and Estella proved no exception. Villatuerta, 4 clicks to the west, seemed largely composed of a houseless grid of roads neatly decorated with give-way lines and zebra crossings, like one of those children's playmats. My 2003 Confraternity guide had been covetously admired for its updated reliability, but even it had nothing to say about the *albergue* I came across while perusing a rare street of completed buildings. A portly señora was reading at a desk inside: she looked both surprised and delighted at my appearance before her, even when it was swiftly and dramatically trumped by that of Shinto. He always followed me indoors at the end of the day, or tried to, and in suitable circumstances this habit could be endearing. It shouldn't have been here, in a reception area that appeared to have been decorated and furnished in the previous two hours, but somehow it was.

'*Eh, burro!*' she cried, rising to her feet with a clap of hands and encouraging Shinto through another door, into a dark and unfinished utility room and thence via the sliding French windows into a yard. In being both tiny and grassless this seemed unlikely to impress Shinto, so it was a surprise to see him half-stifle a whinny of joy and roll delightedly in the clay, particularly as I had yet to remove his luggage.

The dormitory was a small upstairs room crammed with unoccupied pine bunks; the bathroom next door had a marble floor. I deposited my misshapen, clay-clotted bags and set off to find a *supermercado*: with nothing for Shinto to graze on, it would have to be muesli.

In fact it wouldn't, because when at length I found the *supermercado* it was closed. The people of Villatuerte, all three of them, tried their best to suggest alternatives: the lady in the chemist's memorably insisted that the answer was a hefty barrel of baby-milk powder. I laughed, but I'd have taken it had she been a little more flexible on price. Fifteen quid for a donk's dinner? Hee-haw.

There was nothing to do but walk on into Estella, an 8-kilometre round trip. It was 5ish. I should have minded this more, but Shinto had done well that day and for once I was determined to see him right. A dramatic darkening of the sky diluted this determination rather, and I can't pretend I wasn't glad to find myself before an industrially proportioned bakery less than a click up the road. Wheat, rye, barley: it would be a multi-grain banquet for Shints tonight.

Drivers and foremen were in the yard doing what you do at a bakery – milling about. I went up to the one with the least stubble, but opening my mouth I realised I had no idea what to ask for, and that I'd left the pocket dictionary back at the *albergue*. Instead, after a *'por favor'* and a girding cough, I mimed. With upstretched hands sprouting from the top of my head, and a two-tone bray from the back of my throat, I was the unsated ass; when this elicited a small nod of wary comprehension I launched into the life cycle of his comestible quarry, as a barley seedling gleefully piercing the bakery-yard tarmac. The performance had already attracted a semicircle of boiler-suited colleagues, and during my free-spirited interpretation of the threshing process some took a half-step forward in concern; others a full step back in alarm. Breathlessly I scooped together an imaginary mound of grain, before reprising my donkey cameo to effect its histrionic consumption.

Hands on hips and blowing hard, I looked in happy expectation from face to frozen face. 'Come on, boys,' I said. 'Corn me up.' A car sped past with a toot; without turning towards it two or three bakers held up a hand in wordless reciprocation. Then one of them broke rank and placed a gentle hand on my back. *'Peregrino?'* he enquired, softly. *'Si,'* I replied, making a mental note to inaugurate all future discourse with this vital door-opener. *'Peregrino con burro.'*

Slowly he led me towards one of the vans parked in a rank behind us. I watched him crank its back doors ajar and vault in, then rustle out a brown paper bag the size of a mail sack which he motioned me to hold open. I did so and he crouched off to the van's dim depths, emerging with half a dozen stale baguettes. These he dumped in the bag, returning with another load, and another, until my arms could barely encircle its circumference.

He jumped down and waved away my crust-muffled offers of payment.

'*Peregrino, peregrino,*' he said, escorting me to the entrance and thence across the busy road.

'You are a lovely, lovely man,' I shouted over my load as he turned back. Not quite a miracle, perhaps, but certainly a defining moment.

I shed a couple of loaves on the way back, but Shinto still seemed rather overawed by the scale of his nutritional undertaking, piled up before him like some daft inversion of the feeding of the five thousand. I had made a cathedral-sized prannet of myself on his behalf, but I was happy. And also hungry: it was now 7.30, and the dinner my landlady had promised would be cooling on the second-floor dining table.

Indeed it was, a brimming bowl of ketchupped pasta amidst a table full of empties. Four other pilgrims had arrived in the interim, and the one with her head under the formica was Welsh. 'Oh, God,' she said, with a sort of intrigued disgust. 'My big toe is just one huge . . . well, have a look.'

Eight

'Everyone told me that the camino offered those who walked it a love affair,' wrote Shirley MacLaine. 'It was the individual's choice whether to take it.' Well, it hadn't offered me one yet – even though, like her, I'd made 'a conscious decision not to wear a bra'. The same work of academic reference that had detailed those church-bell orgasms (top that, Pavlov) and breakfast erections also incorporated a case study of a Barcelona man who notched up three marks on his staff in three weeks. 'I think my lovers were inspired by natural beauty,' he smirked. Then there was the sixty-year-old German, and the tantalising confession of his experiences as 'a very bad pilgrim'. The author had indeed included a whole chapter entitled 'Increase in Sexual Energy', going so far as to suggest the camino's scallop-shell motif derived from an ancient association with some Venus love-cult. Where were the 'end-of-the-day group massages'? I'm not complaining, not really, but who wouldn't have felt erotically short-changed by a priapic donkey and a faceful of bunions?

Not the medieval pilgrims, at least not openly. Keen to bolster the sin-list, and so maintain a healthy stock of penitent potential pilgrims, throughout the eleventh and twelfth centuries the Church authorities made it more and more difficult to avoid carnal wrongdoing. Sex was proscribed for forty days before a major religious festival, and for five before

113

communion. Ditto on Thursdays (the day Jesus was taken prisoner), and obviously Fridays (when he was crucified). Sunday was clearly right out, and in fact why not Saturday (out of respect for the Virgin) and Monday (in honour of the dead). But hold on to your codpiece, Mr Tuesday Casanova: no unseemliness in the dark, certainly no nudity and none of that foreplay filth. And now I'd like you to stand up, hand on heart and before God, and repeat after me: 'I pledge to douse lustful feelings by practising conjugal relations only whilst extremely tired and ideally half-asleep.'

Yet it could have been worse. The Cathars were a twelfth-century French sect who concluded that Satan, not God, had created the world, and thus reviled procreation with an unusually righteous passion. Forget actually having sex; they couldn't bring themselves even to eat anything created by it, directly or indirectly. No meat, no eggs, no milk. Oddly enough, they didn't last long.

With the sun setting off across a pure blue sky, the second week of my pilgrimage began as had the first. May was bursting out all over: here was a vision of natural fecundity to make a Cathar weep. On the path out of Villatuerte poppies blurted en masse from the well-watered hedgerows, though I could never get Shinto to pose fetchingly before them. He hated pandering to the picturesque, another dogged trait which like his dining habits I had to admire him for. Every time I tried to line him up for a photo by a sun-stippled old horse trough or a walnut-faced widow on her doorstep he'd just saunter onwards and out of shot. If he couldn't he'd very subtly cock his ears and limbs, somehow approximating the symptoms of rickets and abused dementia so effectively that almost every photograph came out like one of the Donkey Sanctuary's 'before' shots.

Welsh Julie walked with me to Estella, and I forgave that appetite-shrivelling dinner-table performance just outside the town, where with her energetic vocal assistance I somehow persuaded Shinto to clatter across a bridge that seemed the very encapsulation of his phobia: a long and steeply pitched arch of wooden slats. I assumed he was off his head on a fearless baguette high, but a couple of days later I read in the *Liber Sancti Jacobi* that this very crossing was notorious for brigands pulling the old poisoned-river horse-flaying scam: 'We watered our mounts in the stream, and had no sooner done so than two of them died; these the Navarrese bandits skinned on the spot.'

We fairly trotted into Estella, laboriously reining Shinto in to stop for a jolly chat with the little and large Dutch couple, rebuttoning each other's epaulettes outside a church containing St Andrew's shoulder blade. The town is known for its ecclesiastical structures, and all adhered to the regional stereotype: Romanesque and closed. 'I went to a wedding in Holland once,' Julie said after we'd left the Netherlanders to their mutual grooming. 'At the reception they played this video showing off the new matrimonial home, and in the bathroom there's the bride and groom, having it off on the toilet.'

Julie was staying on, waiting for at least one church to open, but Shinto was on a roll, a bread roll, and the two of us headed off through the uphill outskirts alone. Though not for long, as a couple of clicks further on the camino passed a monastery, and attached to this monastery was a bodega, and outside the bodega was a little stainless-steel tap, and when you turned that tap red wine came out of it. Free red wine, La Fuente del Vino; the pilgrim's wine fountain. 'Wow!' said the normally restrained Confraternity guide.

On the one hand it was only 11.30 a.m., but on the other, the wine was free. It was already very hot, but the wine was free. Ahead lay a steady 7-kilometre climb (free wine), with another 13 beyond that to the next *refugio* (wine: free). Oh, well. I only had two cupfuls. There. An hour later I washed down my *boccadillo* with the half-litre I'd hosed into a water bottle.

Setting forth into the after-lunch world was a weirdly dislocating experience, a little like coming out of the cinema into bright sunshine. To take wine on a hot morning is to get messed up on drugs; I had changed my brain at the wrong time of day.

Yesterday's mud was already cracking the path into ochred hexagons like the receding foreshore of Lake Chad, and in the wine haze beyond it farmers tended distant vines or bounced towards the horizon on big tractors. A sun-burnished hermitage on a hilltop, the hidebound skeleton of a dog, a peculiar Moorish well. But no pilgrims, and soon no nobody.

It was between the hours of 3 and 7 p.m. that I first properly contemplated the full scale of what I had undertaken: trying to walk all the way across a very large country, with a very large animal who didn't really want to. Shinto rarely went well after lunch, and when the vista ahead opened into a windless, gently sloped enormity of russet earth, he lowered his gaze and his pace until I was barely shuffling along. Geographically accurate as it was to describe Los Arcos, my destination, as the next town up the road, angling my glassy gaze at the fearsome void ahead this statement seemed a graduate of the same school of geographical accuracy as *Krakatoa – East of Brentford*. The heat was cowing, and I was low on water. In all my drinking years I don't think I've ever progressed quite so seamlessly from fuddled vitality to skull-slurried crapulence.

Shinto bore the brunt, of course. He was now stopping for long minutes, and with the little hand nudging 5.00 and Los Arcos still nowhere in sight, I'm afraid I lost my rag. What was this animal's problem? He'd drunk his fill at that Moorish fountain and gorged lavishly on thigh-high greenery at lunch. Come on! Move! Eeeeeuuuwwww! I clapped, I swore, I yanked the rope. I drummed and then clobbered the drinking bowl, the dull, mustardy one that Hanno had selected in preference to the hell-red example I'd taken off the hypermarket shelf. 'A bowl not in a strong colour, or he see it behind and he panic. Panic is the enemy.'

Wrong. Panic was *my* enemy, but his master. I *wanted* him to panic. If the only way to get this animal moving at all was to nurture a low level of constant fear, then the only way to get him moving fast was to ramp that up to blind, mortal terror. Forget a strong colour – I wanted a bowl decorated with flames, skulls, images of slavering wolves with fetlocks sticking out of their jaws. For the first time I thought: I'll thrash him. I'll snap a branch off that dead olive tree and give the stubborn sod a bloody good hiding.

Within an hour I was dragging Shinto along with the rope in both hands and over my shoulder, leaning forward, my face a mask of fatigued fury, soured wine-sweat bursting out everywhere. A low hill took gradual shape before me, and if Los Arcos wasn't behind it I feared I might not be responsible for my actions.

It wasn't. Instead, trailing a plume of dust as it motored unsteadily towards me over the ruts and crevasses, was what gradually assumed the shape of a camper van. 'I think that's a Bedford,' I rasped to myself, to that pilgrim's bootprint, to that thunderstruck tree stump, to anything but that bastard donkey.

A Bedford it was, an old one, and it pulled up before me with a dusted creak. The door opened; a nut-brown fellow in a yachting cap bounded out. 'I've been looking for you,' he said, and not in a way that implied an afternoon spent grim faced before the monitors at PETA satellite-surveillance headquarters. 'I'm John. Would he like a carrot?'

It was beyond odd. This wasn't a road; it was two hours since I'd seen even a tractor. 'How . . .' I began, but John waved his big brown hands about to shut me up. 'I just drive up and down the camino, looking for people in trouble, helping them.' He opened up the side door of his Bedford and emerged a second later with a bottle of cold water. 'Here you go. I was up the top of the Alto del Perdon waiting for you a few days back.'

'Uh . . . ?'

'That wind farm just past Pamplona.'

I nodded vacantly. 'Yeah . . . but who . . .'

'Waited until four. I heard you went over a little later. Biscuit?'

Water bottle pressed to my lips I slowly shook my head, but Shinto had crunched down his carrot and had it instead.

'Now. You're heading for Los Arcos, right?' I cautiously inclined my head. 'OK. It's over the next hill.'

'How far?' I asked, thinly, handing back the empty bottle with a small belch.

He ran his tongue along the underside of a grey moustache. 'About 4 kilometres?'

I'd thought it couldn't be possibly more than 2, and so I'm afraid I said, 'Nunflaps.'

John didn't care. As a possibly non-existent angelic entity he must surely have heard it all before. 'Right, there's nowhere to graze your donkey in Los Arcos, so you'll need some grain. Does he like barley?'

'Does a bear shit on the Pope?'

From a side hatch in his van's red-dusted exterior John procured a large empty fertiliser sack. 'Take this. OK, when you get into Los Arcos there are three large granaries, and if you turn left behind the second . . . '

This was already beyond my current powers of recall, but he went on anyway for perhaps another seven minutes. When he'd finished he patted Shinto's cheek, then took one of my hands in both of his. 'It's gone six. You'd better get going.' And he got back in, fired up the reluctant Bedford and with a wheezy toot bucked noisily away towards the unpeopled horizon.

Nearly two hours later, the pair of us were shambling waywardly down the crippled main drag of Los Arcos, an endless, lopsided parade of grubby whitewash and cracked plaster, big slabs of old wood wedged up against every front door to keep something unwelcome out: dust, mud, rats. It was like the approach to some outsized, downbeat Central American pueblo, which in the circumstances seemed distantly appropriate. I had been across the desert on a horse with no name, or anyway no polite name.

The *albergue* was barely identified, just a dark door next to a bakery, and I'm still not quite sure how I found it. The door opened and I stood there swaying in a coma of fatigue, trying to get a blurred face into focus. The face turned to Shinto and fuzzed out a nod. Soon afterwards he was being tied up to an old bread oven in a shed floored with diesel mud. There was a tiny glassless window high up on one side; a dog shoved his snout through it and barked, and barked, and barked. I could still hear him at it as I blankly retraced my steps towards the granaries.

Improbable as the *albergue*'s discovery had been, it was naught beside the random and empty-headed meanderings that somehow led me to a concrete hangar fadingly emblazoned with agro-commercialisms. No less startling, at 8 p.m. its big sliding door was still open. I went in; it was dim and cool and huge, and smelt like the underneath of a lawnmower. A young woman with dyed maroon hair approached, her expression blending curiosity and wary amusement. John had told me exactly what to say – I think he'd even made me repeat it – but all I could recall was the word for barley. '*Cebada,*' I croaked, proffering my wrinkled sack, happily the one with 'nitrate' printed on the side. '*Cebada. Burro. Peregrino.*'

A querying masculine babble echoed around, and a full-shouldered man appeared out of the shadows. They talked briefly, then she said '*Inglés?*'

'*Si.* Yes,' I replied, trying to remember how to smile.

'You av *burro*? He like *cebada*? You go Santiago?' I kept nodding, and they both broke into beams. The man took my bag and strode over to a conical mound of grain, and began transferring the latter to former with a big steel scoop.

'Is . . . for sheeps,' elaborated the woman, 'but OK I think for *burro*. Is *cebada* wis . . . soya?' Her accomplice dragged the half-filled sack over and heaved it into my arms: this product of peasant industry was the weight of a fat four-year-old. Again the awkward attempts to offer payment, again the ostentatious refusals. When my brain was better I pictured a Spaniard with a big bag walking into a barn in Suffolk, and when I pictured him waddling raggedly back out with it stretched tightly over his head and torso I realised how very wonderful these people were.

The tape-loop barks were now counterpointed by a mournful braying that reached me as I laboured the sack into the relevant backstreet. Shinto threw himself towards the shed door as I unbolted it, and looking at him straining on the rope, the air full of hydrocarbons and dog noise, I knew that I couldn't make him stay in there. Thieving *gitanos* or no, he'd be snuffling up his sheep swill in the open alley.

As I manhandled my possessions to the end of the dim, brownish hall, the *albergue* abruptly opened up into a huge and agreeably rambling edifice, corridors floored with age-worn planks arranged around an enormous central staircase. Everyone was filing to and from bathrooms in preparation for bed: the good news was that I'd somehow once again bagged my own room, a strange trapezoid with over-varnished panelling; the bad news was that I hadn't eaten.

Never judge a Spanish house by its cover, nor a Spanish town by its outskirts. Unshowered I fumbled down into the street, and very soon found myself in an arcaded plaza of confounding beauty. In gathering gloom I squinted about, trying to square this arched and towered Renaissance majesty with what had gone before. And look: there were people, an unpilgrimmed multitude, laughing, smoking, pushing prams. Old men sitting outside bars gamely tapped their feet along to the techno leaking from within, peered down on by nosy old dears perched on precarious second-floor balconies. Friday night it may have been, but this was the first time a small town had been willing to demonstrate evidence of significant inhabitation.

A church filled one side of the square, and I found myself drawn towards its buffed colonnades. The towering doors of the Iglesia de Santa Maria de la Asunción were slightly ajar – an unencountered astonishment that demanded entrance.

Inside was a single worshipper, a bandanna-headed young Spanish pilgrim I remembered exchanging road lore with somewhere near Pamplona. He was genuflecting at the back of the aisle, head almost touching his knee, lips working soundlessly. In other circumstances, ones that would have involved the prior ingestion of equilibrium-restoring calories, I'd have found this spectacle faintly embarrassing. Instead, I looked beyond him to the distant altar, and found myself impressed, transfixed and at length swooningly overwhelmed by a great wall of gold, a Baroque *retablo* sumptuously alive with a profusion of gilded cherubs and virgins and Christ in all his forms. The apostles – could this be right? – returned my stare with eyes of crystal; I lowered myself ashenly into the rearmost pew.

With unblinking eyes I slowly scanned the walls: shoals of scallop shells, gourd-toting Santiagos and a tight mass of screaming, golden souls in purgatory; I turned behind and at the back beheld a glass coffin enclosing a serene saviour. The bandanna pilgrim rose, and crossed himself, and as he passed I felt his zealous, knowing gaze upon me. I thought again of the people who had walked here from all over Europe, stoked by the belief that in doing so they would earn their place in heaven. And just for a moment I thought they might have been right.

Another windless scorcher was well under way by the time I left Los Arcos behind, poppies and cornflowers bright but limp by an undulating camino. The desperate slips and slides of mud-struggling pilgrims were kiln hardened in its surface, like the tracks of a long-extinct species fleeing some now incomprehensible climactic extremity. Revved up by a *cebada* power breakfast, Shinto made good speed through more bark-echo ghost towns, better speed almost than me: my drawn-out spiritual awakening had meant a Mars-bar supper uncomfortably dispatched during yet another Cinderella dash back to the *albergue*.

The camino plaited restlessly about the N111, meaning exposure to more weekend club cyclists – hot and hilly it might be, but there was always breath to spare for a gasped hee-haw – and detours round a couple of poignant Friday-night wipe-outs, roof down in the verge. *Boccadillos* in an almond orchard and an invigorating hatful of fountain presaged what would become the default afternoon pastime: the drawn-out reeling in of one's intended destination beneath a merciless sun. Topping the day's final hill the town of Viana seemed so close that with an effort I might have reached out and tickled its belfries, yet it was three long hours before I could slump messily against a wall in the *refugio*'s panoramic garden.

Beside me the beanpole Australian worked his slow and sinuous way through a t'ai chi routine, cool in the cragged shadows of an ensuite Gothic ruin. In the flat green distance barber-striped factory chimneys announced the presence of Logroño, tomorrow's urban assault course. Somewhere before it Navarra became Rioja – cheers! – and somewhere before that, in fact at the foot of the plain-presiding precipice on which Viana is built, was Shinto, tied to a hunk of reinforced concrete in an acre of wasteland claustrophobically dense with triffidy weeds. My jungly nightmare was his smorgasbord, but it seemed terribly lonely down there. He deserved better: today he'd done well, today he'd been Shints, or Shin Splints, or Shindig, or Shizza, with the more pungent nicknames left in the Los Arcos locker. Still, there was nothing to be done – he'd been dispatched there not by me but by robust decree of the *guardia civil*, whose on-call donk squad had arrived with alarming alacrity at the *refugio* receptionist's telephonic behest.

Viana was an appealing little town, built on the usual model: unhealthy and decrepit tenement outskirts giving way almost without warning to aged, cobbled comeliness. Showered and rehydrated I set off to explore it, sipping ruminatively from what may have been Europe's cheapest can of beer. It was a weekend, but after seven days of tumble-weeded main squares it still seemed odd how much more exuberantly alive were the town dwellers in this part of Navarre. There must be something in the water. Probably gin.

In the town's prettiest plaza, maroon-haired mothers – evidently another regional feature – paraded their flounced-up offspring around the central fountain. The weekend wardrobe of Spain's under tens proved a dependable jaw slackener: boys in sailor suits is one thing, but I passed a trio done up like General Pinochet, with gold bands from dress-jacket cuff to elbow and heavy loops of braid all over their chests. I wound my way through this junior junta, eyes on the flagstones. Somewhere round here, set in the pavement, was the tombstone of an aristocrat whose potted obituary in my guidebook unforgettably declared him 'synonymous with murder, rape, incest, theft and treachery'. I'm thinking, of course, of Prince Michael of Kent. But I'm actually talking about Cesare Borgia.

The Borgias were the Bond villains of Renaissance Europe, and Cesare was the Blofeld's Blofeld. But as well as being a vile and mercenary pan-Continental schemer, he was also, as you'd expect from the son of Pope Alexander VI, a hard-bastard one-man killing machine. At times the plotting must all have seemed a bit much: 'The French, fearing the Hapsburgs, allied with Fernando. The Italians, fearing both but detesting the Spanish even more, backed the Austrians.' And at such times, Cesare sought refuge in a more simple pleasure: taking on a large group of enemies and slaughtering them all single-handed.

It was a hobby that reached its unfortunate apotheosis on 3 March 1507, when having failed to interest the citizens of Viana in joining him in an attack on the fortress headquarters of their besiegers, he set out to confront a whole castle alone. 'Who is that mad man?' remarked the enemy commander, peering curiously from the battlements before dispatching a patrol. After the unplucky Vianans retrieved Cesare's body the next day, they identified twenty-five wounds.

Anyway, I didn't find the tombstone – snidely stuck out in the street so his many enemies could grind his name underfoot – but I did think about him over the course of dinner. I'd met the chocolate *Polizei* and a nice German chap called Simon, and together we'd found a rigorously authentic local hang-out: dark heads thrown back in swashbuckling laughter, the sour smoke of black tobacco, nutshells and fag ends all over the tiled floor. And, high up in a corner, a large telly showing a man in an embroidered pink over-corset waving a tablecloth at a big black animal.

From here on it would be impossible to eat cheaply without encountering a broadcast bullfight, and in consequence I saw one almost every night. As a torture it was a peculiar blend of the cruel and the tedious, as technically complex as pulling the legs off a greenfly and as a spectacle hardly more dynamic. And yet being a televised sport – I was oddly thrilled by the studio experts doodling with light pens on the freeze-frame replays – I felt a duty to my sex and age to find something good about it. The matador's expressions were dependably entertaining – a constipated, glowering pout that German Simon endeavoured to adopt throughout the soup course – but that night there was a very special bonus.

'Look! He has him here!' cried Simon, leaping to his feet and clamping a hand to his groin with the vigour of a young Michael Jackson. And as I turned, the man in pink copped a tusk deep in the loins, before being hoisted, twisted and tossed in one fluid movement. A couple of the girls cheered discreetly, though they quickly stopped when we rewound to the slo-mo. Oh, dear Lord it was grim. But not for the locals. From their titillated gasps you knew that here was a star clip for the next series of *You've Been Gored*.

Bullfights and Borgias: walking back up the cobbles I speculated on the continuities of Spanish life. In the 500 years since Cesare's last stand uptown Viana hadn't changed much on the surface, nor apparently beneath it. And in terms of this enduring celebration of third-party violence, I was still regularly intrigued by the schizophrenic cult of Santiago: Jimbo Peregrino, the open-faced, gourd-bearing shell wearer, versus James the Moor-slayer, a slavering psycho on horseback, his hoisted blade lustrous with the blood of a million Muslims. Perhaps it was a twist on the old nice apostle/nasty apostle routine. (Though the nasty one wasn't really that nasty, being largely a propaganda creation, and the nice one wasn't that nice: what sort of ungodly egotist goes off to pay homage to himself?)

The *refugio* was a faultlessly converted monastery with majestic views, but along with the best points of its genre it showcased all the worst, and these as usual rose to prominence in the hours of darkness. Unexpected confrontation with full-frontal, Pilsner-bellied German nudity was an occupational hazard in any *refugio* bathroom, but in these early days forewarned was not always forearmed. The man trimming his tache in front of the mirror nodded at me in greeting: I'd enjoyed a linguistically compromised but warmly conducted conversation with him and his wife on the way out of Los Arcos. As I recall he'd given Shinto a cup-cake. A good man, a kind man, but a man whose wrinkled pilgrim parts now rested on the rim of the sink I was waiting to clean my teeth in.

And just as the communal claustrophobia of *refugio* life engendered heart-cheering mutual trust – a camcorder charging in a corridor, an unattended six pack on a sleeping bag – so it also catalysed heart-hardening misanthropy. Petty grudges quickly coagulated into destructive loathing: *she* took twenty minutes in the shower, *they* broke one of my clothes pegs, *he* stuck his sandals in the tumble-dryer at 11 p.m. – wait a sec, that was me. The worst, though, were the snorers. And that night we had the phlegm-larynxed, sinus-dredging king of them all.

You recognised them after a while. That grey-maned, conspicuously featured Frenchman at Villatuerta had looked like a snorer, and he was. Generally, if they were round of gut and large of nose, you knew you were in for a bad night, and after a quick silhouette survey of surrounding bunks – this was my first experience of the treble-decker – I knew we'd have trouble from the far corner.

Everyone had earplugs but not everyone could tolerate using them. Certainly one's first time is uncomfortable: a head-filling canal stretcher that I wish I hadn't described in pilgrim public as the cranial equivalent of being fisted. Furthermore, as Shirley MacLaine has noted, earplugs 'obstruct the meridians to the kidneys'. But practice makes perfect, and as a bad father it's now many years since I substituted irksome nocturnal hysteria for the soothing, womb-like whoosh of my own circulation.

Foam technology has come a long way from the ineffectual hole-blockers that distorted rather than dampened, so that 'I think I heard someone downstairs' came through as 'A dingo herdsman's trousers', and 'Daddy! Daddy-daddy-daddy-daddy! DADDY!' as 'Mummy?' Today's earplugs are engineered to filter out everything quieter than a child finding a headless owl on his pillow, but that was many decibels shy of Herr Corner's most troubled inhalations. Was snoring the least appealing human function? So I began to conclude as those obstructed respirations rent the air of a crowded room in which their provider alone slept. With more notorious antisocial excretions there was a personal price for the culprit to pay, a legacy of stench and stain. But the snorer, by definition, slept on and slept well, unaware of the unfolding outrage.

When Herr Corner breathed out, people tutted and swore so bitterly that soon even I could hear them, but when he breathed in, and that great belly rose in the moonlit gloaming, they threw things. Shoes mainly, but also a book. This phase was short-lived, however: the brief hiatus of calm engendered by a direct hit was immediately preceded by a huge orgasmic snuffle, perhaps the very worst noise in the world and as such too high a price to pay. Surrender was the only option for many – the German girls went down and slept on the kitchen floor. When I bleared downstairs in the morning they'd gone. To Barcelona.

I'd been seeing 'Fabricación Logroño' on manhole covers for days, which at least had the effect of managing expectations. It wasn't that bad, but even allowing for the Sunday factor Logroño had the air of a city that never quite got going. A bridge that was long without being grand, a workmanlike cathedral, a main shopping drag whose unavoidably provincial ambience was encapsulated in a fly-carpeted window wherein a largely felled army of Mutant Ninja Turtles laid ineffective siege to a dusty crystal stag at bay. It wasn't hard to see why of the five cities the camino passes through, Logroño was the only one I'd never heard of.

Through the inevitable half-built suburbs – one development floridly announcing itself in Gothic script as the Residencial Camino de Santiago – and out into a big park newly laid out on a brownfield site by the marshalling yards, and now abundantly littered with the detritus of impromptu

Saturday-night gatherings. I punted a pizza box off the Way of St James and looked at Shinto. Was that it? We'd just walked straight through a city the size of – well, all right, the size of Richmond – without even noticing.

That wasn't it, not quite. Presently the camino was joined by other footpaths of recent construction, and on these footpaths were a few people, and then a few more, and soon we were engulfed by promenading families, shifty juvenile shamblers, charmingly love-struck pensioners and a bloke on a big white horse. On a path so populous, the rival presence of this latter pairing should have been towards the fatal end of the awkward scale: when Greek meets Greek, as the proverbial prediction of impending explosive conflict has it, though as a contest this was more a case of when Greek meets Greenfly.

In fact, despite a little low-level bridling feistiness as the towering charger clopped past, Shinto rose to the bait rather than being it. When an acceptable buffer zone had opened up, he began to trot after the horse at a safe distance, mane tossed and nostrils occasionally flared in what I can only interpret as a face-saving expression of defiance. It was rather sweet: I thought of myself and a couple of classmates flicking gleeful V-signs at those taunting skinheads after they'd got off the train and the doors hissed shut. And then what happened after they hissed back open again.

The pacemaker lost us as we approached the climax of everyone else's walk if not ours, a large reservoir encircled by picnic areas. Slightly drunk dads took a break from booting footballs at their cowering sons with raucously mimed demands for photos, rides and, at least once, bestial intercourse. For days the gathering profusion of fly-posters had alerted us to a looming general election, and now a canvassing politician lured me towards an accompanying film crew, bending his head to Shinto's cheek with a look of unholy rapture that said, Kissing babies is for pussies – right, voters? And I was stalked for almost three hours by a middle-aged man with a zoom lens whose telescopic capacity was rivalled only by Shinto's.

If I haven't detailed my donkey's lunch-time performance,

it's because I'd almost stopped noticing it. Actually, that isn't even slightly true. You couldn't not notice it. Perhaps it was just that I usually lunched alone, with no one to disturb, repulse or excite except myself.

As I parked him in the clover for his afternoon graze, Shinto went through a preparatory routine that never changed. First, he would place his rear legs as far back as they would go, tilt forward on tip-hoofs, and let forth a huge gush of piss. This completed, he'd take a couple of steps forward and extrude his suede-look sphincter – stop that – into a neat little dome before squeezing out a couple of dozen warm pellets. The assembly smoothly retracted, utterly unbesmirched, and the first stage, an almost dignified industrial process, was at an end. A faultlessly hygienic one, too, at least until his maddeningly random feeding pattern led him back to that patch of sorrily marinaded grass. Like most sequels, however, stage two was rather a disappointment.

We all like a good meal. Lunch was invariably a slightly wet or slightly stale baguette stuffed with *chorizo* and maybe a crudely flattened tomato, but I always looked forward to it. You rarely found a bar that was open for breakfast, and if you did all they could offer was coffee and a poxy roundel of toast. After five hours on the road, I would be anticipating my footlong sarnie with almost religious fervour.

But for Shinto it was even more than that. With one clap of the gelding bricks, his hierarchy of needs had been narrowed to an obsessive quest for food. It was his only love, his passion, and at lunch-time he wanted everyone to know how he felt. Everyone usually meant me, but today it meant young families and old ladies, and lots of them.

'*Burrico!*' a tricycling tot would squeak, pedalling up eagerly, but that forearm of dark muscle had already parted the sheath and was craning smoothly out and down, and down, and down. Be sure of one thing: here was no ding-a-ling, no winkle, no wiener. Here was the very schlong of Kong.

Childish joy faltered into shock and awe, and as the unleashed appendage began to firm up a parent would stride over and drag trike and infant brusquely away, fixing me with a glare of furious disgust.

'It means he likes you!' I could have yelled, but I never did. I understood. It was a terrible spectacle for any eyes, particularly as the evil bollard's blackened outer casing had of late become flaky and roughened, like the surface of an old inner tube. And bluebottles were now congregating hungrily round the blunt, splayed tip, something Hanno had told me to watch out for. 'If you have too many fly here, you must apply the *crème*.' This was without question the very worst thing I had ever been asked even to think about, and as such I discovered that no matter how many flies there were, it was never quite too many.

We left behind the frolicking burghers of Logroño – the good, the drunk, the pornographically outraged – and followed a once-more empty camino alongside a new motorway, over an old one and then between an immensity of vineyards. Some were clinically technological, thin green shoots trained down mile-long trellises of stainless steel; others small and ancient, gnarled, arthritic stumps on a bald patch of hill.

The ruins of a medieval hospice announced the approach to Navarrete, like Viana and so many others an industro–rural mess with a heart of Renaissance gold. The *refugio* lay happily at the arcaded periphery of the latter, and at 5.45 I'd once again arrived late enough to bag the quieter overspill accommodation on the top floor. My *credencial* was stamped by another of those slightly overbearing young Christians, a beaming youth in a Brazil shirt, who instructed me to stable Shinto at the Centro Hípico: 'Is like hotel for horse.'

Navarrete wasn't a big place, but it took me an hour to find this establishment, hidden over a hill a click outside town. It was a ranch, I suppose, with a big paddock full of horses, and – hey, Shints! – the first rival donkeys we'd encountered. Shinto stopped in his tracks, nostrils flared, transfixed. This may have been because, of the three dark brown donks behind that fence, one was gamely shagging a huge mare.

It was a refreshing inversion of the usual mule-spawning

scenario, and after knocking on the owner's door we watched it unfold to a happy conclusion. A donkey doing a horse is a laudable way-to-go display of pluck, but a horse doing a donkey? That's just wrong. That's . . . mulophilia, or something.

The proprietors were a lovely couple, who ruffled Shinto's mane, refused payment and insisted on photographing him for their archive. It falteringly transpired that Shinto wouldn't be let into the paddock on health-and-safety grounds; this was probably for the best, but we agreed a compromise wherein he was tied up in sight and earshot of his fellow long-ears.

My long walk back was broken halfway by two matching beers, and rounded off with a brisk half-litre of rosé and an overly lubricated platter of fried meat slices outside the bar adjoining the *refugio*. (Note to the lowbrow chefs of Spain: please stop frying *chorizo*. It looks like scabs.) Evelyn was at the bar with a coterie of senior male admirers, and so too were a pair of elderly German ladies, broad faces capped with silvery pudding bowls. They were at least the fourth such couple I'd encountered, and scrutinising them with the enhanced understanding often associated with one's third glass I realised a common link: they were all lesbians. Evelyn later told me that in one *refugio* she'd been awakened in the small hours by some vigorous old-girl-on-old-girl action in the bunk below. I looked at the two ladies, smiling at each other over their *tortillas*. I don't know why the camino should attract so many of their ilk. And unless I ordered another carafe and downed it in one I could hardly ask.

Six fifteen was the earliest I'd been up, but I was still the last out. At some point, I supposed, my body clock would adjust to this idiotic regime; probably when it did, I'd never be able to reset it, and end up booting my kids out of bed in the dark for years to come. Shinto was retrieved – that exchange of farewell brays softened the heart – and it was out into an already shimmering sun.

Navarrete bid us a rather sombre goodbye, in the twin forms

of another impromptu anti-ETA roadblock manned by twitchy, armed youths, and a monument to a Belgian pilgrim who'd been fatally knocked off her tandem in 1986. This was the second such memorial I'd seen, and soon they became commonplace. I suppose if you peg out on a pilgrimage, particularly because having done so you're automatically fast-tracked to paradise, bereaved relations feel an obligation to stick up a stone. But I can't say it did much for morale. One day I saw three: what was this, a big walk or The Long March?

A debilitating stretch through the gutter detritus of our new tarmac neighbour, the N120, was leavened by the colossal mountain range taking shape to the left – I had no idea the horizons of Spain were so generously serrated. Most of the flinty peaks were topped with snow, dispatching a cool breeze to refresh us as the path left the road and ploughed a pleasant, gently rising furrow through more epic vineyards. Labourers were weeding and pruning, and it was good to see that they appeared to be locals rather than the slave-waged North Africans one tends to see out in the fields of southern Europe. But then again maybe they were slave-waged locals.

At midday the advance guard from Logroño whistled up from behind, but unlike most of the speed ramblers these were an unusually communicative lot. Evidently too communicative, because after I'd been asked for perhaps the tenth time in an hour what his name was, and how I'd got him, and what he ate, I felt myself shuffling across the threshold of dangerous boredom. An endless throughput of people I would never see again had presented a persistent temptation for idle deceit, and rendered frivolous by a potent sun I finally succumbed to ennui-related fact management.

Two little German men walked up, conversed, and proceeded towards the russet horizon taking with them the tragic tale of Faustus, found living off chrysalis husks in an abandoned butterfly farm. A lone Frenchman was next to ask the trigger question, and in wide-eyed silence heard of Bjorn's rescue from the grim warehouse where he was due to fight two swans for the entertainment and speculative advantage of Copenhagen's underworld. 'Hugh is one of the lucky ones,' I heard myself telling a plump Dutch cyclist. 'Thirty work donkeys drown every day in Portugal's lobster hatcheries.' After overstepping the mark with the tragedy of little Geraldo, found licking pine sap off his dead mother, I began to cobble together a grand finale.

'Canasta?' repeated a curious husband of Mediterranean origin an hour up the road.

'Card game,' I replied, casting a flinty gaze towards the middle distance, 'and when the Belgians play it, a terrible, drunken one.'

His wife eyed me uncertainly. 'OK, so you win *burro* in dis game,' she began, her brim-shaded brow furrowed, 'but why he eat only paper?'

An indulgent chortle. 'That's the thing, you see. Every time they finished an old pack they'd throw it out the window, and he was tied up in the yard down there . . .' I laid a hand on a hot grey haunch. 'Still loves thin cardboard, but I've got him on to newsprint now.' A wink. 'Isn't that right, Steve?'

Nájera was my destination, and despite the heat I strode towards it with unusual determination. This was a town with a swimming pool you could get into free with a pilgrim passport, and many of whose episcopal forefathers had been convicted of simony – easily my favourite charge of ecclesiastical improbity. And the *refugio* was next to a church I simply had to see: the choir-stall carvings included mermaids seducing monks, crossed circumcision knives and syphilitic beggars baring their bepoxed buttocks. A ruby looted from its statue of the Virgin now adorns the Queen's crown. That's the Queen of England, QE2.

It should have been under five hours to Nájera, but confrontation with a certain sort of river crossing near a cement works just outside town made it over six, incorporating a detour across a sticky acre of poisoned industrial leachate that the coroner at my inquest might want to be aware of. I'd been alone on the camino for a broiled age when red earth finally evolved to pavement; having endured a further foot-dragging, alley-shambling eternity I found myself cruelly finished off by the old one-two.

Thwack! Church closed for hours. Smack! *Refugio* already full. From behind a huge desk the bearded *hospitalero* shook his head in apology and despair. He was French, and spoke in damning terms of the '*contre-la-montre*' walkers who yomped in before lunch-time and yomped out again before dawn. His disposition suggested that with a little wheedling I could have bagged myself a space on the floor, but when I mentioned Shinto the shutters came down.

It was absurdly hot now, easily the hottest yet. I tramped out to the lamp-post I'd tied Shinto to, gave him a weary pat on the jugular groove and got the books out. It was bad. The next town was Azofra, 6 parched and lonely clicks away.

I stooped to pull the snake back out of the well, and as I did so noticed a small, weeded yard, right next to the *refugio* and contained by a rusty gate. I stumbled over: it was locked. So I ran back inside, and blatheringly endeavoured to describe this little garden with some grass for a donkey. The beard rose and fell, but the eyebrows above it sloped down in sympathetic dismay. '*Oui, je comprends,*' he said when I'd finished sounding stupid. If the garden was his, of course . . . but it wasn't, and the owners would never allow it. Who were the owners? '*Les Franciscans.*'

It wasn't until I was almost back out the door that I assimilated this information. The disciples of Francis of Assisi, the ideological descendants of Christianity's Mr Animal, every beast's two-legged friend and a man who had done this entire sodding pilgrimage in 1214 on a pigging donkey . . . ? Oh, how my hot blood boiled. A thick gobbet of righteous, visceral outrage began to fill my chest and throat, and it might even have come out had not a man with a towel round his waist then appeared at the top of a distant staircase. He saw me and his fearfully familiar face lit up. 'Please! I have some nice thing for Steeeve!'

A donkey isn't the ideal getaway vehicle, but I have to say

Shinto did a pretty good job. It was almost as if he didn't want to be force-fed *El Mundo*.

We were packing up after a very late lunch, Shinto still snout down in a pile of mown grass at a little park out the back end of Nájera, when Petronella walked past. She'd been turned away at the *refugio*, and I was glad to welcome her into our convoy. Shinto's post-lunch trough had become an ordeal of cake-stamping frustration, and the guidebooks were of one accord: it was tough ahead. Saddling Shinto up that morning I'd allowed myself to think that for the first time I was running a pretty tight ship. But we all know what happens to tight ships. That's right – they're so tight that they suddenly crack and get all smashed in and sink and everyone drowns.

I was up front; Petronella got the tail end. After a short, sharp climb we found ourselves at the far end of a broad *meseta*, flat and fly-blown, the camino bisecting vineyards the size of Suffolk. At first it appeared no worse than dull, but there was no shade and after an hour the battering sun seemed to soften bones.

Sweat burnt my eyes. I blinked it out and squinted around in a vain quest for something that wasn't the blue sky or the combed red earth or those rows of big-leaved shrublets that filled the gap between the two. Everyone else would be stretched out on a cool, dark bunk, but here I was once again, out in the igneous afternoon with the crickets and lizards. And if this was mid-May, what broiled lunacy went on here in mid-August? It was too hot to talk, and soon to think.

A yank on the rope snapped back my limp and useless head and left it wobbling about atop a rubbery spine. By now I could gauge the strength of a pull-back and assess with reasonable accuracy its cause. The hierarchy, in descending order of induced whiplash potency, was as follows: the presence, on or alongside the path or road, of rival donkey dung; of wild alfalfa; of a funny shadow; of general equine dung; of hairy barley; of all other dung. When my skull had stopped moving I turned back: there was nothing. Shinto just stood in the middle of the path, gazing at or through my midriff. Petronella's crimson countenance registered as much bemusement as it could.

I hauled him back to life but five yards on it happened again. And again. I felt a new sensation in my right palm and when I held it up to my leaking face, sweat dripped agonisingly into three great splits in the flesh. I already had rope burns on six fingers, and my left fist was bound and taped like a boxer's. The perpetual turning back and heaving forward had neurones in both shoulders dispatching urgent messages to the brain; the brain nodded quickly and told the eyes to watch out for a flaming breaker's ball. And in the short time since the rain had stopped I'd been dramatically flash burned on every exposed area of south-facing skin: forearm, ear, cheek, half a nose. West, west, always west. The only way to guarantee a non-comic, all-over tan was to turn round at Santiago and walk all the way back.

Our pace dropped further: in the next hour we covered less than 2 kilometres. To maintain the illusion of progress I reduced the length of my stride to that of an infant penguin's, and soon my entire body ached, as if all that pent-up motion was curdling in the muscles. Hare and tortoise teamed in a three-legged race. It was a little like walking your great-grand-mother to church; exactly so if you were in Chad, and the church was 500 miles away, and you'd just nicknamed her Fucko.

What was going wrong? I looked round again and saw Shinto contort those hitherto inscrutable features into an alarming gurn, wobbling forth a jowly lip before the neck slumped down-wards and he began scraping his mouth horribly through the red gravel. Was he hungry? The extra weight of the *cebada* sack certainly can't have helped – I untied it, poured some out into the bowl and wedged the remainder into my day pack. Without enthusiasm he lowered his head and snuffled down a few mouthfuls. Then he eased upright and began pawing feebly at the earth like an infirm bullock going through the motions.

'I think he would like to roll,' rasped Petronella, who'd just inspected my crevassed palm and noted a lifeline cut short by the longest weeping gash. Hanno had urged me never to deny Shinto a roll in the dust, and because I'd apparently passed this information on to Petronella in some previous life last week, I stumbled over to him and unloaded everything.

He watched me detach all the panniers and carrier bags and bowls and pile them messily up either side of him. He watched me drag them to the edge of the path. Then, for perhaps twenty minutes, he just watched me. I watched him back for as long as I could bear, then feeling sympathy and restraint evaporate in my bubbling brain I robotically reloaded him. What the Teutonic sink-bollocks was he playing at? Maybe the donks at the Centro Hípico had been getting at him, filling that empty head with filthy asinine propaganda.

'Every day?' came the shrill bray through the fence. 'He makes you walk *every day*? That is *precisely* the sort of odious fascist exploitation my grandfather went through under Franco.'

'You're being sacrificed, brother,' whinnied his colleague. 'Sacrificed on the altar of human sloth.'

And Shinto would blink his big lashes, then turn to the third, sauntering languidly up to the chain link. 'Hey, Frenchie,' he'd begin, in a deep and sugared neigh. 'You wanna stick around here. Man, you ain't *lived* till you done it with a horse.'

'Come on.' The crack in my voice gave notice that Shinto was drinking at the last-chance trough. A fearful scenario was forming in my mind – what if he decided that was it, that he simply wouldn't take another step? We both knew there was nothing I could do if he did. He made the rules; the law was indeed an ass.

On cue he dug his hoofs in, and when I pulled harder strained his head back and bared those jaundiced tombstones: a hideous whites-of-the-eyes display that I would later dub his El Loco look. In that one moment I understood, in stark and vivid detail, why donkeys have acquired their unfortunate reputation, an impenetrable, illogical inertia that for 2,000 years and more has been propelling decent men to the edge of reason, and then off it.

'EEEEUUUWWWW!' In one quick but ragged movement I stooped to claw a hand through the path-side scrub: it emerged with a foot-long frond of yellow-budded oilseed rape. My jaw tightened along with my grasp round its stem. I threw down the rope and stamped to Shinto's rear, my boiled red head filled with badness, a terrible determination to do things to a donkey that even Basil Fawlty wouldn't have dared do to an Austin 1300. If he didn't work, there was no point having him. With a small noise that was more fear than protest, Petronella scuttled round to the front and picked up the rope.

I'm not ashamed to say I brought that bouquet down upon him. What am I saying? I'm horribly, cravenly ashamed. Out there under an angry sun, punishing the doe-eyed pride of many an infant bestiary in a rush of ugly, primal exhilaration: it wasn't really a postcard moment. Up front Petronella went very quiet, head down at the hot earth. All it needs for evil to triumph, she was no doubt reminding herself, is for good people to do nothing.

And it didn't even work. The frail buds and tendrils thwicked against Shinto and sent the relevant haunch into a reflex flinch; the first time this was followed by half a dozen trots, but the second time it wasn't. Hanno's three-day authority deadline had long since expired: I'd spared the rod and spoilt the donk, unlocked the stable door too late and found the would-be bolter asleep. For a mad minute the black heart of a pitiless Dark Age drover thumped within me. My hot tongue darted across blistered lips – what I'd give for a goad. A stick with a nail, blood on that dumb brown rump.

I was pondering an upgrade to a juniper switch when a noise like a peacock being castrated screeched out and there was Petronella, waving her sticks above her head, wheeling round to Shinto's rear with a fearful ululation tearing from her throat. Those long ears flipped back and he ran. That now bent and flaccid stem dropped from my whip hand and I just stood and watched him go, already haunted by the awful probability that my miserable, beastly conduct might be the closest I'd come to recapturing the zeal of the wayfaring medieval fanatics. After 100 yards he shifted down to a brisk walk, and when his pace lowered to a saunter that grating shriek and those wind-milled poles instantly fleetened his feet afresh.

It took me twenty minutes to catch them up. 'You must remember that we expect to go faster, because we are now getting fitter.' Petronella's voice was abnormally muted. I had been bad, and now she was going to go all rational and Dutch on me.

'Why isn't *he* getting fitter?'

'Maybe he is. But this is not usual for him.'

'Yes, it is! He spends all summer going off on . . . on . . .' On three-day hikes. I thought back, and contemplated an important and shaming truth: Shinto's average speed had been in gradual decline since day four. This was unknown territory for him. I was pushing the donkey envelope, and I was obviously pushing it too hard. There was nothing else to say. Nothing I hadn't already said with flowers.

Azofra took the whole crumbly, dusted shambles thing and ran with it. This time there was none of that nancy nice stuff at the middle, just two long streets of rude deprivation, the unsteady, dishevelled houses like old winos propping each other up. The roads converged near a scuffed-up church that also accommodated the *refugio*, described by my guide as 'in poor condition'. Just beyond were two bars, the walls of each hung with desiccated haunches of pig. Outside one sat Evelyn, encircled as was presently the norm by her adoring entourage. 'The whole town just ran out of water,' she called out. 'And the refuse-io is completely overrun with Belgian kids.' Well, she was wrong there! They were Dutch.

A babbling senior señora invited Petronella to share the church's overspill porch with her teenage compatriots, a week into a school trip rather more roundly edifying than the dank Welsh festivals of tent-bound masturbation I wish I didn't recall. The church was surrounded by toothsome undergrowth, but also by steps. '*Burro no passa*,' I mumbled, as the house-coated *hospitalera* gamely urged a bridling Shinto towards a small stone flight. She looked at me with withering condescension, then snapped the top off a dead sapling in those tiny, gnarled hands. 'No!' I yelped, jumping in front of her as she flexed it approvingly. 'No, that's . . . wrong. *Gracias*.'

Half an hour later I was stamping tent-pegs into a rock-strewn, ant-happy triangle of semi-desert near a bus-stop just out of town. Before me, through a grove of fluttering beech trees, the sun was settling down to kiss the hard plain, as if in apology for what it had done that day. Twenty yards to my rear, two trilbied old farmers stood either side of a fountain in whose fitful, shandy-hued expectorate I'd later be cleaning my teeth. Every time I looked up they were staring with blink-less fervour, one at me, one at Shinto, up the top of the apex dentally pruning some big shrub. This was an agricultural settlement of desperate poverty, the first I'd been to where donkey theft might be the product of practical necessity rather than juvenile boredom. (As the perpetrator of many far less imaginative wrongs committed in the name of adolescent entertainment, I always held this as my dominant fear for Shinto's overnight safety.) Yet I needed food, and access to mankind's full gamut of bottled fluids, and when the tent was semi-erect that meant leaving the pair alone with Shinto. I approached with a manic smile and a lofted hand. And when that didn't seem to work, I stopped between them and crossed myself at each in turn.

Nine

'We found a woman weeping bitterly,' I read aloud to my donkey as he stood saddled up by the fountain, hock deep in morning mist and nose down in a basin of barley. 'We followed her into a nearby field, where she had two asses stuck in a bog. We offered her assistance, whereupon she began laughing.' I scratched a mosquito-ravaged forearm, uncertain what I was trying to achieve beyond vaguely unsettling him, a job frankly better left to my mud-washed, camping-haired dishevelment. 'Not my words, Shinto,' I said, wedging the book into a pannier, 'but the words of seventeenth-century pilgrim Dominic Laffi as he walked out of Azofra.'

I had camped, and so it had rained. The world beyond Azofra was a drizzled fuzz which occasionally offered up a medieval gallows, or a dead deer, or – sorry, madam! – a full pair of pilgrim buttocks caught in an ineffectively shrub-shielded comfort stop, before quickly engulfing them back behind us. Small groups of walkers plodded past every hour or so, and generally checked their pace for a little verbal byplay. All the English people I'd previously encountered, admittedly a modest sample, had been the sort who'd said things like 'the bods up at Confraternity HQ' and referred to their heads as 'the old noggin', so it was a frank relief to meet one, the loud and cheerful Sara, who didn't.

An infuriating detour round a huge new golf course – surely

a recipe for heavenly-wrath-induced lightning-related fairway fatalities – then slowly up and slowly down to the conclusion of another stage. In terms of clicks Shinto and I were 20-a-day men, but it was only 15 to Santo Domingo de la Calzada and we passed the big potato warehouse on its outskirts at half twelve.

I liked Santo Domingo before I'd even got there. The name helped, of course: St Sunday of the Causeway in my dictionary, St Dominic of the Cooking through that peerless Internet translator. But it was more than that. Somehow the history of Santo Domingo was a microcosm of the history of the entire pilgrimage: a tale that combines piety, endeavour and winningly surreal cobblers.

It's not many a fifteen-year-old, unfortunately, who strides off into the forest resolved to the life of a hermit, but Domingo Garcia was a special character even by the standards of the early eleventh century. Inspired 'to improve travel conditions in the Rioja region', apparently by a dream rather than an infra-structure-development press release, he set about upgrading a nearby stretch of camino. Domingo hacked out a road through 37 kilometres of dense forest, and laid a stone bridge over the mighty Oja, the Rio that gives the province its name. He built the pilgrim hospice and the church that were the kernel of a new town that would later be Santo Domingo – and he did all this alone, or at least with a handful of spirited volunteers and the odd angel who took up the slack when everyone stopped to pray.

Domingo dies in 1109, his apposite final act the literal digging of his own grave, and having been canonised is interred in his own church. Life goes on in Santo Domingo – a steady stream of pilgrims, a fire in the church, the series of vicious regional disputes that sees Navarre and Castille swap owner-ship of the town six times in one twenty-four-year period alone – until some unknown point in the mid-twelfth century, when a family of Germans en route to Santiago stops at a Santo Domingo inn.

The innkeeper has a beautiful daughter and the pilgrims a

handsome son. Well, you know the story: boy meets girl, chastely eschews lewd congress, spurned girl frames boy for theft, boy is strung up by furious locals and left to rot. One of the perennial attractions of these tales is the bereaved family's nonchalant acceptance of tragedy.

'I don't know if you've looked out the window this morning, Heidi, but there's a corpse swinging from the gallows that looks an awful lot like our Wolfgang.'

'Let's see . . . Honestly, why do they always have to spin about like that? I can't get a proper look at him.'

'Next time he's facing our way try and imagine him without that big purple tongue lolling out.'

'OK. Here we go . . . Know what? You're absolutely right: that's the tabard I had to stitch up after that business with the donkey.'

'Oh, marvellous. Some bloody pilgrimage this is turning out to be. Anyway, best crack on – you nip down and get his shoes off and I'll bring the cart round the front.'

They reach Santiago and pass back through Santo Domingo a month later. But when they go to pay their respects to the fly-blown bird table that was once their little boy, instead there he is, waving happily at them from the gibbet. St James has held his weight the whole time, presumably with one hand, leaving the other free to lob earth-bound scraps of sustenance into his mouth. The newly unbereaved couple rush to inform the local town clerk of the miracle. 'If he's alive,' he snorts, 'then so are these roast chickens I'm eating.' Cue flying supper.

The enduring upshot is that to this day a coop in the west transept of Santo Domingo's baroque-towered cathedral houses a pair of noisy white cockerels. The curious pilgrim can still today take a rather high-risk Baguette Challenge: chuck a lump of bread in the cage, and if they eat it, his pilgrimage will reach a successful conclusion. If they don't, he'll find progress to Santiago impeded somewhat by his own death.

I don't know who'd been fattening up their cocks that day, but the Santo Domingans were evidently happy about something. As the street narrowed and the buildings aged and grew, so my fellow pedestrians swelled in numbers and effervescence. There were groups of men in matching neckerchiefs, children in lace caps and harlequin-hued plimsolls. Suited dignitaries with religious medallions covering their tie knots and red-haired wives in tow. An audibly complex commotion echoed towards me off the aged walls and was presently traced to a brass band in polka-dotted boiler-suits, half of them parping enthusiastically into cornets and the rest extracting flamboyant refreshment from those chemistry-lab wine-spout things, arms aloft, stained and gaping mouths to the sky. A gang of teenagers roared and honked past in an elderly Peugeot with its roof sawn off and the rest painted like a Friesian. And after all the checkpoints and separatist graffiti, all the bilingual roadsigns and furious defacement of public buildings, it was frankly a relief to see red-and-yellow banners and ensigns draped in merry profusion along the old balconies. After nine days of Zubiris and Utergas, here was a town that didn't sound like a Bulgarian moped; a town that was Spanish and happy to be so.

But we all know what can happen when you leave a donkey alone in a town full of partying Spaniards. I tightened my grasp round the rope: lose Shinto here and the next time I saw him he'd be cowering under a hail of tomatoes with the fattest trainee priest in Santo Domingo sitting backwards across his withers. It was almost a relief when the slightly harassed *hospitalero* explained that because the magnificent old *refugio*'s usual stabling area was currently alive with banqueting revellers, Shinto would have to be locked up in a quiet yard round the back.

I did his feet, then my laundry, and after a particularly important post-camping shower went out to hit the streets. There was a dense throng in the square outside the *refugio*, gradually organising itself behind half a dozen boys carrying a huge crucifix decorated with crêpe-paper cockerels. A proper religious procession: under the list drawn up by British pilgrim William Wey in 1456, participation was worth forty days off purgatory; two hundred if I could find a mitred bishop some-where in the ranks.

Well, I haven't had such fun on a Wednesday afternoon since Margaret Thatcher resigned. In a dilatory conga the parade led me past cartwheel-girthed vats full of garlicky mushrooms simmering outside a bookshop, past fairy-lit silhouettes of Santo Domingo and those two chickens, past a church whose tower was conspicuously home to half a dozen flapping storks. More colour-coded kids in their hilariously illegal gangmobiles: loudness in all its forms. Rainbow dungarees aside, the keynote fashion items – an integral part of some earlier procession and sadly now only on view in photographers' windows – was the daftest millinery it has ever been my pleasure to hoot at in deranged appreciation: lacy, flowered cylinders the size of Michael Schumacher's rear wheels, somehow balanced atop the veiled heads of the young flower of Santo Domingan womanhood. Here, at last, were the people who invented the upside-down exclamation mark.

I sidled off the end of the parade along a street between whose pavements a funfair was in the latter process of erec-tion, and sat outside a bar with the first of three coffees, watch-ing the mad, mad world go by. Boys in berets and their grannies' shawls begged for change: mindful that they were doubtless collecting for unstable pyrotechnics, I gave generously. One talked a little English, and in so many words, and then so many more, explained that each gang represented a suburb of Santo Domingo, often focused round a bar. He jogged over to rejoin his blue-capped companions, and watching them chant away between the bingo booths and airgun galleries, I felt warmly infused with a sense of continuity and community, by this free-spirited display of tribal anarchy. And then, drain-ing my cup for the last time, I thought how sad it was that we'd lost all this, and that any attempt at recreating the spec-tacle before me in small-town Britain would be sourly compro-mised by an undercurrent of beery aggression.

The plaza outside the *refugio* was still alive, pilgrims and locals jiggling about to the brass band's now rather fibrillated rhythm. 'Special night tonight!' shrieked a Frenchman, one whose hysterical girlish giggle had enlivened many a bunkhouse on previous evenings. 'They keep open ze door to ten surty!' He handed me a plastic beaker of marinaded mushrooms and a brimming wine spout, both of which I tackled with the reckless chutzpah of a man wearing black clothes. 'Viva España' segued messily into 'Brown Girl in the Ring'; a trio of Brazilians mamboed lithely about while along with my fellow North Europeans I jerked to the whim of some inept puppeteer. It was good to be with pilgrims but not talk about clicks and bunks and blisters, not even to have thought or cared whether my laundry would have dried in the lingering misted humidity. But when the curfew drew near, and my fellow travellers trailed back through the mighty *refugio* doors, I thought of Shinto, a four-footed Cinderella shut up under a carport with a bucket of barley while his ugly master lived it up at the ball. A minute later I was clambering about a building site, uprooting huge armfuls of alfalfa and wedging them into a bin-liner.

Shinto seemed very nearly moved by the unexpected bounty I upended at his loud (or louder) end, settling immediately into its enthusiastic ingestion. For a moment I surveyed his steady jaw work with proprietorial content, the concrete at our feet sporadically illuminated by an aerial pyrotechnic flash whose retort hit us a second later. The trumpets whined and blared distantly, a fading jeer after every off-key parp.

I smiled, happy in at least two different ways. And soon in at least three, because groping my way out through Shinto's yard and back to the *refugio*'s rear entrance, I immediately blundered into a wire cage that twittered and gobbled in shrill protest. The occupants, starkly so even in the uncertain half-light, were a dozen or so white chickens, strutting jerkily about in aimless alarm. I stooped to the cage and could just make out 'CATEDRAL' Dymo-taped to the top of the frame. The cathedral had naturally been closed, this time at least for festival preparations, but here were its fêted avian inhabitants: evidently the pairs were subject to squad rotation. I nipped quickly back to Shinto's enclosure, brushed up a handful of spilt barley from around his bowl, then breathlessly emptied it into their cage. 'Eat,' I hissed, and in a great chirpy flap they instantly did. The holy roosters had spoken: I would reach Santiago alive.

Evelyn attended the odd mass, the bereaved old Chicagoan did so every day, so too a few of the big snorers and those wide-eyed young Hispanics. That was largely it: in the soundtrack to this pilgrimage, the droning chants of the pious went largely unheard, unless you count all that Enya I had to put up with in the evenings. But though the judge of all men might not have pointed our way to Santiago, someone had. This was still somehow a sacred undertaking: even if you didn't talk the talk, you had to walk the walk.

The golden rule was this: you got to Santiago under your own steam. 'Pilgrim' was derived from the Latin *peregrinus*, a cross-country walker, a wayfarer. The power ramblers might not have understood much, but they understood that. Yes, many lacked the holiday allowance to do the camino in one go: two weeks' walking a year for three years was a popular option. But if you said you were going to do it, you did it – all of it.

The road to Santiago was for centuries plagued by what medievalists call 'false pilgrims', usually thieves or fraudsters dressed in the requisite hat and cape who'd inveigle themselves into a pilgrim convoy for the purposes of covert or violent plunder. They came from all over Europe, attracted by the compelling opportunities presented by a ceaseless through-put of tourists wandering through lonely woodland. They particularly came, I'm afraid, from Britain: in 1318 'John of London' ransacked pilgrim hospices throughout Navarre, and twelve years later an unnamed Englishman was hanged for drugging and robbing travellers in Estella. Even before William Wey's ship landed in Spain, a light-fingered fellow pilgrim had snipped purses from at least two belts.

But the modern breed of false pilgrim comes with a more

malignant deception in mind. He wears the shell, and bears the pack, and carries within his papers the imprinted cipher of many a humble hospice. But when the human tide sets forth each morn this man tarries. And then when the coast is clear he nips down the taxi rank and bungs his stuff in the boot of a Citroën Xantia.

It takes one to know one, of course, but for me all the short cuts were blocked off well before those 'Moral Dilemma Ahead' signs. Even a Spanish bus driver would probably baulk at a donkey, particularly when his owner refused to pay full fare for a nine-year-old. And hitch-hiking was out of the question unless I happened upon a driver with the stunted quadruped-detection faculties of Little Red Riding Hood. I'll never know if I would have cheated if I could have. But because I couldn't, I galloped Shinto up to the moral high ground and sat impressively astride him, seething with righteous indignation.

How could you come on a pilgrimage and cheat? And lie about cheating? To do so, I decided, was a symptom of terminal soul cancer, a corrosion of human decency that should by rights be detected by some kind of inner spiritual alarm. And punished by some spectacular psychosomatic malady: spontaneous combustion gets my vote, but syphilis would do for a first offence.

Pilgrims passed me as I led Shinto over the Rio Oja, storks beaking up nest sticks on its flood-rubbled foreshore. They passed as I startled him along the hard shoulder of the N120 with a four-foot length of reflective plastic, salvaged from a shattered marker post and waved semaphore-like through his rearward peripheral vision. And they passed as we plodded out from another wheaten prairie and into the town of Redecilla del Camino, home to an enormous Romanesque font and a euro-in-the-slot weighbridge.

I saw him as I manoeuvred Shinto on to its platform. He was sitting on a shaded bench, shirt aggressively creased, outstretched boots smugly unbesmirched. He'd slept in the bed two away from me at the *refugio*, and in fact had still been asleep when I left. Because that never happened, I remembered.

He hadn't passed me, yet now here he was, spoiling my silly fun.

'Hey – does he need to diet?' He spoke in a complacent, untraceable Eurodrawl. The coin went in and a strip of dot-matrixed ticker-tape spooled out. I have it here now: '14 MAY 2003. 11:52 PESO: 200 KG.' Less than a third the telly-captioned weight of a doomed bull.

I appraised him again. The books had talked about a 'pilgrim look', and with 200 kilometres under our sweaty belts I knew what they meant: a dusted, windswept ruddiness, like a Midwestern farmer at harvest end. It is fair to say that my friend didn't have the pilgrim look. With him it was more of the golfer look. A Scottish *hospitalero* I met later said he'd been given a tip on how to detect a suspected cheat: pat a hand on their back in welcome, and if you don't hit sweat start asking questions. The figure before me would have failed that one straight off. His pastelly polo shirt was crisp and dry. Simply put, the man was a wrong 'un.

'Bus or taxi?' I said, flatly.

He looked at me, and I suddenly noticed his resemblance to the pudge-faced, shiftily insolent mechanic who accompanied Bonnie and Clyde during the best-known celluloid depiction of their criminal rampage. He looked but he didn't speak. I nodded at him significantly and, with as much portent as you can muster leading a donkey off a weighbridge, walked slowly away.

A merry, lightly bearded Frenchman stopped as I was fending two insistent yappers away from my lunch-time *boccadillo* under a tree in some shut-up siestaville. 'You are from . . . ?' he said, and when I told him he extracted a large and densely annotated ledger and made a note. We walked together that afternoon, across the provincial border into Castille-León, and as Jean-Michel told me of his journey – early retirement, the full-strength pilgrimage from Le Puy in central France – it became gradually apparent that as a metaphorical donkey-prod, conversation was more effective than exhortation. Shinto's asinine curiosity was aroused by any debate: a comparison of Anglo-French primary education systems, last night's festivities, the Ford Focus. He'd feign indifference during the opening rhetorical stages, lagging nonchalantly back. But when we got to the crux, even if that meant rear-light clusters, he could bear it no longer and that big head would nuzzle brightly up between our elbows. 'Chin-chin, chaps, what's it all about?'

The Dutch kids were all over the grass out the front of the churchside *refugio* at Belorado, and that meant an *albergue* up a grubby alley just past the John Lennon bar. Each of the small rooms upstairs was crammed with bunks. The official *refugios*, particularly the overspill accommodation that was my default experience, were well meant but spartan and vaguely awkward – one might imagine oneself being put up by sandally beardos at a traditional-instrument weekend. But the private *albergue*, as here and at that place with the Welshwoman's bunioned feet, was a very different gig. A dark patch of wallpaper where a picture had hung, a child's plastic boat in the bathroom cabinet, a pair of patent stilettos in the bottom of a wardrobe: everywhere were reminders that off-season this was a family home. And the home owners were largely doing this out of the goodness of their Catholic hearts – I think I paid 3 euros at Belorado. Somehow we were like resistance fighters secretly billeted with a plucky sympathiser.

In the act of unpacking, a ziplock bag of almonds appeared, donated by that American art historian on the first evening ('Bought more than 5 pounds,' he'd said, awed by his own folly). I was eating them by a trellis of wet socks in the little garden when a gaunt and lightly bearded German walked briskly up. I'd seen him many times with his wife.

'Your monkey is maybe a little curious,' he beamed mysteriously.

'Oh, yes?' I replied. The only suitable place I'd been able to park Shinto was by a tree at the edge of the grass outside that first *refugio*. Perhaps he had eaten a Dutch teenager's shoe.

'Oh, yes. I should say that.' He fingered the bottom half of his face sagely. 'Yes. But perhaps too curious?'

I sat forward in my plastic chair. Perhaps he had eaten a Dutch teenager. 'I don't understand.'

'Soon your monkey is finding his own pilgrimage.' Another Confucian smile. You don't find many lapels to grab en route to Santiago, so instead I stood up and addressed him with a crispness that bordered on the forthright.

'What are you saying? Has the monk— the donkey done something?'

He closed his eyes and nodded, opening them along with his mouth perhaps two seconds before the time came to have almonds crammed up his nose. 'He is not attached to the tree. I am Tum-Tum the Daddy Groon.'

Actually he might not have said that last bit, because with the word 'tree' still hanging in the tepid, socky air I flew out of my chair and charged through the *albergue* and up the empty alley like Ewan McGregor at the start of *Trainspotting*, only with sandals on.

It took me less than a minute to get to the church, but that was easily long enough to imagine Shinto legs up in a river, legs off on a hard shoulder, legs akimbo under a lust-blinded stallion. Long enough to imagine walking alone in a donkless world.

A nicotine-tached Frenchman had Shinto by the ring on his head collar, leading him confidently back towards the tree watched by a happy semicircle of Holland's youth. I placed both my hands on Shinto's dusted withers. 'Thank you,' I gasped, surprisingly close to tears. 'Um . . . *merci beaucoup*.' Squinting through his cig smoke, he said it was nothing, then, in tones of light admonishment, explained that the knot had been inadequate. As he stooped to demonstrate a more secure alternative, the young pilgrims encroached, exchanging muttered gutturalisms. I told you: the donkey man knows nothing. Can't even tie a knot. The sandaled oaf.

Half an hour later I was outside a bar in Belorado's Plaza Mayor, a big mixed salad and a jug of rosé on the table before me and beyond it another tantalising glimpse, a tapas-sized appetiser, of the small-town good times that got into gear as we tossed about in our snore-torn bunk-house. It was well past any infant bedtime that I was familiar with, yet children as young as three or four were careering about on their big brothers' bikes, or punting footballs against the brutally coppiced plane trees. Half a dozen more were up on the central bandstand energetically trading Pokémon cards, and on the benches around young couples gazed moonily at each other's tilted faces. A well-kempt wino loped irregularly by, and I thought how much better off he was here than in whatever the British equivalent of Belorado might be – a town with 2,000 souls in the impoverished middle of rural nowhere. *Buenos días*, I had of late realised, meant not good day but good days, plural.

The sun eased down behind the arcade of shops opposite – half nine and you could still buy yourself a pair of wedge espadrilles – and as a bull died on the screen behind her the teenage waitress brought over my steak and chips. I hoisted a glass at a distant table of familiar faces, then sat back to enumerate my successes and failures as tourist, drover and pilgrim.

Well – we were both still alive, I hadn't seen a cockroach or had a single stone in my boot, and in ten days I'd spent less than 70 quid. In the square here at Belorado there was even a price war: €6.60 for three courses on that side of the plaza; €6.00 for two courses with wine on this. More pertinently, I was becoming a very slightly nicer person. I'd started leaving tips that staff didn't interpret as a calculated insult, at least not always, and had made an effort to stop describing fellow pilgrims as 'that ugly Austrian', 'the pointless gnome' or 'those pudding-bowled lesbos'.

But then I had also beaten a donkey with a bunch of flowers, still couldn't tie a knot and despite that malnourished epiphany in Los Arcos didn't yet believe in Our Mister. Shinto now had a scabbed sore where the rear strap had chafed into his rump, and my feet hurt when I didn't have boots on. My electric razor, a burdensome luxury denied to the donkless, was now operating on a voltage so diminished that the present shaving experience was as comfortable and effective as one carried out with a rusty wire brush. And no matter how often I told myself what a special experience it was to see a country and a story unfold like this, step by thoughtful step, there was still a pang of melancholy whenever we trudged past one of those blue signs. 'A1 MADRID', it might say, or 'A68 BARCELONA', and for a moment I would see myself reeling in the clicks towards an exciting and distant metropolis, left elbow out the window, right foot to the floor. One of these moments had lasted for two hours.

A night untroubled by anxiety-related donkey ponderings was rare, and that night wasn't one of them. Passing back via Shinto on my way home – *home?* – from dinner I'd found three boys, none older than ten, throwing bottles at the wall just by his head. To Shinto's credit, it hadn't put him off his weeds. I clapped my hands and barked out a park keeper's 'Oi!', then stooped to redouble the knot at both ends. They watched me steadily, the oldest fingering the lip of a Heineken empty, and I stared back with a look that gamely attempted to merge the threat of retributive violence with pious entreaty: devout yet stroppy, like St Jim showing both his faces at once. And then, because it was already gone 10.00, I'd had to leave them there.

So for the second time in less than twelve hours I was gratefully astonished to see my donkey present and alive, a sensation that waned slightly when I plonked the saddle over his back and he bit me on the shoulder. '*Attention!*' cackled a nearby voice. It was the Frenchman. He said that as a smoking insomniac he'd been able to keep tabs on Shinto throughout the night, and I held out my hands in helpless gratitude: for every taxi that sped past with a thin-lipped cheat crouched down in its foot wells, there were at least a dozen saintly Samaritans. The next time I saw the smoking Frenchman, weeks later, he was walking towards me – one of only three pilgrims I encountered doing the return trip.

The day's recommended stage was a 23-clicker, conspicuous for the ascent of the Montes de Oca, Goose Mountains. At nearly 4,000 feet its highest point was the most vertically conspicuous obstacle I'd encountered yet, higher than the road over the Pyrenees; an eminence so considerable that it steered the rivers on its west flank towards the Atlantic and those on its east to the Med. People got lost up there: Dominic Laffi in 1670, the fêted pilgrim–diarist Walter Starkie in 1950, and others far more recently. The bandits that once preyed on pilgrims had gone; but the wolves, I'd read, had not. For all these reasons it had seemed prudent to stop short of the final, lonely assault on the summit, overnighting at Villafranca Montes de Oca, 12 kilometres from Belorado. One of the strictest *refugio* diktats was the rule restricting pilgrims to a single night's stay, but if I couldn't give Shinto a whole day off, at least I could give him a free afternoon.

I set off with Maria, a jolly little Brazilian who via the mutual exchange of undistinguished gesticulations had indicated that 12 kilometres was more than enough for her. In fact she didn't even make that. She'd slept in the bunk next to mine and in the morning I'd noticed eight of her toes thickly swaddled in blood-blotted bandages. Maria hobbled through Belorado, but an hour into the still, sweet countryside beyond pulled up, unable to continue even in sandals. Shinto and I waited a while but she summoned up a smile and waved us on. 'Is OK, is OK, is OK.' I never saw her again.

The odd facial hot spot in that now rather alarming farmer's tan, a little rope-burn scar tissue – my only genuinely worrisome physical corruption was a sharp knee twinge, the sort of impacted, internal bruise that suggested recent participation in some marble-floored hopscotch marathon. How had I got off so lightly? Because the Lord looks after his own. And because my feet weren't pinned to the earth by a backpack the size of São Paulo.

A sombrely ruminative half-hour ensued, leading us into a hamlet with an elderly church: looking at the map now I can't remember if it was Tosantos or Villambistia. The path curved down to a little patch of unkempt green in the heart of the village, and on it were a set of swings, a rusty slide and a very large, very dark donkey.

The donks at the Centro Hípico had been behind bars, but

here was one Shinto could rub noses with. I thought of those twelve absent friends in their Pyrenean paddock, and beckoning his new acquaintance with little clicks of the tongue led Shinto to the edge of the grass.

What happened next cleaved Shinto's pilgrimage in two, before and after. The division was as dramatic as it was sudden, like two paintings crudely spliced together in the middle. One second we were ambling across a Constable. The next it was *Guernica*.

Their snouts were about 4 feet apart when it happened. Shinto stiffened, and stared, and the stare bounced back, and in the blink of a large brown eye the hierarchy was established to his disadvantage. The rope rasped through my flesh and he was off, round the swings, under the slide, then straight up the hedgerowed lane with that satanic beast in audibly close pursuit. It was the title sequence to *When Donks Go Bad*.

Shinto hammered round the corner and I hammered behind him, at a speed I hadn't thought him capable of and one I'd certainly never have managed two weeks previously. Bags were bucking wildly about on his back, smacking me in the head and chest as I fought to keep the end of the rope in both hands. Up a short straight, round another uphill left-hander – and still that bastard came, his heavy hoofs drumming ever closer. If I'd thought he just wanted to defend his turf, I was wrong. He didn't want to scare us. He wanted to kick us, and keep kicking until our protests faded to a phlegmy, defenceless gurgle. Then he wanted to eat us.

The snorting huffs were at my elbow – I could hear them and so could Shinto. From somewhere he found more speed, shifting up into a full gallop, 200 kilos of raw panic on the hoof. The rope was tightening; Shinto was getting away from me. My brain began spooling out ever more desperate contingency plans: try-line escape dive through the brambles, fist-in-the-stifle counter-attack, prayer. And then, with fearful finality, Shinto ran out of gas. He hit the wall, and pulled up in abrupt accordance, steaming head lowered in submission, surrendering himself to a one-sided assault.

'Nnnnnnnnnnnnnnnnnnoooooooo!'

I didn't know what I was going to do until I did it, but there I was, baying at the ragged edge of human capacity with my arms and legs outstretched, like a skydiver after a fruitless yank on the reserve cord. I held this pose and spun round to face the donk of death, finding that huge black head just a foot from mine. He'd stopped, but he didn't take even a tiny step backwards until I flapped my arms and somehow screamed louder, a valley-shattering explosion of spittled, bestial decibels. There was soon nothing left in the throat locker, and still he filled the path behind, two yards back, side-on and staring with intent. The stone I picked up was rather larger than I'd have preferred but I'm afraid I threw it anyway. With a taut thump it bounced off the meat of his shaggy thigh. He didn't flinch, and for a moment I wondered where all this would end. Then, with studied and impudent sloth, he turned his head away and plodded slowly back to hell.

Barbed vegetation had ripped into both legs and an arm and torn half the collar off my shirt, and though I didn't know it yet my Dictaphone had spoken its last 'Eeeeeuuuwwww'. But Shinto was a broken donk. I looked at his craven, lowered gaze, at the sweat seeping through the saddle blanket. He'd trotted into that playground with the eager innocence of a lonely child finding a playmate, and the playmate had tried to kill him. That quivering anus swelled and unpuckered and what was left of his morale spattered horribly on to the Way of St James.

At that moment I wouldn't have cared if Villafranca had been a forsaken pocket of hell relentlessly bisected by roaring 32-tonners, but by the time we got there, and found it was, I did. 'Not staying here, Shints,' I said as we ate our respective lunches outside a cemetery on a hill overlooking the town. Suits me, his look said: procuring brief respite from the flies now clustering his loins meant kicking himself in whatever was left of his bollocks. The upper reaches of Villafranca's domed church tower were engagingly festooned with really quite large bushes, but even up here the traffic was deafening, and the *refugio's* grimy windows had it all right in their face. My mind was made up, but if it hadn't been, a glance at the sky would have settled the decision. Bridging the blue expanse were wisps of clouds, warped by some extraordinary whim of nature into celestial chevrons, arrows pointing due west, up over the big hill behind us and on to Santiago.

These days no one's going to get lost on the camino, not badly anyway, but there were times in the hours ahead when I wondered if I'd missed some vital yellow arrow and erred into the wolfish wilderness. The climb itself was hefty and meandering, but it was also movingly winsome, painterly foothills dense with ancient oak, their upper reaches dotted purple and yellow by broom and heather, and all of it smiled on by a billion-watt sun. Iguana-sized lizards green as tree frogs scuttered off the path and into the piny undergrowth as we approached the brow.

Only there wasn't really a brow. The path peaked but didn't fall away, instead ploughing remorselessly across a yawning, heathery moor on holiday from Cumbria. Shinto had been withdrawn and lethargic since the pursuit, and I knew this vista would spark off what I was beginning to think of as his agoraphobia.

I nursed him onwards, with conversation, and when that inevitably palled, in song. This was always a risk, as in addition to an abysmal taste in music he was implacably demanding. Like the back-seat howler demanding a nineteenth rewind to the start of 'On Top of Spaghetti', if he didn't hear what he wanted he wouldn't cooperate. And what he wanted to hear – I will never know what initially possessed me to mumble the intro – was 'We are the Champions'.

'"And WE'LL keep on FIGHTING", till the . . . Look, Shints! We're going downhill!' And so we were, but before we could go uphill again there was something to cross, and it was made of planks. That was a blow, and though we soon found an acceptable concrete alternative just upstream this proved the straw that broke my poor donkey's back. Back up on the hot and shadeless plateau, in a landscape purged of man and his creations, Shinto gently lowered himself to his knees, then eased over on to his side like a cat being put to sleep. There was a noise that I'd later link to a buckling saucepan lid, and then another, a terminal wheezy groan.

We were in a bad place, and Shinto seemed bound for a better one. For thirty minutes I thought he was about to die, and for at least five of those that he actually had. I pressed my water bottle to his flaccid lips, and gathered what grass I could in this . . . oh dear, in this bewolfed and gradually darkening nowhere. I heaved the barley bag out from under him and he accepted a little from the bowl. But only a little. And then, as I pictured myself scooping out a huge shallow grave with a bent saucepan lid, I did what I suddenly remembered seeing a Scottish shepherd once do to a similarly stricken sheep. I paced out a run-up, then charged at Shinto, rodeo yee-hahs rasping from a Queen-ravaged larynx.

He leapt upright when I was almost upon him. And just over an hour later, with the mist already beginning to coil out of the dim and cooling fields, we were being cheered and applauded into the extraordinary, marooned monastery of San Juan de Ortega, site of 114 recorded miracles. Make that 115.

Before they set off everyone has a mental image that they build their expectations around, an encapsulation of their pilgrimage, and mine was something like San Juan de Ortega. The situation was exceptional: a stolid, mighty Romanesque pilgrim–fortress bursting out of this remote and lumpy pasture-land, its neighbours a token handful of forsaken farm buildings. Largely unroofed and surrendering to nature, like Roncesvalles the monastery had been saved by the camino's renaissance in the eighties. The galvanised canopy keeping the rain out spoilt the profile somewhat, but what it encased was the most authentically medieval experience of my pilgrimage to date.

The cheers, being many and youthful and Dutch, meant that I'd be sleeping on the refectory floor, though I was lucky even to bag that. Peering through from the hall I could see mattresses and rucksacks stacked all along the refectory's splendidly panelled walls. The *hospitalera* was a bustling crone who stuck her head out of an arch, saw me, saw Shinto, barked 'Camping!' and disappeared.

That wasn't going to happen, so to give her the slip I tied Shints up in the grass, hid the tent bag in a bush and went up the big stone stairs in search of a shower. Modernisation here had evidently been pursued with less than the usual enthusiasm, but the aura in consequence was more captivating: this was where they had slept, you felt, and there was where they had eaten, and here was where they had prayed.

The dormitories were arranged round a cloister, huge peeling halls full of metal beds like a hastily established military hospital. 'Consistently reported as unhygienic,' said the Confraternity guide, and though you could see why it seemed a little churlish. I didn't even mind, not really, when it became apparent that the showers, as well as being wreathed in a miasma of sewery badness, were cold – hard-slap-across-both-cheeks cold. This, after all, was what I'd imagined as the default scenario. This was life at the pilgrim coalface. Loo paper? Pah. Who needs loo paper when you've got . . . water.

It wasn't going to be a Camay advert in there, but a shower was no longer optional. Shinto's habit of shitting on his own doorstep, and then pissing through the letter-box above, meant the long night rope was now impregnated with a swoon-inducing putridity that clung to everything it touched. In essence this meant my hands, which I'd often hold out before me in appalled disbelief, like Lady Macbeth, or maybe Ron Weasley. So foul were these spots that a quick splash under the tap was never going to suffice.

Two young Dutchmen had just stepped out of the cubicles, and even though both were now peeling their sunburnt noses in the mirror I was glad of the company. Communal bathing allowed me to gloatingly display my sumptuous donkey-borne toiletry ensemble while everyone else was coaxing a worm-cast of toothpaste from Superglue-sized tubelets. The downside was the risk that they'd notice I was washing my hair, and my body, and that evening the bramble-shredded clothing stamped underfoot beneath the muscle-cramping torrent of hail, with the contents of the same vast bottle. Let's just put it this way: I was hoping it would be kind to a lot more than just hands.

The pilgrim hordes had been filing out of mass when I arrived and while shivering out obscenities in the shower I missed another San Juan ritual: Father Alonso's garlic soup, solemnly doled out at the head of a great table. In fact, I never even saw Father Alonso. But this place was a tradition sanctuary, and rubbing life back into my limbs as I came down the stairs again I was presented with another – my debut encounter with a *refugio* honesty box.

I'd never warmed to the euro, partly because it seemed to snuff out a little more of the already waning romance and adventure of Continental travel, and partly because I forgot to take those sodding escudos down the bank before it was too late. In consequence, pre-departure I'd imagined cultivating a haughty pride in my status as a euro refusenik, curling a lip at the bland and faceless banknotes, perhaps even slamming a stoutly regal pound coin on to a tapas counter and declaring, 'Now *that's* money.'

But I never did. On day one, at Roncesvalles, I'd watched all the Germans and Dutch and Spaniards and French pooling their shrapnel to buy a round from the bar, and immediately felt ashamed and a little silly, a muttering eco-Luddite alone in the corner with a pocketful of groats. The euro was so plainly a giant stride forward in holiday efficiency; also, Santiago cathedral was on the back of the smaller Spanish coppers. But though one of the small triumphs of previous days was an acquired ability to think meaningfully in kilometres, I'd yet to demonstrate a familiarity with the fiscal denominations.

Hence the word I now uttered; the word 'buttocks'. Instead of the intended 5 euros I'd just wedged a 20 in the San Juan box, fixed to the limestone in the gloomy entrance hall. Twenty! That was almost two days' budget. I pinched my face up in agonised frustration, but then, in the uncertain light, noticed a tiny corner of blue still sticking out of the slot. Now, if I could just . . .

'*Eh! Eh! Eh!*'

It was the harridan, elbows out and striding towards me.

'It's . . .' I began, whipping the probing hand away.

'*No! Eh! No!*' She grabbed my arm in a way that said she wished it was my ear, and led me the short distance to the back of the door. There was a multilingual notice staple-gunned to it, which she nodded at before propping a bony fist on each bony hip. The laminated English page was headed 'READ CAREFULLY'. I did so.

'This shelter don't receive no subvention . . . show your respect for the other people . . . obey the shelterkeepers indications . . .' And then, right at the bottom, a horrifying caveat. 'The Pilgrim Identity Card can be taken away from you by using it wrong.'

In a second I saw it: my camino hung in the balance. The truth was too hard to explain, and even then a little compromising. There was nothing else to be done. I went up to that box and folded another 5 euros into it. 'You better remember this, Jimbo,' I hissed after her breezy departure.

Because this was Spain, there was a small bar attached to the monastery, and while everyone else was spooning down Father Alonso's holy starter I nipped in there for the usual wine-partnered fry-up. I was just finishing when they all piled in, eighty people fighting over two dozen chairs. The solitary waiter was a young man with the build and voice of a sultan's eunuch, and when I went to pay I found this poor, put-upon fellow hunched sweatily down behind the bar counter, pretending to look for something.

In failing light I wandered over to the church door. It was closed, but there was a barred window in it through which I squinted in vain search for San Juan's alabaster tomb. His earthly representative had just bled me dry, but after the events of the day I still felt I owed him one.

A follower of our friend St Sunday of the Causeway, Juan

had pledged to devote himself to pilgrim welfare after surviving a shipwreck on the return from his own holy excursion to Jerusalem. It's him we have to thank for hacking out a path over the Montes de Oca, and of course for the hospice which was to blossom into this monastery. I thought how rejoicingly relieved I'd been to come down from that moor and find this place, and how that feeling would have been intensified in the days of robbers and rather more wolves.

Hunkered up as I was in my sleeping bag with a torch, head under a table, full moon outside the window, it wasn't that surprising to read of the perfumed clouds of white bees emerging from San Juan's tomb, of the Irish couple who'd knelt before it with an offering of apples and looked up to find their dead daughter munching on one, of a congregation gathered round the alabaster hearing a cripple's nerves and bones stretch and straighten and heal. Nor was I unduly taken aback when I clicked the torch off, straddled my bagged feet awkwardly round a defunct wood-burning stove, and heard the nocturnal orchestra tune up with the watery wobble of a fat man's larynx.

Every morning now I'd wonder if Shinto would simply refuse to move, and it almost happened the next day. The *Ben Hur* donkey-derby encounter had evidently exacted its toll, and as the Dutch children filed lankily past – yes, somehow I'd beaten them out of the breakfast blocks – he began to drag his hoofs. And his perennially cautious approach to constricted passages was gone: blundering complacently through a narrow gate beside a cattle-grid he ripped a great hole in one of the panniers. It was almost a relief when the great massif ahead was abruptly darkened by pewtered clouds as we entered the village of Atapuerca, encouraging me to sit out the encroaching storm at a café with Shinto tied to a drainpipe under the eaves.

It was busy in there, and as the thunder came down the hill it got busier. Conspicuous among the existing clientele was one of the Dutch girls, her face horribly bloodied, slumped bonelessly before a cooling cup of hot chocolate and her own shattered spectacles. A teacher pushed through the circle of concerned classmates with a roll of Elastoplast; engaging one of his colleagues I heard how the weight of a backpack could transform the slightest stumble into a headlong poleaxing. 'This also happened to an Italian girl yesterday,' he said. 'It is a serious danger. But for you . . .' I followed his gaze out of the window and over to Shinto's sheltered, panniered loins. 'For you this will not be a problem.'

The wind that had been gently teasing the election banner strung across the street was now savagely assaulting it. Pilgrims started to run in, blowing rain drips off their noses, and the lone young barmaid struggled to keep the cappuccinos coming as her infant son patrolled the premises on all fours. I took a heavily milked *café con leche* to the corner, assessed the sky through a window, then got the books out.

Atapuerca seemed in no way remarkable, and in terms of the pilgrimage it wasn't. San Juan had built a small bridge just before it; there was a church worth five words. But in the hill just beyond, the massif currently being pelted with thunderbolts and which at some point I'd have to cross, there was a cave. And in that cave, during the summer of 1994, archaeologists found some human bones. They were old, and there were lots of them. So many, in fact, that in five years the team had amassed what amounts to over 90 per cent of all the pre-Neanderthal remains unearthed in this continent. The youngest was 127,000 years old. But the oldest – by some considerable distance the remains of Europe's most senior citizen – was a million.

A million. With a confounded grin I slowly shook my head, like a tourist loud-shirt told that in fact *all* of those candlesticks were older than Texas. There was so much history round here – big, hairy-chested, million-year history. Almost every town had Roman origins: you'd lean against the outside wall of a bar sipping a Coke, and notice that the block near your shoulder was marble, and then that it was chiselled with the second half of a Latin inscription. A lot of places were Iron Age or older. And now this. It was the sort of discovery that suggested there was something about the camino that went back beyond Christianity, back beyond even the Celts who walked on to Finisterre.

The rain cleared reluctantly, and so did the café. Everyone else was aiming for Burgos, 20 clicks distant, but after the previous day's alarums that was way beyond our capabilities: following a long, damp trudge over the massif we opted to stop short, overnighting at an unlovely ring-road motel.

With Shints lashed to an old fridge in a grassless yard round the back an early start was obligatory, and with a laundered blue sky above and the tyre factories behind, our final approach to Burgos proved an agreeable one. Ahead lay the camino's second major city, and by general accord its loveliest. 'Staggering', said the guides, and 'extraordinary', and 'wearers of shorts may be refused admission'.

Burgos was the last outpost of cosmopolitan urbanity before the camino headed off across the *meseta alta*, 200 lonely kilometres of prairie unabundantly studded with modest settlements. The *meseta* farmers brought grain and wool to Burgos, whose merchants were travelling as far as London by the end of the thirteenth century. Burgos was rich, and the holy tourists made it richer: with thirty-two hospices in the fifteenth century, no city accommodated more pilgrims. The first mahogany brought back from the New World was used for the doors of the largest hospice, the Hospital del Rey. Nearly all of the silver Columbus returned with was fashioned into a huge cart that once a year would accommodate the consecrated host in a parade through the streets. It still does. On the Thursday that follows the eighth Sunday after Easter.

The showrooms and superstores gave way to real shops, and as they did the streets began to bustle: it was a crisp Saturday morning, and Burgos was in skittish, uptown mood. And of course I had a donkey, which heralded the now traditional scenes – fathers hoisting offspring aloft for a beaming overview, ladies of great age blocking the pavement to pat and pet and often to deliver moist-eyed recollections of their rural youth. The defining moment came when a young John Travolta swaggered across the main drag, sneering choice arrogances into his mobile: he saw Shinto, stopped right in the bus lane and some blustering anecdote trailed off into a tiny, dumbfounded *'Burro!'* Shinto took it all with an air of practised celebrity – he didn't want to show it, but he loved this stuff. He loved it so much that he tried to walk into two supermarkets.

Boulevard into avenue into street into alley: the camino was routed, as ever, through the old town's most cramped and antiquated thoroughfares, but here in Burgos these were home not to stained tramps and vermin but the purveyors of unforgivably priced evening wear. The windows were all full of fancy hats and Bang & Olufsen – after more than two weeks of shabby privation I was rather overawed. I stopped by a souvenir shop for a reassuring fix of puerile tat and instead saw it stocked with fully featured suits of reproduction armour.

This was the first time since Roncesvalles that I'd encountered tourists who weren't pilgrims, and Shinto's photographic appeal swelled accordingly, particularly when the yellow arrows led us up an unremarkable rise of cobbles, past a gang of street cleaners hosing away bits of Friday night, and smack into the back of Burgos cathedral.

For a confounding moment everyone around was a dumbstruck peasant up from the sticks, gawping heavenward at the multi-spired profusion of lacy stonework, those two dozen filigree ladders to paradise. Following the substantial but rather stodgy Romanesque fare we'd been fed on so far this was like a sugar rush: a party-sized pavlova after two weeks of stale wholemeal. I dawdled up to the façade with wonder smeared across my face – the embellishment was almost pathological, as if the architect had been given the Lego Gothic DeLuxe super set and challenged to incorporate every last pinnacle and finial. And it was there that I took my most cherished picture of Shinto, a compliant, cock-eared gaze into the lens, a blandly contented tourist snapshot that said, Oh, and here I am outside the cathedral at Burgos.

The *refugio* was out the other side of town, a pair of log-clad oversized trailers in the sprawling parkland behind a military hospital. It didn't open until 2.00, which meant an hour's wait behind the queue of early risers who'd left San Juan at 5 a.m. It was the first time I'd been in that position, and it would be the last: the dour lack of camaraderie in this pilgrim sub-group was palpable. When I tried to engage the golfing-capped Italian behind in conversation, he shot me a nettled glare and immediately pushed in front. A Spaniard sauntered up, and in whispering tones of doom punctuated with chiding tuts grimly let it be known that the picnicking family behind those trees were *gitanos*, and as such Shinto would be dog food by dawn. And then he pushed in front. It was ridiculous: there were no more than thirty of us queuing for ninety-six beds. When the round-bellied little *hospitalero* waddled up with the keys there was an immediate, elbowing free-for-all, as if the quarry wasn't a bottom bunk near the loos but the very last place on the very last chopper out of Saigon.

I left Shinto browsing happily at the edge of a sun-feathered floral meadow, tied to a big chestnut tree just inside the *refugio*'s corralled perimeter. The plan, one with which I was quietly pleased, granted him a day off while I returned to inner Burgos for an afternoon of urbane, donkless peregrinations. This plan, however, was contingent on the use of Spanish municipal transport.

I've only ever sat in a bus shelter for a whole hour once before, and this time it wasn't down to tequila-related semi-consciousness. An hour! Later I discovered that many Spanish routes are operated by this number of buses: one bus. A week or so later, I walked for eight hours within sight of a railway line, an intercity line, a line important enough to be marked on my Michelin map of Europe. I knew whenever a train was approaching, even when the track was right on the edge of the horizon, because before I'd heard or seen it Shinto would have bolted off across the road in blind, unbridled terror. In almost any other developed country this reaction would have occurred often enough to have proved our fatal undoing. But because this was Spain it happened once before lunch, and once afterwards.

All that said, I can't blame anyone but myself for opting to allocate so many of the remaining daylight hours to a gormless dawdle round the sprawling food hall of some airport-sized hypermarket. I emerged with a lobotomised consumerist glaze on my face and a huge sack of vinaigrette crisps in my hand, depleted of the cultural stamina that was apparently required to tackle the cathedral's interior. 'Allow at least six hours,' one of my guidebooks urged, 'and bring a flashlight and binoculars.'

Knowing I would never do any of that had left me feeling aesthetically inadequate before I even went in, and though it was grandiosely immense, I couldn't catch a sniff of the sombre majesty that had very nearly had me on my knees in Los Arcos. There was too much stuff – fifteen chapels encircle the naves – and, on a late-spring Saturday, too many people. I spotted the carved image of a peeing angel on the choir-stalls and that did for me. A shame, really. I somehow completely missed the thirteenth-century life-sized Christ upholstered in buffalo skin, a figure that even sceptical medieval pilgrims saw move, and bleed, and have its nails and hair clipped. Stick that in your dummy, Tiny Tears. And I also appear to have stepped blithely over the tomb of the man who stole my epitaph by riding out of the gates of history and into legend.

Burgos is known as the City of El Cid, stamping ground of the eleventh-century Castilian noble played so memorably, or so some muttering loon at a pub quiz once told me, by Charlton Heston in the eponymous 1961 bio-pic.

I've always liked El Cid, largely on account of his name. It was almost a shame to discover it derives from the Arabic for lord, but I perked up at the revelation that he was christened Rodrigo, because El Rod is even better. Other than that, and not even having seen the film, I knew absolutely nothing about the man.

It was an education, the very best sort in fact, to discover that there was almost nothing to know. Yes, El Cid fought in battle before he was a teenager – show me an eleventh-century European who didn't. A heartless mercenary who sold his services to the

Moors – is that good? – and ripped off the Jewish moneylenders of Burgos by selling them a treasure chest filled with sand. Brilliant, and truly heroic. 'He could write, though his spelling was awful . . . he ruled Valencia from 1094 to 1099.' You can imagine Charlton thumbing through the script with a furrow across that great bronzed brow: When do I get to the good bit? And the bad news, Chazza, is that you don't. Or rather that when you do, you're a fortnight-old corpse strapped to a horse, leading troops posthumously into battle.

Outside was better. In the square just below the cathedral a transvestite stag party was press-ganging female tourists into acts of photographic tomfoolery, and just beyond I discovered a representation in bronze of a seated pilgrim nude, almost proudly displaying the symptoms of advanced leprosy. I was prodding his most intimate lesions when a cry of welcome turned my head: seated outside a proximate bar were Evelyn, Petronella, two auburn-haired British Columbians whose names I've forgotten and an as-yet-unencountered Australian couple in their fifties. The wife, as I soon learnt, had done her knee in on day two, but they weren't giving in: he walked on, she took the bus and they met up each evening. Every pilgrimage needs at least a couple of Australians. How novel it was, and how refreshing, to hear an irksome stretch of road recalled with feeling and volume as 'total shithouse'.

We all went off to find somewhere to eat, and suddenly there were pilgrims everywhere. You'd walk past a bar and hear someone saying, 'You can see the linguistic connection between Jacob and Iago, but how do you get from there to James?' With a keen ear I could even spot the Spanish ones: '*anti-inflammatoria*' was a certain give-away. And in the restaurant we ended up in – like every other devoid of local custom until after our curfew – our sole fellow diners were a couple of German greybeards we knew well enough to nod at. 'As a pilgrim I feel almost guilty to enjoy food,' one called over earnestly as the starters arrived.

'What, even when it's so bloody cheap?' Total Shithouse bellowed back.

Though in fact that night it wasn't: we'd all gone for Saturday specials like langoustines and rib-eye, and somehow it just didn't work. I'd have been so much happier with my standard pilgrim meal-deal – mixed salad, *lomo* and chips, and 'flan'. *Lomo* was pork escalope, and flan wasn't flan. Flan was crème caramel, and came in two varieties: a viscous and slightly acrid magnolia discharge, or foiled and potted butter-scotch tofu straight from the supermarket chill cabinet. But I always had it, simply to reward the alarming way they barked the word out as an upper-case exclamation. 'FLAN!' – a blunt, nasal syllable, a wedge of Yorkshire amongst all that hacking, hissing Latin.

Since Santo Domingo we'd been in the lisp belt, and all of us agreed how much more fun it was saying 'grathias', so much so that it usually became 'grathiath'. In fact, I'd been nurtur-ing an enthusiasm for the Spanish language ever since it was explained to me that Don Mueble, regularly encountered writ large on the hangar-sized flanks of an out-of-town commercial concern, meant Sir Furniture. I'm not quite certain why I loved that so much. All I know is that at least twice a day, more if there wasn't much to look at, I'd bend my head to Shinto's ear, and in a low, bandito rasp demand that he bring me the head of Don Mueble.

Smart but extremely young children were still finger-painting in their own breath on the designer-store windows when we headed back out into the tepid, dark streets. Evelyn was doing what a lot of walkers did in the cities, and had booked herself into a rejuvenatingly well-appointed hotel on the other side of the river. Like a true pilgrim she stole from the filthy rich to give to the filthy: it took her two weeks to disperse the cosmetic booty looted from that en-suite toiletry cavern. For the rest of us it was a stroll back to the *refugio*, past the old riverside mansions, a stroll that became a jog when one of the Canadians looked at her watch.

The *hospitalero* took no prisoners, other than the ninety-six of us. At 10.00 on the nose he clicked off the light and slammed the door shut: in the morning we'd find almost a dozen haggard, bleary stop-outs who'd turned up a little late and been obliged to bed down on the picnic tables. I found myself recalling the fourteenth-century Burgos assistant abbot who, infuriated by perpetual overcrowding in his monastery's pilgrim wing, poisoned the soup and so granted one hundred guests a short cut to paradise.

Mutiny was inevitable, and almost instantly a pilgrim clicked the light back on to a round of defiant cheers. But an outside force would destroy this hard-won solidarity, and the rebellion had long since been superseded by darkness and slumber when it attacked.

In the bottom bunk nearest to the window, I bore the brunt. An extraordinary noise blared in through the earplugs and seemed to come out of my eye sockets, blasted open by a decibel grenade. Groans and lethargic confusion, ninety-six unhappy mumbles. Then another huge if somehow quavering retort, hard by my head. Every window was open in a wooden bunk-house still torpidly haunted by the day's accumulated heat, and if I looked out of mine I would see an enthusiastic but helplessly drunken novice huffing into a didgeridoo. Before I could do that something butted through the net curtain. 'It's you he wants!' I very nearly shrieked, preparing to fling myself door-side of the little Spaniard top-to-toe in the conjoining bunk. I didn't, though, because the something was Shinto. Or at least the tips of his flared and trumpeting nostrils.

A minute later, the most hated man in Burgos stood outside the fire-escape door in his pants. 'What are you why is it how time?' I said, slurring out the gaps between words as I blundered sockless through predictable donkey awfulness. In the urban moonlight I could see those nose holes dilate and quiver, as sure an indicator of loud and imminent drama as a wobbling infant lip. But when this came it came in fearful harmony, the desperate, toneless orchestra of dreadnoughts lost in fog. I saw a mobile shadow at the other end of the corral. It was another donkey; a bigger, darker donkey, a donkey that even in this light I could see bore a chilling resemblance to our fiendish pursuer. 'Shite,' I probably said. At least he was tied up, though

I wasn't at all happy about the let-me-at-him strain being applied to the rope.

'Out in the woods, Shints,' I said, fumbling at the knot, or rather the macramé football it had been ever since his Belorado break-out. But then I stood up. The woods; the *gitanos*. I'd dismissed the warnings, but how to explain the sudden appearance of old El Ned here? There was a thick-skinned, long-eared Romany if ever I saw one, a graduate from the school of hard donks. There was only one thing to do: leave absolutely everything exactly as it was, then get up at 4.30 a.m. and hit the road before my under-slept pilgrim peers could mete out any properly coordinated punishment. It wasn't a bad plan, and I managed half of it.

'Is your donkay?'

There was a man at my bed, but he didn't sound as though he was about to smother me. I opened my eyes: once more, almost everyone had left. The man had kind but terribly furnaced features, the face of an amiable wino. 'I have also a donkay outside. If you come to the garden we can be talking.'

Twenty minutes later we were, across one of the pub-garden trestle tables out the front. Another ass-hauling pilgrim! This was an auspicious encounter: Donkey Livingstone, I presume?

Jean was from Belgium, and in the early stages of an extraordinary undertaking: from his home near Brussels he would lead Pilou to Santiago, then to Rome, and finally to Jerusalem. The pilgrim hat-trick – I was dumbfounded, and utterly humbled; in that moment I confess to coveting my neighbour's ass. 'Yes,' he coughed, rolling up what even at 7.30 was evidently not his first cig of the day. 'But I have five years.' He lit it, sucked in, blew out. 'This is the best thing I can do. That anyone can do.'

It wasn't a good time to expect positive reciprocation of this statement. The nocturnal goings-on had merely supplemented the groaning catalogue of bad things that were still better than what I was doing, a catalogue which when Shinto had started up again at about 2.30 was updated to include borstal and getting your face stuck in a badger set. Instead, I said, 'How do you get him over bridges?'

Jean smiled, deepening a dozen already deep creases. 'It's not so much a problem. I attache the long *corde*, and I walk to the other side, and I wait.'

'Wait?'

'For fifteen minutes.'

'Right, and then you pull like buggery.'

Jean might have been Belgian, but he had a Frenchman's flair for facial outrage. 'No! He come across after five minutes.' He straightened his back, intimidating me just as Pilou had intimidated Shinto. '*Never* pull a donkay.'

There was an awkward silence here, but I'd learnt by now not to fill it with a blurted enquiry into what had inspired this epic mission. It was bad form to ask someone what their pilgrimage was about, on a first date at least. Particularly so in Jean's case: I found out later that the year before his wife had died. He'd had Pilou ever since, and despite knowing nothing about donkeys had trained him up himself.

It was odd the way information passed along the line, a Chaucerian chain of news, tittle-tattle and, yes, slanderous, unfounded rumour. But at my speed you never heard who or what lay up ahead, only what was coming from behind, Chinese-whispered on by passing pilgrims. In the previous week I'd seen rival donkey crap on the camino and Shinto had certainly smelt it: the reason I hadn't heard about Jean and Pilou was that until the day before he'd been ahead.

'You're saying I'm *faster* than you?'

'Of course,' said Jean. 'I have five years. But also I don't walk on Saturday so much, and today, on Sunday, never.'

More than that, we weren't alone. There was a German woman, said Jean, who he'd seen a few times. She had two donkeys and two young daughters. 'You think it is *sympathique*, yes?' he said, before elaborating in ostentatious detail exactly why it wasn't. The mother believed in eating only what she could find in the fields, which at this time of year meant living on grass. 'And also for her children! Grass!' Jean extinguished his tiny dog end with an angry boot. 'I see her some days before. She is looking like this at a wall in the *refugio*.' He held a horny-handed palm to his nose and fixed it with moronic intensity. 'For three hours!' That grizzled, ruddy head shook with bewildered rage. 'The teeth of the children . . . '

It all sounded horrific, but at the same time I really hoped he wasn't exaggerating. Because if he was, what might he say about me? Especially now he knew I was a donk-puller.

Pilou tried to get at Shinto one last time, but the knot held and after a very self-conscious loading procedure – 'Oh, he has not so much: Pilou is with 40 kilo' – we said our farewells. I picked up the rope and clicked my tongue, endeavouring both to affect easy professionalism and encourage Shinto out of the blocks at a healthy, face-saving pace.

'Oh, but he is slow,' said Jean, because I failed.

'Yes,' I said.

'But then he has hunger!'

'Yes?' I said.

For fifteen minutes we watched Shinto browse the high grass, which at least allowed Jean the opportunity to inspect his hoofs. 'It's enough food,' said Jean, once he'd pronounced all four fully roadworthy. 'Now you see.'

I led Shinto back out to the path. After fewer than a dozen despondent paces I was ahead of him and the rope was taut. Jean surveyed Shinto evenly, then did the whole *pah, bof, sacré bleu* thing with his hands. But it was important that as the sole bearers of the donkey flame – sole sane bearers, anyway – we parted friends, and so we did. '*Eh bien*, all donkays are different. I know only Pilou.' We shook hands – ow – and with a heartfelt '*bonne chance*' I turned to the west and left him.

We passed through the brief western outskirts of Burgos at a crawl, Shinto's ears splayed flat in the 'fuck you all' handlebar position. A dead mole on the path, a French motorist whose photographic eagerness almost drove us into a river, a huge motorway viaduct over our heads. Abandoned factories; a distant, watch-towered prison. Sunday cyclists.

Then an hour of torpid nothing until I stopped to eat a tin

of pimientos by a bus shelter, whereupon an old man in a flat cap came up and called me a fascist.

It's funny, or rather grimly shaming, to think of the blithe holiday larks many of us enjoyed in Spain during Franco's long tenure. Thirty-six years he ruled: I still can't quite believe Western Europe had a fascist dictator in 1975. How could Abba and General Franco have overlapped?

'*Falangista, Falangista!*' the man croaked animatedly, poking a vague and shaky forefinger at Shinto's head. There was no audience, but I can't pretend not to have been a little alarmed. He stooped effortfully to pick up Shinto's rope, then held it up to me defiantly. '*Falangista!*' he cried again, before casting it haughtily into the dust and heading across the road towards a bar. For a brief but vivid moment I imagined him re-emerging through its dangling fly curtain at the head of a heavily armed death squad masked in the long-eared balaclavas of the Donkey Liberation Front. But then I looked again at the rope, which was striped red and green, and realised the green was very dark, dark enough for a man of many years with short sight and a long memory to have thought he was looking at the red and black of Franco's army.

If feelings run a little strong in this part of the world – I'd certainly advise Dennis the Menace to think long and hard before agreeing to that tour of the region's old people's homes – it's perhaps not surprising. Franco swore in his first fascist government at a monastery in Burgos, and that prison I'd passed had incarcerated many of his political enemies. Crossing the Montes de Oca I'd seen a memorial for the unknown thousands of Burgos republicans abducted, murdered and buried in lonely mass graves that are still being discovered. But, and there's no way of saying this without causing grievous offence, I still can't understand how the people of Spain never rose up and overthrew Franco. They waited until he got really old and died, buried him with due pomp, then quietly adopted parliamentary democracy. I mean, I could understand their trepidations in the unstable post-war climate, but – well, he was eighty when 'Waterloo' came out. An eighty-year-old dictator with no credible possibility of being survived by his odious regime. It's not great, is it?

Pensively I trudged forth, pondering that even in Franco's absence Spain still seems oddly rooted in the fifties: the shameless love of private transport, the heavy industry nudging right into town, those blaring election tannoys. And all this rural poverty – I was now passing through towns that seemed to be shedding wealth and sophistication in layers, each scrappier and more rustic than the last. There were new cars, then old cars, then no cars. We turned an uphill corner out of a farm and there, mercifully in the distance, was the first working donkey I'd seen: incredibly, taking on the collie role at the rear end of a column of sheep, nudging the slackers into place with his snout. Donkeys, I now saw, were neither lazy nor agelessly stupid. Some donkeys. Over a distance Shinto's ears were a lot more use than his eyes, but he still did a double take.

The sheep donk was a clear indication that we were entering the parochial periphery of the great *meseta*, but not as clear perhaps as a rather bleak ascent through an unremitting expanse of corn, and the epic covering of the same that filled the prospect from atop the climb's conclusion. But wasn't the chalky descent from here unusually severe for what was supposed to be a prairie? It certainly looked so: halfway down I could see a dismounted cyclist scrabbling perilously for purchase as the path split into a dozen pebbled gullies.

'Moment please!' It was another cyclist, a German, approaching from behind and holding up a wiggling forefinger in what I could now spot at 100 paces as the universal sign for 'I would like to photograph your monkey.' Shinto was already nose down in the corn; I shrugged in assent. As he extracted his camera from the bag on his handlebars, I saw inside it an unfamiliar guidebook, long and thin and English. 'Could I have a quick . . . ?' I asked, as Shinto pushed out his fifth leg into a pose that perhaps at this very moment is bringing a Bavarian slide show to an early and ignoble conclusion. 'For sure. It's most useful. I believe from Canada.'

I skimmed through the relevant paragraph with what began

as mild curiosity. Rural road . . . uphill through cornfields . . . Ah. Here we are. 'On reaching the highest point of the plain, continue for a short distance, before beginning the sharp descent down the "Cuesta Matamulos" (the "Mulekiller Hill").' Not since that terrible business with the encyclopedia shelf have a pair of brackets been asked to bear such a burden. How many good animals had met their ends on this crumbling escarpment? Breathing loudly through my nose I let the cyclist through, and allowed Shinto a . . . a last meal. Then I eased him back to the path, patted his neck rather too hard and took the first auspicious downwards step.

Well, butter my donkey's arse. You know what? We beat that cyclist. We caught him halfway down as he stopped to negotiate a gravel-filled scoop in the limestone, skipped neatly by and beat him down to the bottom and all the way to the door of the *refugio* in Hornillos del Camino.

I liked any village whose name officially declared allegiance to the pilgrimage, and after that triumph I especially liked Hornillos. It was a tiny, rather neglected settlement, all rough stone and dusty wood beneath a rolling sea of cracked pantiles, but the bar was open, the *refugio* was new and most of my friends were in one or the other. 'Hail the conqueror of Mulekiller Hill!' called Evelyn through the fly screens, bookended by the jolly faces of Anna and Janina, two Dutch ladies who'd cycled from Holland to St Jean, and been on foot since then. 'Yeah, well . . .' I sighed airily, tying Shinto up to the churchyard gate. It would have been about this time that I accepted the escarpment's nickname was of course derived from the debilitating efforts required to ascend it.

The bar did us the full salad-to-flan-via-*lomo* deal, and when I was done the quietly welcoming proprietor arrived with a snifter, a small alcoholic balloon, bearing an imprudent volume of Veterano brandy. I'm not sure why I asked for this, but when the bill came I was sorry I had. I was sorry because this treble-measured troublemaker cost but a single euro, and that meant it would be very difficult from now on to end a day without one. So difficult, in fact, as to prove impossible.

175

We took our *digestifs* outside, and dispatched them on the church steps in a diminishing triangle of low sun. A distorted and amplified voice approached, and we turned to see an electioneer pulling up outside the bar: all this way for half a dozen votes. Two widows of great age sat on doorsteps knitting (it was startling how many of their populous ilk actually did this), oblivious to both the hectoring entreaties of the Castilian Nationalists and our presence.

I'd often been struck by the benign indifference with which most of these places regarded pilgrims, even here where the twenty-eight of us might easily have outnumbered the villagers. In some ways the lack of interaction was a matter of time-keeping: we walked while they worked, and ate while they slept, and slept while they played. But in socio-economic terms ours was a strange symbiosis, and I suppose an ancient one. They fed us, and we brought some much-needed money into a deprived community.

But time and again we were all struck by how rarely any locals seemed willing to offer any lucrative extras: an à-la-carte menu, a nice private room, a kid selling sun cream and lemonade on a table in the shade. There seemed to be an unwritten code of honour – it was a religious and civic duty to see a pilgrim through your town amply catered for, but no more. You gave him some hearty walking fuel but never thought about ripping him off – even if he was a middle-aged North European with the economic wherewithal to take a great long slab of holiday and spend it on some self-indulgent quest for his inner student. I suppose it's what you expect in a country where the Miss June on garage calendars is typically depicted in oils, swathed in a blue kirtle and cradling a haloed baby.

I'd bagged a bottom bunk, beneath an ominously big-nosed Dutchman. Soon the latticed mattress springs were bowing towards me, each creak giving way to a steady, contented and in fact not disagreeable low wheeze. Outside, no doubt silhouetted against the moon, Shinto issued what was now his standard midnight reveille: five doughty, reverberating foghorn blasts fading into a weary, piteous snuffle, like some aged farm-hand concluding a belaboured act of love. It was a fitting end, somehow, to what I realised eighteen hours later had been my birthday.

Ten

The clouds were still wisping past the moon as I buckled the saddle, frogmarched from slumber by swishes and shuffles and the slam of the big front door. When at length the sun nosed above the horizon it was the first time we'd cast long shadows up the camino, into the wheaten wilderness ahead, instead of back down it.

There was sun and wind and photosynthesis, and the haunted song of unseen, cowering birds, but there was nothing else. No sane soul would have located a *refugio* out here, so it wasn't an especial turn-up to find the inverted eggcup of Arroyo de San Bol under the management of a scarily blank-faced young German. He was standing solemnly at the doorway when I arrived, lured by the promise of elevenses and a bathe in a spring that my Confraternity book credited with healing powers.

'You English expect magic water,' he said slowly, addressing himself to the little red book in my hand. 'But it is not magic. It is only water.' His gaze moved sluggishly towards Shinto. 'Last year one monkey like this ate here a young tree.'

'He won't do that, honestly. It says here you have coffee?'

'Yes. But it is not magic. It is only coffee.'

The *refugio* was a marvellously idiosyncratic structure, and scrutinising it I was able at least for a moment to view its

178

caretaker's auspicious behaviour in the same light. The domed interior had been painted as a star-clustered night sky, and each of the half-dozen beds beneath was immaculately topped with a crest-adorned blanket.

'So – how many pilgrims did you have to stay yesterday?' I enquired brightly as my host stooped silently over a camping-gas stove. No electricity here; and, as the Confraternity guide had stressed, 'NB: there are NO sanitation facilities.'

'One.' He sounded as if he'd much rather it had been none. My coffee was ghosted on to the low table before me. What a time of it the two of them must have had together, out here in a million acres of inky nothing, either side of this table with a packet of Marie biscuits and a candle.

'I am here all the summer,' he said, pacing behind me as I desperately urged my coffee to cool. 'Every summer.'

For two minutes he paced as I puffed and stirred and sipped. Then he sat down on the floor beside me, cross-legged beneath the dome's apex. 'My name is Udo,' he whispered, and struck a match. He was still watching it burn at the end of an outstretched hand when I upended searing caffeine painfully down my throat, tossed a couple of euros on the table and marched briskly out into the sun.

I was reasonably eager to put some camino between me and Udo, and for once Shinto seemed to pick up on the urgency. On we scuttled, through a silent town wedged in a hole in the plain, along a hillside Monet-spattered with poppies, to a lunch spot beneath a Gothic arch of heart-stopping scale and splendour.

I read as we ate. Around and above us were the ruins of the monastery of San Anton, whose roofless remains somehow expressed the full scale of the medieval pilgrimage infrastructure more vividly than the restored showhouse that was Roncesvalles. Here we were, out in the definitive middle of nowhere, yet by the fourteenth century this hospice monastery had its own mill and orchard and dovecotes, and was merely one of the 369 such establishments the San Anton order controlled along Europe's pilgrim routes. A lot of hard cash had gone into the construction of this place, but also more than a few pints of the milk of human kindness.

The order's mission was to tend the many sufferers of St Anthony's Fire, a disturbing ailment epidemic throughout medieval Europe. What we'd doubtless now call SAF was no less disfiguring than leprosy, but the physical symptoms were typically preceded by paranoid hallucinations; a double whammy that explains why many victims were expelled from their home villages. On the road, as honorary lepers, they were forced to warn others of their approach by ringing a bell or banging two boards together: theirs was a pilgrimage less about reaching heaven in the next life than getting out of hell in this one.

It was a happy surprise to learn that the monks were able to cure many sufferers, and without even knowing why. It's now widely accepted that the symptoms of SAF (see how easily that slipped out?) are consistent with ergot poisoning caused by the long-term consumption of mouldy barley. In the twelfth century, eight out of ten consumed calories came in the form of bread, most of it at best stale. Because the monks had more money their grain and bread were fresher; stay long enough in a monastery, and a complete recovery was almost guaranteed.

I found myself almost uncomfortably affected as I stood under that great, pointed arch and let the guidebooks direct me to two little niches set into its base. Every night the monks would fill these with loaves of bread, untainted bread, lest any hungry pilgrims arrived after the big doors were heaved shut at dusk. And as I stood there, contemplating all the hideousness and beauty of the medieval pilgrimage, I heard the telltale taps and scrapes that heralded the approach of a serious, pole-pushing walker. Two of them in fact, walking up to and straight beneath that glorious arch without ever once raising their eyes from the tarmac.

Castrojeriz was known to the old pilgrims as 'long town', and certainly embraced the tenets of ribbon development more tightly than any town of 1,200 souls should ever dare. It was half four when we ambled past the first church, and half five

– sixty whole, hot minutes – before the *refugio* revealed itself. An airy gymnasium filled with incense and tinkling instrumentals, this was an establishment under the languid stewardship of two terrific middle-aged hippies – brothers, said Evelyn, poofters, said our old friend Total Shithouse. The younger took an instant shine to Shinto, carefully inscribing his name and age in the *refugio* logbook, and then insisting I accompany him on a quest for suitable donkommodation.

This involved a brief reacquaintance with some of the forgotten pleasures of motorised transport, but also with every one of its obscurer elemental terrors. He piloted his elderly Renault in a manner inconsistent with its braking system, a largely external affair involving piles of sand and pliable roadside vegetation. It was perhaps fortunate that plenty of both edged the driveway to a farm additionally blessed with charitable owners and a surfeit of uncultivated land. There were good people in this town. I returned there with Shinto and shuffled back alone, warmed from without by that ever-blazing sun and from within by the spirit of San Anton.

'Hey – where's the donkey?'

I turned to see an American woman, fiftyish, in racing-driver shades and a white beanie hat, and crossed the pan-fried tarmac to join her. A swift résumé of recent travails revealed that she had also taken coffee with Udo, and our walk back to the *refugio* was accompanied by a breathless account of her experience. 'Like, it was just *so* theatrical,' she said, her pursed and painted lips working furiously, 'though as an actress, from Hollywood, I really have to say I found the whole experience totally amazing.' This sentence was delivered in perhaps two seconds, and I was still trying to pick through its many salient features when without warning she grabbed my arm and abruptly adopted a tone of low, urgent confidentiality. 'But he hated me. That man *hated* me.'

'I think he was just generally odd,' I said when she'd let go. 'To everyone.'

'He wouldn't even let me use his toilet! Can you believe that?'

'There wasn't a toilet.'

She fixed me with a cold, suspicious stare; I had the Confraternity book in my hand and read from it: ' "NB – there are NO sanitation facilities.' " Watching her walk briskly away up the *refugio* steps I wondered why I'd said those capitals so loudly.

I had dinner in an uplit, dandified cellar with Jean-Michel and a female compatriot of his who spoke Spanish and at my behest wrote down what I felt to be a key phrase on a napkin. I have it before me now, that plump and gracious Continental calligraphy sorrily furrowed and wrinkled: '*Limpiará la suciedad de mi burro.*' How oddly rewarding it was to pick up the sort of holiday vocabulary that substituted pleas for beer with a pledge to clear up the mess of one's donkey.

'I met a very interesting lady from America today,' whispered Jean-Michel as we picked our way up the dark *refugio* stairs. He described her and we both nodded in confident recognition.

'The actress from Hollywood,' I gently confirmed.

'Ze children's book right-air from Philadelphia,' murmured the Frenchwoman, more slowly.

Jean-Michel eyed us as carefully as the gloom permitted. 'Ze artiste from Connecticut?' And that was the story of how Baroness von Munchausen got her name.

The farmers weren't around to thank again when I released Shinto from the old bedstead I'd tied him up to the afternoon before. As I surveyed his environs in the light of another wide blue morning it was apparent that he'd spent the last fourteen hours up to his hocks in wild alfalfa, and for the first time I had to loosen the saddle straps under his gut by a couple of holes each. Guffing queasily he allowed himself to be led out of town, and even over a long wooden bridge, but came to a bilious halt halfway up the hill that followed – an eminence far more grandiose than that eponymously charged with mule murder. I got him to the top in the end, but as we stood there in the lee of a weathered pilgrim monument, Shinto gazing dolefully down at Castrojeriz and me across at the windfarm on a distantly opposite *meseta*, I knew it had taken a lot out of him.

Evelyn and Petronella, the former at least unusually late on the road, caught me as we plodded funereally down the gentle descent. Company always shifted Shinto up a gear, but that day he seemed oddly withdrawn, settling immediately into a full run-through of his favourite stalling tactics: the frenzied nibbling of that suddenly unbearable gnat bite on his ankle, the elaborate olfactory encounters with even the most inconsequential dried turd, the abrupt, prick-eared halt which had us all scouring the landscape for a non-existent threat. After an hour I told them to go on ahead. I was beginning to accept this dreadful, torpid sloth, or at least to tolerate it with nothing more than the occasional resigned obscenity, but welcoming as companionship always was I couldn't expect any other normally fit human to put up with it for long.

The path was undeviating and I watched Evelyn and Petronella pace steadily away for some time. They were halfway to the horizon when I was overtaken by a quietly polite Norwegian lady I'd lent – perhaps even given – some toothpaste to the night before. Then, as the comely silhouette of a compact 800-year-old *refugio* took shape, and beyond it the rising hump of a 1,000-year-old bridge, the two more distant figures were joined by a third: small, hunched, male.

The three of them walked together awhile, then stopped and seemed to converge. I narrowed my eyes into the heat haze: the man, hatted and of advanced years, had an arm tight round either waist and was hungrily kissing each face in turn. For the first two minutes or so the women seemed to find it very funny, but when the comic appeal waned he was eased aside and walked off to the right with an unreturned wave. Poor Evelyn. It was only a couple of days since she'd shaken off the most unwholesome of her coterie, a Dutchman who, in her memorable description, 'just sat there rubbing his legs together like a cricket'.

After a while the old feller turned about, and shuffled back to the camino. I had a feeling I knew what was going to happen next, and so did the Norwegian lady, because when he came up to her she said something loud and pushed an outfacing palm hard into his throat. When I passed him a few minutes later he was still standing there, stroking his tender gullet and looking sad and bewildered. I don't understand it, you could see him thinking. I've waited seventy years to be old and shrunken enough to get away with this.

A sign on the other side of the bridge welcomed us to the Tierra de Campos, land of fields. 'This country abounds in fodder,' said the *Liber Sancti Jacobi*, 'and it has plenty of bread, meat, fish and honey.' I read it out to Shinto but it didn't seem to make him any happier. Big flatness he hated, and the gradient profiles of the days ahead were like brain-activity readings from an overweight narcoleptic listening to John Major count in binary.

Somehow the horizon behaved itself, hiding behind a couple of false summits, throwing up a diversionary hillock on the right or a copse on the left. Lunch went fairly well, though after his alfalfa blow-out he didn't eat much, and at one point caused me a violent stab of panic by lying down in a patch of very tall grass when I wasn't looking.

Soon after we'd hit the dusty camino once more it speared unwaveringly up an incline substantial enough to be named on the map. Near the top we passed a young girl sitting on her rucksack at the side of path, crying. 'OK?' I said, stooping down. She pressed the fat part of a hand against the moister eye and smeared it down her cheek. 'Please,' she beseeched, quiet and German, craving only solitude. I was to see her about half a dozen times, in the company of a portly youth I learnt was her new husband. Few ever heard him speak, and that tiny imploration was her solitary reported utterance. The camino is many things: a religious duty, a voyage of personal discovery and shared experience, a test of spiritual and human endurance. Perhaps, in many ways, it is like a marriage. But a honeymoon it is not.

Shinto seemed a little downcast after this encounter: his

presence had, perhaps uniquely, failed to cheer a doleful stranger. Then the Otero Largo reached its gentle summit, and there it was. Sky of blue, sea of green – the true *meseta alta*, a sweeping continent of wheat that has been the bread basket of Iberia since Roman times. Three or four distant towns struggled up out of the haze, each crowned by a shimmering, wobbly church tower. And that was it. I took a picture, but when I look at it now it's hard to tell what it's of. That's no landscape: that's just a flag, a big, dull flag, top half blue, bottom half green.

'The grain in Spain grows mainly on this plain,' I said, flatly, then turned round to Shinto.

Donkeys always look slightly hungover, but this was the first time mine had looked drunk. His head was all over the place, straining back and erratically darting forward, then swaying left to right, then jerking up again. The eyes were in whites-up El Loco mode, lolling back into his big skull. And great God Almighty, that mouth: lips stretched tautly back like a shrivelled Pharaoh's, yellowed teeth gnashing at the heavens. It was like Mr Ed cursing in tongues.

'Come on, Shints,' I said, in a voice very unlike a man's. I cut him some slack, and with the rope paid out to its limit turned to continue. In a second he'd bounded up, and I looked back just in time to see his teeth clamp around one of the straps of my daypack. 'Shinto!' I shrieked, jerking it out. But his eyes were now slits of restless hatred, the ears pinned back with sociopathic intent. He went for me again, gnashing at a bare elbow, and the chase was on.

On and on we ran and scrambled and panted, trailing a column of bad words and dust across that epic panorama. Sometimes he'd slow down, then catch me off guard when I followed suit. Only after an hour, with the sanctuary of Boadilla del Camino approaching at unencountered speed, did I happen upon a strategic solution. Keep the rope taut, and maintain a steady jog keeping it at full length. And when it slackens, young pilgrim, run for your sorry life.

The presence of other human life had a policing effect on

Shinto, and he strolled through the scrub-dusted, tractor-jammed streets of Boadilla with his demeanour settling into an approximation of repentance. The uneasy truce was for once accompanied by mutual understanding: we both knew that he hadn't been himself, that he had in fact just been Berserko, the Mad Donkey.

I could probably call Boadilla horrid, and was certainly in a mood to, but folded up in my back pocket was a little brochure that meant I wouldn't. I passed the official *refugio* and was uncharitably relieved to see it comfortably the most wretched yet: a sort of abandoned post office, with broken windows and fluorescent tubes emitting unwanted light and an insistent monotone. There were pilgrims glumly manipulating their laundry in its filthy yard, but I didn't know any of them. They were out of the loop on this one.

It was Petronella who'd found the brochure, days back somewhere before Burgos, and on many an evening since we'd all gathered round to scrutinise it with hushed reverence. '*Oasis en el Camino*' was the catchline presiding over images of a pilgrim Shangri-La, lawns like golf greens, parasol-sheltered tables, a wall of bougainvillea, sculptures, fountains. It was a twenty-first-century update of those orchard/dovecote monasteries that must regularly have reduced our medieval forebears to tears of grateful joy. One of the British Columbians had dubbed it Club Med, and the forty-eight-bed bunk-house aside it did indeed seem the sort of place you'd book for a real, normal holiday. So much so that I'd made a real, normal holiday booking, over the phone from Castrojeriz.

The walls of the new pride of Boadilla were square up next to its old one, a magnificent Gothic *rollo*, a sort of giant and ornate limestone sceptre stood on end. I walked Shinto round it a couple of times, admiring its carved scallop shells, flowers and animals. 'The *Rollo* shows with dignity the judicial autonomy the village had in the times of Enrique IV,' read the brochure, which didn't quite tell the whole story. Erected by the Boadillans in the fifteenth century, the *rollo* served both to celebrate and expedite the town's newly acquired right to

hang its own criminals. The deluxe gallows stood at the edge
of a doornail-dead plaza, a strangely unpeopled realm dominated by a sombre, foursquare church whose big, cracked bell
tolled out as I stood there, a ponderous, hang-'em-high tocsin
echoing tonelessly off the shuttered houses.

'Yes!' I looked round to see a young man with a huge pony-
tail grinning brilliantly in the *albergue's* gateway. 'Here we
kill de killers!'

He stood there impressively as I walked Shinto over, fists
on hips, black-leathered legs planted distantly apart, perhaps
debating whether to do something complicated with a sabre
or catch a willowy swooner in the crook of his elbow and press
his lips roughly to hers.

Edouardo was his name, but he was more than that. I was
looking at the King of Boadilla. He had done everything that
I said small-town Spaniards didn't do, ruthlessly targeting the
pilgrim euro with a success whose visible trappings multiplied
throughout our short walk to Shinto's overnight field: the
Burberry pullover on the back seat of the big car, the pair of
haughty white stallions prancing magnificently about in an
adjacent pasture. Shinto surveyed them glumly – in the equine
attraction stakes, he was now up against a couple of babe
electro-magnets. Edouardo's farewell to him, a belittling sonny-
boy slap on the rump, can't have helped.

'It's a good life,' breezed Edouardo as we walked back to the
albergue. Too right: 14 euros for half board in a bijou country
club might seem a ludicrous bargain, and indeed was, but when
you multiplied 14 by the forty-eight beds that meant a lot of
cash in Edouardo's manicured hand, seven days a week for
seven months a year. Great weather, cheap property and guests
you can lock up together in a big room at 10.00: I know I'm
tempted.

I hadn't dared expect the *albergue* to live up to its promotional billing, but oh, how it did. Within its walled grounds
pilgrims were prostrate on the velvety lawn with books over
their faces; a woman, who was of course Edouardo's put-upon
mother, walked out from the main house with a tray of beers.

When I noted that these were delivered in frosted glasses I could have fallen back into Edouardo's hairy forearms, but it was just as well I didn't because they were full already. 'I had a girlfriend from Canada one time,' he was crooning, his hand round Evelyn's shoulder. 'What happened?' she asked, gazing at him wondrously. Edouardo shrugged cheesily, a parodic homage of the Fonz. 'I love de ladies too much.'

I'd never thought of Evelyn as a simperer, and when Edouardo followed these words by brushing his knuckle gently down her cheek with a sickening wink I waited eagerly for her to empty that frosted glass into his leathered crotch. Instead, she giggled like a schoolgirl. 'That was a lot better than the kissy old granddad this morning,' she said once she'd recovered. I find I'm now obliged to point out that as a Spaniard, Edouardo was by no means a tall fellow.

For this performance and so much more I should have despised him, as should everybody else, but because he had created heaven on earth he got away with it. If Edouardo loved his job just a little too much then he was also very good at it: bantering with each and every guest as he took our evening orders, and supplying me with FLAN! even though it wasn't on the menu. After we'd all sat up late, sprawled on huge sofas in the candlelit, wood-stoved antechamber guarding our dormitory, he brought in all the stuff we'd forgotten on the lawn: books, shoes, saddles.

And the next day there he was at 6 a.m., or in my case 7.15, serving up *café con leche* with a toothy Wham! smile. All things considered this made up for the in-between bit, which was rather besmirched by a German woman accusing me of cheating ('But with a monkey this is an *easy* way to walk') as we brushed our teeth, a vast spider on the wall by my pillow, and a pair of French boots under the next bunk that assaulted the senses so savagely they might just as well have snored.

All morning we walked along the Canal de Castilla, an appealing but grandly over-ambitious civil-engineering project, inaugurated in the 1750s and rendered redundant by the railways long before its completion. Every few clicks we passed

a comely little classical gazebo, one of the original mainte-
nance huts; the flight of locks just outside Frómista was more
like a centrepiece water feature from the grounds of Versailles.

Frómista was about as diverting as you'd expect from a town
named after the word for cereal. Dominic Laffi had seen the
locals engage a swarm of locusts with wooden clubs, and it's
occasionally suggested as the birthplace of San Telmo, better
known as St Elmo, patron saint of awful films my wife loves.
As far as I could see that was it, so it came as a surprise to
encounter a large group of pilgrims waiting about by the busy
crossroads. Amongst them was Kathy, a quiet and erudite
Australian I'd met at Club Med, who today had formed an
unlikely walking alliance with Total Shithouse.

'Waiting for some church to open, mate,' he said, before
issuing a magnificent belch.

Kathy's eyes twitched behind her little glasses. 'It's one of
the finest examples of Romanesque architecture in this area,'
she whispered, with a brave smile.

That didn't sell it to me, I'm afraid, so instead Shinto and
I headed off into an already hot morning. The canal was
replaced by a rather fetching river, and we picnicked delight-
fully between the trees on its sun-mottled banks, the lazy,
shallow water alive with flailing trout that because this was
Spain nobody could be arsed to catch.

As would later become apparent, almost straight after rejoin-
ing the camino I missed an important arrow. Instead of dog-
legging left–right and up to rejoin the road, I continued along
the river bank without sensibly pondering why the vegetation
seemed a little wilder, the path a little vaguer and the arc of
its hesitant progress a little too far to the north.

The oilseed rape and poppies hemmed and encroached until
I was having to part a way through them with one hand, ensuring with the other that they didn't whiplash back into Shinto's
eyes. The path dipped down to the dried bed of some kind of
flood-relief trench and reared immediately back up: a small
roller-coaster which Shinto rather enjoyed. A little while later
we swooped rashly down and up another. With the sun now

at its punishing apogee I was delighted to find a water tap, so delighted that I gleefully emptied out my unpalatably tepid supplies without checking whether it worked.

It didn't, of course, but that setback was soon forgotten. Round the next meander I heaved back a great bush of oilseed and there was another culvert affair, this time bridged with a door-sized slab of concrete. 'No fun this time, Shints,' I said, and walked across. The rearward anchors dug in; my head snapped back. I looked round and he'd stopped with his front hoofs an inch from the concrete.

It was the first time he'd been seriously put out by a solid bridge, and here was one of especial poxiness. In fact, I thought, a perfect trial for Jean and Pilou's no-stress long-rope waiting game. Out came the stinking night cord, and with it tied to his head collar I paid out the full length and sat down in the weeds opposite. For ten minutes we contemplated each other mildly, like two commuters on opposite platforms. Then he twitched a fly off his rump, briefly assessed the proximate vegetation and stuck his grey head into a thick tuft of something.

As I watched those jaws slowly working through the under-growth I felt my own tighten. Then, working quickly, I tied the short cord to the end of the long one, dropped to my stomach and slithered backwards until I was out of sight, paying out rope throughout the retreat. It didn't take long. After a minute a plaintive, bereft honk filled the hot, still air, followed by four more and that distasteful granddad climax. I hunched lower, quietly smiting away an ant the size of three olives, and was soon rewarded with an unmistakable thunk, the sound of hoof on concrete. Extrapolating from previous experience that where one foot trod the others always followed I jumped up from my hiding place in exultation. A poor tactical decision, which as I watched had Shinto reversing back off the bridge and away.

Neurologists speak in awe of the human brain's ability to process information at tremendous speed in a crisis, but as someone once told me before I begged them tearfully to leave me be, a fast processor is nothing without a bug-proof operating system. The logical options here were to clear a bridgeless path down through the culvert by pulling up a few small bushes; to tie Shinto up and search for an acceptable detour; or to calm him down, let him graze a little, then try Jean's method once more. My brain riffled through the consequences, logistics and probabilities in a breathtaking flurry, then announced its assessment. Bollocks to all that, it said. Jump up on that donkey's back, boy, jump up there and ride him!

I inaugurated plan D, of course, by ripping my shirt off. Twirling it wildly overhead and with a throatful of noise I hammered over the bridge; Shinto naturally turned smartly about, but already seeing myself up on that panniered saddle, clattering to an exultant halt in Santiago's Plaza del Obradoiro, I launched into my vault regardless.

It was an unhappy spectacle, this star-crossed marriage of lunatic resolve and malcoordination. A take-off boot missed its appointment with the ground; suddenly I seemed to have far too many limbs, and none where they should have been. An arm threshed through a thistle, an ankle buckled, and somehow there was my head, or at least its left side, making jarringly stout contact with Shinto's robust hindquarters. Then I was down, a knot of twined and twitching appendages, a dying spider on the path.

I could hear Shinto's hoofs drumming off through the neighbouring field; I got up because I had to. My ankle yodelled with shrill pain, and a lens had been punched out of my sunglasses. No time to find it, or whatever was left of the shirt – he was bolting swiftly away through the corn like a wild palomino, the long rope scuttering behind him.

If he'd kept going that would have been the end of the story, but righteous outrage was mercifully overridden by the panic alarm that always went off when Shinto's radius from nearby humanity topped 100 yards. Shirtless and one-eyed I staggered through the crops, grabbed the rope, and breathing hard began to haul myself along it towards him. Just in time I saw those ears flatten back in a reprise of yesterday's Evil Mr Ed; my sidestep was quickly followed by a double-footed buckaroo back-kick, aimed right where I'd been standing. And so, I'm afraid, we had a fight.

He turned about, bared his teeth and snorted, and I filled my lungs with hot, wheaten air and bellowed back the worst things you could call a donkey, or at least the worst things that came to mind, an anthology inauspiciously launched with 'big-eared crap-sniffer'. When I could shout no more his ears went back and his eyes narrowed. We faced each other across the still green corn: only one of us would get out of this field alive. Stay out of it, Frank Assisi – this was between me and him. I was ready to kick some ass.

Shinto charged and I swayed and feinted like a matador; then I chased him; then he chased me. Mad donks and Englishmen. Round that field we went, thrashing through the thigh-high wheat until we'd flattened out a drunken crop circle. I paused again to turn the air blue, then Shinto swivelled his rear round to face me and turned it horribly brown.

Hands on knees, torso tarred and feathered with sweat and dusted vegetation, I watched those off-kilter panniers rise and fall with each of his huge breaths. Slowly he turned back, looked at me, at the trampled earth, at the now distant line of trees bordering the river, then raised his head and brayed into a flawless sky. Seven low, steady blasts, like no noise he'd made before: the all-clear klaxon, an end to hostilities. Then stillness and silence. That was it. We were both done in. Neither of us was really sure what we were doing here, but whatever it was we were in it together. I needed him; he needed me. And good God we both needed a drink.

Heart booming in my neck and head I blundered up to the field's highest point. There was a spire, and dragging myself cross-country between cereal crops but mainly through them I went straight at it. After two fields I was a humid, saline fly magnet, but after two more I didn't care. As the town beneath the spire took shape the buzzing faded, and I became dimly aware that my eyes had stopped stinging. The soggy cornflakes and pretzel sticks pasted to my arms and chest were drying up and falling off.

I had stopped perspiring. Every body fluid that could have been reprocessed into sweat had been: every joint seemed rustily ungreased, and my tongue was that crisped-up old sponge down the back of the bathroom radiator. Kidneys brutally wrung out by a fat-armed washerwoman, then fed through her sandpapered mangle. Only my socked and booted feet had escaped the desiccation, and somewhere down there they stumbled off the crumbled clods and on to tarmac. Creaking my unshaded eye shut I squinted at the sign: 'VILLALCAZAR' it read, meaning we were somehow back on track. A paragraph of lunchtime reading inveigled itself out of my skull's shrivelled core, and I slowly turned round to share it with Shinto, his head at half-mast, a grubby, crusted streak leaking from each huge nostril. 'The church in Villalcazar has the tallest porch in Spain,' I announced, in a dry gasp that gave out halfway through. And if there hadn't been a fountain outside, we'd have been looking up at it for eternity.

It was another 5 clicks to Carrión, which was a long way to keep the jokes coming, but rehydrated and at peace with my donk I got there in under two hours. The Monastery of Santa Clara looked like a prison of the sort Butch Cassidy might have blown a hole through to escape, but it was a proper, working nun-house and I'd been looking forward to staying there for days. There were three sheets of corrugated cardboard wedged through a barred window by its hefty arched entrance, and each bore a message. 'NO STAMP' said the first. 'COMPLETO – FULL' said the next. And at the bottom: 'GO TO THE OTHER'. Nay, nay and thrice nay. After my miserable experience at that monastery just before Pamplona, I suppose I shouldn't have been surprised.

'Christ, mate!' It was Total Shithouse, walking out of the gate and gawping with raw consternation. I'm surprised he recognised me: on top of everything else a sudden lust for cold alcohol had reduced me to perhaps half my normal size. 'We had a . . . a race,' I said, belatedly appraising the more conspicuous aspects of my appearance and their suitability for the monastic environment. 'No room here, right?'

'There's some funny feller in the office. He found me a place in the bunk-house. Check this out – there's a machine in the courtyard that sells beer. A convent with beer . . .' I watched his long, weathered face crack into a gurn of carefree depravity; it was a shame that no one would catch even a glimpse of the fourteen nuns said to be in residence.

I dropped my dead sunglasses in a street-side bin, effortfully unpacked a replacement shirt and walked in and across to the office. He was right about the funniness of the feller. 'No, no – no room here,' the man jabbered into an open drawer, fussing about behind the desk like Mañuel.

'I don't mind sharing,' I said.

'With a nun,' called out an Australian voice from outside the door.

'No, no – no room.' He stopped suddenly, and looked straight at me. 'Only private room, one bed, 16 euro.'

'Hey!' cried Total Shithouse.

'Too late,' I called back, peeling a damp pair of tens from my money belt.

Accessing my room involved three keys and a long walk. I followed the little man up many stairs, along a covered balcony overlooking the ancient courtyard and down a succession of immaculate but grimly spartan corridors. 'Here,' he said, ushering me into a tiny whitewashed chamber. A cupboard, a barred window, and over the narrow bed a framed depiction of Mary keening over a flayed Christ. It was a cell, really, but it was a nun's cell and I had it all to myself. And that was before I opened the cupboard door and found it contained a bath.

I secreted Shinto behind some trees up against the monastery's rear wall, half-filled his bowl with barley in a spirit of Christian forgiveness and returned to my room, via that vending machine, with an armful of baggage and as much of a spring as my step could conjure up. And a minute later there I was: drinking beer, in the nude, on a nun's bed! Drinking beer, in the nude, in a nun's bath! Drinking beer, in the nude, in front of a nun's mirror! And – oh, filth and buggery – seeing a tick attached to my throat.

Eating was going to come next, but by the time I'd twisted that little bastard out of my flesh I felt an unstoppable back-wash of fatigue dragging me under, and my beery aperitif evolved into a nightcap. It didn't feel as if I'd been out for all that long when some night train of thought crashed into the buffers and my eyes blurted open. In fraught and sweaty retro-spection I lay there, watching the moon diced and sliced through the curtainless bars, piecing together the clues to Shinto's recent behavioural problems. I smelt a hot sack of grain fermenting on a clammy grey back, I heard the banging of planks, I saw four burly monks pinning a screaming, nose-less freak to his bed. Shinto wasn't just a bit pissed off. He was medievally unwell. This was ergot poisoning. My donkey had St Anthony's Fire.

'Initiation occurs through a spiritual awakening while making the camino, which is divided into experiential parts,' read one academic overview of New Age pilgrim motives. Stage one, from Roncesvalles to Burgos, was described as representing universal spirituality, and the final stretch, from the Cruz de Ferro, as spiritual resurrection. As a non-Catholic European (age twenty-five to forty-five), I apparently fell smack into the category the author declared most vulnerable to such beliefs. Ha ha ha! But today I wasn't laughing. Today was the start of stage two. Carrión to Astorga, symbolic death.

Carrión was stubbornly unbustling as I walked through and out over its long bridge, no kids en route to school, no postmen, no one willing to suggest this wasn't Sunday except the usual scattering of labourers listlessly half-building something on the outskirts. Shinto seemed more placid, but I was taking no chances: the *cebada* sack was untied as we passed a stagnant construction site, and with Shinto watching in gormless, impo-tent protest – his Stan Laurel look – I heaved it into a skip.

In the newspaper forecast Iberia was plastered with yellow circles, and as well as being cloudless the early morning was ominously still: I stripped down to my T-shirt at 8.30, two hours earlier than the norm. A couple of big roundabouts, the farewell petrol station, and then, right before us, the landscape laid down and died. We'd set out across a lot of giant green tablecloths in the last few days, but this was the first that had been ironed: ahead the track rulered its way through a treeless, 2-D world of heat and supine agriculture. 'IMPORTANT,' said the Confraternity, and for once I'd paid heed. 'Before leaving Carrión buy some food and plenty of water. Between Carrión and Sahagún (43 kilometres) is an arid plain.'

An hour, two hours. We were getting nowhere. By 11.30 Shinto was already beginning to paw at the orange dust and rub his bottom lip through it, a symptom of fatigued delirium that didn't usually kick in till around 4.00. At 12.00 we passed a broken fountain; at 12.15 a tree. I lunched early, rigging up an abysmal parasol with my poncho and two tent poles. Hunched at the pathside in this tiny rhombus of shade I repelled the relentless earth- and airborne assaults on my bulletproof *boccadillo*, the most notable led by a droning, clumsy blue-black bugger the size of a prune. Out in the bean field Shinto was being horribly bullied by horse-flies, and armed with that reflective strip of marker post – still an invaluable humane goad when the sun was in the right position – I raisined four against his loins. Oddly, he seemed to understand why I kept hitting him. Or perhaps he was just too sun-fucked to bite me more than once.

It was worse after lunch, a donk-day afternoon. 'There are no minutes or hours,' I rasped, remembering what someone had written somewhere about something. 'There is no time. There is only space.' The geometry was merciless, and rather than look along the road to nowhere I dropped my gaze to the dusted gravel. This was beyond any earthly concept of solitude: I felt like the *Voyager* space probe. We both dragged our feet and occasionally stumbled; I allowed my head to flop and loll in ragged sympathy. At one point, and I'm hoping my motor insurers don't hear about this, I jerked my neck up and realised I was ten feet off the path: I had actually fallen asleep whilst walking.

Soon after this scare I looked behind and saw an approaching figure on the rear horizon; over the coming hour it evolved into a human, then a pilgrim, then a male. 'Heard about you,' he mumbled through his black beard, a full-on Beirut hostage job, when at last he drew level. 'Sam and Tonto, right?'

Joe was the youngest pilgrim I'd yet encountered, though his eyes betrayed the remoteness of someone who'd seen slightly too much of the world. 'Started out from home in New Mexico,' he said, scanning what may have been a familiar landscape. I'd had enough of the horizon, so I rubbed sun block into my ear tips as Joe took stock of the full desperation of our surroundings. 'Must be Roman, this stretch.' I nodded. Somewhere out in the fields were the finest remains along the camino, the mosaic floors of great villas doing battle with the sun and the odd errant tractor.

Joe wiped his face with the sleeve of his T-shirt, then, after an obstructed sniff, loudly voided his nostrils into a bare hand. He appraised the discharge dispassionately, then with a wristy flick dispatched a viscous skein to the dust at our feet. 'Yeah, been pretty ill,' he said. 'Three days' sick leave in Burgos.'

If his complex mid-Atlantic vowel sounds were the first indication that Joe had been away from home a long time, then that nasal cameo was the second. The third, and handsomely the most compelling, occurred during a consideration of what brought him here, when without breaking conversational stride he hoicked down his waistband and passed water loud and long, directly into the small gap between us. 'But aren't you a bit young for a mid-life crisis?' I croaked, meaning, Mummy, that man done wee-wee on my shoes.

'Not at all,' he said, shaking off the drips and palming everything back into place. 'I'm twenty-one, halfway.' His eyes locked into mine, and in that fearful moment I'd have gladly let him crap in my panniers. 'I'm going to die when I'm forty.' With a half-smile Joe turned and walked on. For the next hour I watched as he strode into the unsteady distance until at last it absorbed him.

A pilgrim who walked through Calzadilla de la Cueza in 1974 walked on streets of dust past largely stoved-in adobe shacks, and found the handful of villagers queuing to raise buckets of brackish sludge from the only well. They've piped water in now, and paved a couple of streets, but house martins were still nesting in the wattle and daub and a powerful sense of deprived isolation prevailed. The rumour I later heard was that all the land I'd walked through that day, and would walk through the next, was owned by four men, and not being one of them made you a serf in all but name. Shambling gratefully towards the *refugio*, I passed a gap-toothed, boss-eyed villager sitting on a kerb, blankly tracking a large woman as she wobbled down the street on a tiny child's bike, knees out, dinging the bell to announce something important: end of siesta, death of Franco, arrival of four-legged solution to the sausage famine. It was a scene that somehow encapsulated a favourite Jerry Springer caption: 'Slept with cousin's boyfriend and had his child.'

The *refugio* was compact, and nearly full, but it had a drinks machine on the porch and bordered a patch of grass shaded by rude barns. That was the two of us sorted out. I fumbled and tugged my horrid boots off, then slumped against the cool wall by the door with the first of many Cokes upended to my tilted head, watching familiar and new faces come and go. Foremost amongst the latter were an oldish Japanese couple, the husband shuffling behind his wife with an outstretched hand on her shoulder. 'Almost 100 per cent blind,' whispered German Barbara. But no Joe. Petronella had seen him walk past; the next *refugio* was unthinkably distant.

'*Eh, burro!*'

It was the *hospitalero*, young by the standards of Calzadilla and short even by the standards of Spain. I gathered that his name was Antonio and that he liked donkeys, but was then happy to hand over translation duties to Australian Kathy. Antonio prattled away theatrically, sizing absent donkeys with his hands and mourning them with his eyes and forehead. Kathy tried to keep up. A many-assed upbringing on his grand-father's farm, the improbable agricultural tonnage a *burro* could haul, the cruelty he saw inflicted on donkeys in neighbouring farms, and the strict edicts that now proscribed this. 'He says donkeys are very rare now in Spain,' said Kathy. Well, I knew that. Antonio blurted a couple of loud words as he walked off. 'Only fifty,' Kathy translated.

I gawped. Could that be right? Was I really responsible for 2 per cent of the Spanish donkey population, and by inference around 24 per cent of all proscribed cruelty? It was a thought that preoccupied me throughout my unpacking procedure, after which a Chilean–German chap in the bunk opposite announced that Antonio had earlier told him of his grandfather's recent death. At the age of 131.

There was only one place to drink and eat and we all went there, thirty of us lined up either side of a long table. After a day of authentic pilgrim suffering it was always good to enjoy an authentic pilgrim debrief. 'Hey, remember that tree?' called out Evelyn as the *lomo* arrived. And we all did.

Many bottles in we relaxed into stereotypes. Jean-Michel announced that life was short, and in a voice unsteady with philosophical melodrama urged us all to welcome each day as an opportunity to experience new adventures. A man I knew as Gunther started taking his pedometer to pieces. Petronella launched into an enthusiastic celebration of Shinto's fearsome endowment. I ate everyone's chips. Poor Kathy had been handed the short straw down the end next to Baroness von Munchausen, and passing by en route to the loo I heard her small voice enquire politely, 'So, um, how did you disarm the hijacker?'

I was by now accustomed to being woken at an hour that could not be described in numerals alone – quarter to sodding five, half bloody four – but that night was disturbed from an unusually early stage. At twenty past twelve there was a great convulsion of stomps and snorts, and I eased out an earplug to hear a German male hissing a multilingual list of furious grievances. The English portion was issued as he swished the last of his belongings into his rucksack: '*She* reads viss the torch, and *he* makes some sounds like a dog who dies, und everybody smell und I vill NEVER stay in zis places again!' And out he went, into the night, taking two pairs of somebody else's socks and leaving behind a compass.

No one slept much after that, or no one else. By the time I woke again, night still held the upper hand; yet in the gloaming, shapes moved to and from the bathroom and stooped over rustling backpacks. I still couldn't understand it. Evelyn had already left a penknife and a pair of sandals under various dark bunks, and that day paid the heftiest dawn tax yet. Walking by torchlight out of Calzadilla, she mistook a roadside reflector for a yellow arrow and headed in the wrong direction for two hours. As she retraced her steps there was a twanging snap so loud she heard it above Edith Piaf's Walkmanned warblings. Her left leg buckled – a ruptured tendon. I'd have given up, ended it all, stuck my head in Shinto's mouth and yelled 'Cheese!', but Evelyn carefully strapped herself together and hobbled on. So laboured was her consequent progress that a couple of clicks outside Calzadilla I caught her up, yet still she refused to let us – him – shoulder even a tiny part of her burden. I don't know what made that woman tick, but if you listen hard enough you can probably hear it.

We walked together into the next village, where the baker sold us fairy cakes and a hot baguette before slipping off his white coat and opening up the shop next door to weigh out our tomatoes. Just beyond, Evelyn waved us on. 'Never thought I'd say this,' she said, coaxing her wince into a smile, 'but that *burro* has me beat.' It was an awkward situation, but by this stage traditional chivalries had long since been abandoned.

Freed from a diet of hallucinogenic poison, Shinto was indeed burning up the road: what a difference a day makes. He always went better on asphalt, and this was newly laid and clean swept. Crucially, it was also bordered by an unbroken guard rail high enough to keep any edible vergeside distractions at bay. Without access to loop tapes of stampeding carthorses and the means of their amplified broadcast I couldn't have designed this stretch better myself.

And that morning we had the N120 all to ourselves. Three cars in the first hour and two in the second: someone told us the traffic had been sucked away by a new *autovia*, but when those broad sweeps of shiny tarmac swung round towards us they were silent. This was as close to a no man's land as we'd been through: it was no surprise to read that in the sixteenth century the belligerent Moors of Andalucia were forcibly resettled on the Castilian flatlands. Nowhere to hide, no one to kill.

We clopped past the marker posts at 4 clicks an hour, for the first time since day one. Lunch banished all memory of that endured beneath the previous day's fly-blown bivouac: a tap, a shaded bench by a church, a yard full of alfalfa. As I sat there, watching the snowy seed-fluff from the big white poplars pile up in drifts by the porch, the usual steady flow of pilgrims passed with a wave or a word. Evelyn, walking much more easily, Baroness von Munchausen, gabbling cobblers at some whey-faced unfortunate, and a shrunken clockwork Dutchwoman in her seventies who without stopping called out that she'd walked from Eindhoven averaging 45 kilometres a day.

We had almost been done for by 19 the day before, but with 25 on the meter and the little hand shy of 4.00 we entered the not overly appealing outskirts of Sahagún. Just beyond the station stood the flaking concrete ellipse that housed the Plaza de Toros. 'Fancy a night in the bullring?' I chirped at Shinto, just before a train – sorry, *the* train – clattered deafeningly past and sent him careering madly over a bridge and through two red lights.

The *refugio* wasn't just next to a church, but actually in it, upstairs, below the mighty beams: it was in one of its cubicled, nautical-style bunks that my friend Nicky had enjoyed her very nearly mystical experience, lying there after lights-out with haunting yet heavenly choral ululations seeping up through the floorboards.

Behind the desk was a jolly young *hospitalera*. I explained the situation with Shinto; she smiled and made a phone call. '*Bombero*,' she announced after putting down the receiver. As a stand-alone statement this sounded fearfully alarming, and the ensuing wait allowed ample time to colour in the image of Shinto meeting his end in a controlled explosion.

After ten minutes a bristled, silver-haired man in a stained yellow shirt sauntered merrily in, and at the *hospitalera*'s behest I followed him back out. There in the street was a fire engine. It was a surprise to see him clamber up to the door with 'BOMBEROS' painted in fading white on sun-bleached red; he certainly didn't look like a fireman, and during the introductory process I'd been made unavoidably aware that he was slightly drunk, with the suggestion of having recently been prodigiously so. With a discoloured grin he beckoned down from the cab, and after untying Shinto there we were, following a drunk fireman through the streets of Sahagún, back over the railway, over to the right and . . . and up through the back entrance of a building we'd passed on our way in. A round building with no roof. My donkey would, fantastically, be spending a night in the Plaza de Toros.

The bullring's shambolic interior complemented the decrepitude suggested by its scabbed outer walls. Grass and dandelions had pushed through the sand of the ring proper, and it was evidently some months since a pair of Sahagúnese buttocks had burdened the amphitheatrical terraces. A ramshackle VIP pavilion looked across the weeds: I tried to imagine it sheltering the mayor's over-rouged wife, clapping her plump hands at some preening matador, but instead saw a bored Falangist major with his boots up on the rusty barrier rail, overseeing the execution of political prisoners.

This was a donkey photo op I couldn't possibly pass up, but no sooner was one hoof on the sand than Shinto lost it, bucking about crazily and doing the whole Mr Ed thing at the sky, at the royal box, at me. '*Fantasma, fantasma!*' chortled the drunk fireman, and once I'd brought Shinto under control we followed him into an area once given over to bull pens but now a sort of open-air municipal warehouse. Corroded street furniture nosed through the succulent weeds, and the drunk fireman splashed an oily hand through a bath full of lichened rainwater: '*Agua por burro,*' he said, before brazenly folding back

Shinto's top lip and appraising his teeth with a gypsy's cocksure showmanship. His verdict: '*Harrrrgggh!*'

Enclosed by walls, Shinto could at last enjoy a night of untethered browsing: he was happy, and once the big gate slammed shut so was I. The drunk fireman vaulted theatrically up into his tender, and giving him a wide berth I set off in search of Sahagún's nice bits.

I knew I'd find them, because though the town's quiet streets now exude an air of bypassed provinciality, Sahagún was a big noise back in the Middle Ages. Surrounded by wheat and rivers, and linked to the world by the camino, it prospered after the Moor-ousting Christian *reconquista*, both as an agro-commercial hub and a stronghold of the Catholic fundamentalism that underpinned it all. A charter of 1085 listed residents born in England and Germany as well as every corner of France. There were nine churches; a university was established in 1348. Its Benedictine abbey was the most powerful in Spain, controlling ninety monasteries across the land, and Sahagún's monks became pioneering New World missionaries. One, Fray Pedro Ponce de León, devised the first sign language for the deaf; his brother Juan discovered Florida.

No other sizeable town along the camino demonstrates quite so dramatically how abruptly the liquid assets dried up when the pilgrim tap was shut off in the seventeenth century. The Lord gaveth, then tooketh away. I ambled down a pleasant but studiously unremarkable commercial thoroughfare, past windows half-full of bad shoes and electronic appliances from the pre-digital age, and at the end found myself dumbfounded before an almost overbearingly vast baroque arch, fulsomely embellished with crests and statuary and dwarfing the delivery vans passing beneath it. Amongst the foot-dragging schoolkids and mini-marts, its domineering presence was as out of place and scale as a dreadnought in a boating pond. Further perambulations laid bare further contrasts: a straw-chewing, straw-hatted shepherd ushering his grubby, bell-necked flock past some formless ecclesiastical substructure, a wall and half a Romanesque window flush up against a strip-lit discount supermarket.

The brandy club dined opposite the *refugio*, then adjourned to a bar in the oblong piazza. We were half a treble Veterano to the good when a man with the leathered, weathered face of an expat appeared behind me. 'Please tell me to piss off if you want,' he said, 'but I'd really like to talk English.' Rob was his name, and he wasn't an expat at all, but a cyclist. Apart from the odd on-the-road donkey discourse I never talked to the cyclo-pilgrims. No one did – they were a breed apart, travelling 90 clicks a day and too far down the authenticity scale to bag a bunk in most *refugios*. 'Decaff pilgrims' someone had called them back at Roncesvalles, in withering belittlement of their watered-down pilgrimage; I cringe to recall my subsequent claim that by that token, Shinto made mine a treble-espresso camino. German Barbara and her husband Walther had done the camino on bikes ten years previously, and claimed they'd found it harder than walking – largely due to the absence of companionship. Such at least was Rob's apparent ailment.

The poor man had a lot of pent-up conversation to get out, and so in a long, unpunctuated sentence we learnt that he was thirty-four, from Derby, and had engineered his own dismissal as a museum designer to make this trip; he'd enjoyed comprehensive sexual congress with a rather plain German girl in Logroño, and was going to set fire to his tent the next morning because he'd been drinking since lunch-time and camping was shit. He elaborated on these themes and others for some time, and when next he paused to draw breath I quietly reminded everyone that it was five minutes to curfew. Rob necked his vino, then looked across at two footballing infants with a ruddy fervour. 'Does anyone know how the name of this town is correctly pronounced?' he said slowly, enunciating with the elaborate precision of the very drunk. We didn't. Sahagún seemed so tantalisingly homophonous to 'shogun' that many pilgrims couldn't be bothered to clutter their skulls with the extra word. 'It's all on the last syllable, the emphasis is.' This latter couplet proved troublesome. 'SahaGOON. I got that from a priest I drank with earlier. SahaGOON.'

We heard him at it as we walked back through the promenading families. 'Saha GOON! Saha GOON! Will you DO THE FANDANGO?' Everyone else cringed, but I smiled. It was what Shinto would have wanted.

The drunk fireman wasn't there when I turned up at 8 a.m. outside the Plaza de Toros as arranged. Or rather he was, but this time as a drunk road sweeper. Same shirt, same blithe befuddlement, same crazy-veined eyeballs, but now in charge of a broom and a trolley. The civic multi-tasking never failed to endear: more than once we'd finished our meal, ambled to a distant bar and had our brandy served up by the very waiter who'd taken away our half-finished flans.

After a great wrenching clank and a kick and a tirade of latch-directed abuse my grizzled associate heaved the iron gate ajar, then, breathing heavily, snatched out a pen from his top pocket and handed it to me. 'Souvenir, souvenir,' he said, effacingly. Three weeks before I'd have spurned it in suspicion, but I'd been a pilgrim long enough to recognise a humble and heartfelt offering. It was a genuinely affecting moment. And a nice pen: it's still the pick of that carefully marshalled jar by the phone.

I found Shinto hiding behind a sheaf of rusty no-left-turn signs with a mouthful of wild roses, and after a shoulder-clutching goodbye with the drunk fireman we headed out of town through the Saturday-morning market. The preponderance of accessible produce made this a poor choice of route, though the pace certainly picked up after the guy from the cucumber stall went at Shinto with a pallet. Waiting at a red light we were caught by a large group of photographically inexhaustible Swiss pilgrims, and then, on the dull roadside haul past the edge-of-town campsites, by an Englishman on a bike.

'That's where I stayed last night,' said Rob by way of greeting as he wobbled alongside, nodding at a field of canvas and caravans. I'd been scraping the marker post behind me through the hard-shoulder gravel, a durable auditory donkey prod, but now raised it as a conversational courtesy. 'It's the same place that Charlemagne's army camped before a big showdown with the Moors.' It was as if he'd been talking to himself ever since we'd left him. 'That yours then?' Belatedly, but with minimal curiosity, he took stock of Shinto's existence.

'It is,' I said. By not asking the usual questions, Rob oddly inspired me for once to consider the answers. Most pressingly, what to do with this great big animal if – or as was beginning to seem possible – when we made it to Santiago.

'Right. Anyway, the night before the battle they stuck their lances in the ground, and in the morning they'd all sprouted branches. A miracle!' He raised both palms from the bars and briefly clasped them together in a display of mortal gratitude. 'Though not a very good one. By the end of the day 40,000 Christians lay dead. That forest is supposedly . . .' He'd been gradually moving ahead, as even the most lethargic pedestrian did when alongside Shinto, but carried on his soliloquy regardless. 'Mozarabic' was the last word I picked up; I called out his name in a querying tone but he didn't look back. As he moved away I noticed that amongst his modest panniered possessions there was no sign of a tent.

The divide between town and country was marked by a huge motorway and a confusing but critical pilgrim junction. I was very keen to avoid the more authentic path to the right, which as well as being longer, incorporated a 22-kilometre stretch that my red book described thus: 'No shelter, no shade, no water, no food, nothing.' Two jolly Dutchwomen took the wrong fork, and when I saw them days later they were jolly no longer; someone said they hadn't spoken to each other since. So too did a grey-haired little German woman who always wore gloves. She didn't come out the other side. The word was she'd done her knee in. I hope that's all it was.

It was hardly a carnival parade the way I went. A chiding side wind whipped across the *meseta*, carrying low cloud and the drone of toiling goods traffic from the distantly parallel *autopista*; the few villages were moribund and largely derelict, adobe walls eroded by the elements into termite mounds. (Mains water arrived here in the mid-seventies, and phone lines ten years later.) Everything suddenly seemed rather sinister. Why was a man digging a trench in that copse, and why did he look at me like that when our eyes met? I don't know what that armless, toga-wrapped shop dummy propped up in the next field did for the crows, but it scared the piss out of me. And just outside the second village there was half a freshly savaged fox in the path. What could do that to a fox? I got one answer when I read a bit of Dominic Laffi, hunched over my *boccadillo* in the lee of a squat water tower: 'Past Sahagún we came across a dead pilgrim. Two wolves had begun to eat his body, so we chased them off.'

The long, lonely gaps between settlements had been sporadically endowed with young trees and concrete-benched picnic areas, but the former were shrivelled saplings old before their time, and the moss-stained latter were being steadily reclaimed by nature – inevitably so considering their stubbornly ill-thought locations, clustered just after a town where most pilgrims would have had breakfast, and just before the one they'd be having supper at. This was El Burgo Ranero, and improvidently harried down its main drag by two unhelmeted nine-year-olds on trials bikes, I got there just in time to bag the second-last place on the downstairs floor.

The *refugio* was an adobe structure of recent construction, and after the modest physical rigours of a short stage its inhabitants were in skittish mood. The wash house was thick with whistling launderers; someone had opened a bottle of wine and at 5.30 it was being passed round. On the inside of the loo door was a cautionary line drawing of two male stick-pilgrims in the act of urination, one standing up and partially obscured by a large red cross, the other happily seated and crowned with a green tick. At some point in the late afternoon this image was effectively adulterated to depict the sedentary fellow energetically soiling the floor with a very different excretion.

For the last few days we'd been working our way through the salad-less bean-and-pulse belt, which didn't do much for the vitamin and mineral situation but opened up a new world of multilingual menu entertainment, principally because the

Spanish for beans was *judías*. As soon as I spotted 'Jews With Ham' on the English bill of fare at the restaurant over the road I knew it had been a mistake to share a table with Total Shithouse. Sure enough, he very nearly swallowed his tongue.

Mrs TS nobly endeavoured to curb her husband's ribald excesses, but with a bottle of wine a head thrown in as part of the meal-deal it was an uphill battle. 'I read that El Burgo Ranero was named either after frogs or wheat,' she said brightly as the flans arrived.

Her husband briefly scanned the frogless world of grain on display beyond the window. 'Well, that's bloody stupid,' he barked in disdain. 'That's like saying Melbourne is named either after an old Prime Minister or a . . . cow's arse!'

There was a brief but profound silence, one interrupted by a defeated voice from Baroness von Munchausen's distant table: '*Ja*, but that is faster I think than the vurld record.' It was almost a shame that our paths were never to cross again. The last reported sighting had the Baroness dramatically brandishing a small canister containing her mother's ashes. In the one before that, she'd been seen putting her earplugs in it.

A dripping shower and a tiled floor were effective discouragements to restful slumber, and the sky was full of constellations when I reluctantly rustled myself upright. But yawning at the window, a new day nudging the next horizon, I saw Shinto as I would like to remember him: nobly silhouetted against an orange dawn, head bent down to the grass. 'Beautiful,' whispered a backpacked Frenchman, en route to the exit across a floorful of rustling snufflers. And as we watched together, Shinto raised his tail to the fading stars and flopped out a big wet sack of crap.

It was another day across the void, another day of prairie madness, seeing a town taking shape at the edge of my world, and knowing that in the half a day or more it would be before I walked amongst its spires and telegraph poles and pantiled roofs I would know and loathe them all with a contempt born of familiarity. Here the barley was hip high and its ears crisping gold, but after showing its face at dawn the sun responsible was soon just a light patch above the swift, low clouds, like a torch in fog. Yesterday's side wind had shifted and now swept snidely into our faces, carrying the smell of farms and flowers and the occasional knockout whiff of fox piss. For the first time since the big rain it was cold, and I found myself warming my hands on a donkey's hot neck.

It was always good to bolster the perception of Shinto's utility with an additional function. Whenever we stopped he would rotate his anus to face the prevailing wind: the weather-vane feature. If my laundry hadn't dried and the sun was out, with a string round the panniers and a couple of pegs he was a clothes-horse as literal as any you'll find. And at Carrión I'd purchased and blended the ingredients of a titanic reserve of vinaigrette dressing, guaranteed to moisten and revitalise even the most wizened *boccadillo*; this conspicuous addition to Shinto's burden, along with a burgeoning fruit store, certainly warranted the honorary title of mobile canteen.

Since I'd discarded the Devil's Barley his behaviour had been no worse than truculent, but weather and outlook were both dispiriting and by mid-morning Shinto's locomotive rhythm was down from 'We are the Champions' to 'Michelle'. The marker-post dragging had proved only sporadically effective, but was granted a new lease of life when teamed to the 20-foot length of chevroned hazard tape I'd found flapping, uselessly I decided, from a roadside pylon. One end of the tape round a saddle horn, the other distantly anchored to the trailing post, and the whole wildly animated by the elements: the first big gust filled Shinto's peripheral vision with multicoloured danger and sent him clattering off for a good quarter-click. So too the second, and to an extent the third, but within an hour he was once again demonstrating that any fear created by his master, in contrast to those thrown up by Mother Nature or indeed anyone else, could with time be rationalised and thus conquered. Despite my early start I was soon once more falling back through the field, and tying three plastic bags and a small bush to the tape didn't help. 'That's not a donkey,' said Evelyn as she passed, 'that's a carnival float.'

The *meseta* had never been a more disheartening treadmill, but if there was one thing this pilgrimage had taught me it was the value of simple pleasures. Ambience and old bread should by rights have made lunch a dire ordeal, but there was salad dressing, and a bench, and the sum of these meagre parts was happiness. A small, bright-eyed woman approached as I agitated my vinaigrette; a hesitant exchange of conspicuously accented '*buen camino*'s revealed our shared nationality. 'It's great this, i'n't it?' she said, the wind gusting her Lancastrian words away across the drab flatness. Ten minutes earlier I'd have thought she was mad, or from Blackburn, but with smooth concrete under my bottom and the flavour of the Mediterranean in my glistening chops I found myself nodding in hearty assent.

Mansilla de las Mulas was so named for its mule market, and I suppose for that alone I should have stopped there. Certainly everyone else had: walking through its largely intact medieval walls and past a galleried church I spotted the blind Japanese chap following his tiny wife into the *refugio*, and looked up to see laundry and familiar faces in every window. But even though progress was now down to the agonising end of the sloth scale, and it was gone 4.00, I didn't. I couldn't. León, the last city before Santiago, was 19 clicks off and I didn't want to get there late the following day.

There were two reasons for this. One was that I had a bed waiting in the Parador San Marcos, the palatial former HQ of the Knights of Santiago now transformed into what the Confraternity guide called 'one of the great hotels of the world'. The meter would be running from noon tomorrow, and I'd clearly need all the hours God gave and I'd paid for to re-appraise those simple pleasures before dispatching them one by one down a marble bidet. And the other was that my bed was a double, and next door were three singles, and that these remaining berths would, by late afternoon, be occupied by my wife and children.

Total Shithouse had supplied the inspiration. By walking on

to the next town while his incapacitated wife got there by bus, and meeting her with apparent success every night over a long period, he'd shown that a two-speed camino was logistically feasible. It was Birna who'd first raised the possibility of a half-term family pilgrimage, during a phone call from Burgos: I can't pretend I wasn't slightly surprised by her enthusiasm, but I did pretend my money was about to run out when she asked how many other paradors she could book us all into along the way. A hire car and ruinous mobile telephony would be required, and the sort of head-melting to and fro associated with that riddle about the farmer crossing a river with a fox, a chicken and a bag of grain. But it could and would be done. This was more than just a slightly odd holiday story to tell in the playground. There were four young souls at stake here. How's a chap to enjoy a gilded afterlife knowing his wife and kids are down there in the fires of purgatory?

The route out of Mansilla was fairly wretched, sometimes separated from two lanes of baying traffic by a strip of brambles but more usually by nothing but a fading white line. Horn-happy Sunday drivers shot past, almost grazing Shinto's ears with their wing mirrors. One shrieked to an oblique halt 100 yards down the road and began reversing waywardly towards us; I saw the French plates and was ready with an appropriate gesture before the camera appeared.

The N601 sliced rudely through a town with neither appeal nor accommodation, picked up more traffic from a busy tributary and headed towards Puente de Villarente. Just before the twenty-arch bridge that introduced the town, I was joined on the hard shoulder by a little old man in his Sunday best. 'Hotel?' I asked, and promptly found myself being chivvied up to a decaying façade embellished with topless neon cowgirls. It was twenty minutes before he'd tottered out of sight, and so twenty minutes of foolish loitering before I could politely begin my search for more acceptable accommodation.

An hour later, having passed the bridge and a hotel with a pool full of yesterday's guacamole, I was wondering if I ought to turn back to the fly-blown bordello. I was still wondering when I peered through the window of the Hostal Montana, finding myself presented by another of those oppressive bars full of droopy-lidded card players flicking nutshells on to the floor and drinking hard spirits at inappropriate times of an inappropriate day. But I didn't, because by now I knew better.

I knew that the passage to my room would involve the ascent of a grubby and windowless stairwell, its navigation dependent on a big round switch which when depressed procured a brief period of illumination: just enough, in this case, to leave me fumblingly marooned on a half-landing with a donkey saddle over my shoulder. I knew that resolving this situation would involve fear, pain and a fight with a pot plant. I knew that logic demanded that when at length I shouldered open the door to my room I would find the bed filled by a squat and sprawling hairy-back in a string vest, who would slowly roll his red eyes and budge grudgingly up to one side. But I knew also that logic has no place in a Spanish hotelier's lexicon, and that instead I would find myself strutting regally through an air-conditioned realm of gleaming mahogany and vitreous enamel.

It was a rear-facing room, which gave me peace from the traffic and a view of Shinto, who I'd smuggled round the back and tied up by the kitchen door. I looked down as I was stringing my laundered socks out the window: there he was, gazing wistfully across a broad field of fallowed something or other. I turned the telly on as I wrung out my underwear in the bidet – that election had finally happened and the votes been counted, but I couldn't make any sense of the pie-chart analysis. It was odd to feel so completely out of the geo-political loop. Huge and important things were happening – lawlessness and violence in Iraq, Britain scoring no points in the Eurovision – but somehow I seemed to have dropped out of the world they were happening in. This was what my life had become: a donkey in the yard and a sink full of pants.

When I returned carrying a wet T-shirt, the sun had made a belated appearance and Shinto was rolling in the dust with unbridled abandon, raising a cloud that showed up the low-angled rays. I guess it would have been about this time that I noted the large green dome to which I had attached my donkey, evidently with impaired vigilance, was a recycling bin. Had we been in almost any other European country I might not have found myself hammering erratically down the stairs and outside, but Spain, like Britain, is still at that stage of environmental awareness where citizens patronise such facilities to recycle old bottles not into new bottles, but into violent noise. The detritus associated with this pastime is predictable, and Shinto was now energetically working it into his flesh.

He cumbersomely righted himself at my loudly vocal approach, and though agleam with diamante shards, emeralds in the dust, his hide appeared miraculously unpunctured. I brushed Shinto down and led him to the nearest alternative tether point, miles off in the field but otherwise safe. Regardless of their age and experience, my family's impending arrival could only dilute the witless incompetence that still threatened my pilgrimage with a premature and tragic end.

You don't want to linger in a *refugio*, and indeed can't even if you did, but because this was a hotel, with a telly you could watch from the bath, I didn't get off until well after nine. It was only a dozen clicks to León, but my self-styled 'short day' was off to a poor start.

The usual suspects who'd stayed in Mansilla were already striding past when the path veered away from the road, and did so in steady profusion as Shinto stopped in his tracks by a large earthen yard enclosed by a tall chain-link fence. Ears at 12 o'clock, head and body taut and immobile: I knew that expression by now, and I knew that it meant we had entered enemy territory.

I scanned the rising, convex enclosure for some time until I spotted a small head approaching from behind the brow. The head was followed by a long neck, a really very long neck, and then a disproportionately hefty torso. It was an ostrich. Most birds are a little stupid and ostriches famously so, and I was not surprised to see this example strut about randomly, bobbing and stretching at nothing and no one. Shinto obviously felt he knew better, though, and tracked his opponent in unblinking earnest.

And how right he was to do so, because as I idly surveyed the map the ostrich abruptly charged us, pistoning those spindly legs to dramatic effect, wing stumps fluffily outstretched. Shinto had seen enough, and with the now enormous freak-beast ten yards from the fence he legged it. Happily in the right direction, but once we were over the next hilltop his head dropped and he slowed almost to idling speed. Beaten again, boy; beaten by a bird.

That wasn't nearly as bad, however, as the truly awful stuff that happened an hour up the road, at the top of a hill with León happening right down there before my eyes. The yellow arrows had been letting me down all morning, ordering us right across a huge highway and then back across it 50 yards later, and I scrutinised with a degree of scepticism the one that pointed pilgrims straight over a four-laner. The brow of a hill and no green men or zebras: it was like a circle-all-the-dangers illustration in a road-safety leaflet, particularly as the furious traffic throughput provided the answer to where everybody in this part of Spain had got to. There was, however, a police car on the opposite hard shoulder, and seeing both front seats occupied I waved and yoo-hooed above the whooshing flow of fast metal.

The window was lowered, exposing a pair of aviator shades and a big, lazy smile. A smile that didn't say, Stay there and remain calm, sir, while my colleague halts the traffic, so much as, Ready with the shovel and bin-liners, Luis – and if they make it over, the flans are on me. I waved again, motioning at the vehicular onslaught in helpless imploration. The smile became a laugh; the window smoothly closed. Proffering gestures that in Spain's less enlightened recent past would have had them truncheoning the soles of my feet for a week, I set off down the hard shoulder in search of an alternative crossing.

The traffic intensified and our tarmac safety margin narrowed into a merging sliver of dirty chevrons, off-white streaked with the cataclysmic skid marks of someone's last moment on earth. There were hoots and snatches of bellowed Hispanic reproof; the four lanes became six and now there were slip roads and ramps and those big blue signs that say 'No pedestrians', 'No mopeds', 'No tractors', and 'Get that fucking donkey out of here NOW'. Yet Shinto always gave of his best in heavy traffic, cheerfully incapable of acknowledging a clear and present danger to his continued existence when, who knows, there might be a puddle or a flamingo or something round the corner.

When after perhaps half an hour the hard shoulder finally disappeared we scrambled down an embankment, to be met by a series of crash-barrier hurdles and an underpass. Cars and huge trucks were now roaring past above and below: I could hardly hear myself swear. It was a bad place, a place where no man had stood in this highway's active lifetime, and here I was, standing in it with a donkey. We would have to go back.

Six legs make a lot of footsteps to retrace, and I was almost in tears by the time we were looking at the empty space where those evil policemen had been parked. Shinto had blithely jaywalked all the way back up the motorway, and having utterly exhausted my nervous and physical resources in laborious restraint, I blindly shuffled alongside as he sauntered across those four lanes. In a cacophony of horns we made it. Quite why my donkey opted to cross the 100-foot wooden bridge we encountered almost immediately after I will never know, but if he hadn't it would have meant a hearse or a horse trailer. A truly Bunyan-esque ordeal was at an end.

Shinto continued to excel himself as León gradually took shape around us. The schedule was all shot to hell, meaning his lunch was half a loaf and a packet of biscuits eaten from my hand in a car park, but snorting the crumbs off the long, rogue hairs on his old lady's chin he ploughed doughtily onwards. He paused by a gate and let the immaculately presented kindergarten inmates on the other side force their little hands through the bars to pet and tickle. He waited patiently at zebras between the executives and shoppers, kept his nerve as the arrows led us down sour-smelling alleys I could touch both sides of, and haughtily ignored the jeers of students vocalising what I now accepted as the last dregs of an age-worn cultural reflex to taunt any passing jackass. And when we found ourselves in the square before the great Gothic cliff of León cathedral, he allowed himself to be rather aggressively appropriated as a photographic prop by the many tourists waiting for its towering doors to open.

I wasn't about to join the queue, but the cathedral's exterior featured all I desired in such an edifice: a huge rose window and flying buttresses. For no good reason that I can think of, flying buttresses have ended up lodged in the sieve-mesh of my mind, along with other random reminders that I once went to school. An ox-bow lake, the vas deferens and Venn diagrams: it's an elite club, and a sighting of any member in print or in life always raises an inner cheer.

A Pacman route through more tight alleys, a few more high-profile road crossings and finally across the manicured plaza gardens – sorry about those petunias – to the frankly astounding Parador San Marcos, a great block of gilded history crowned by a proudly regal St Jim. Here was the longest Renaissance façade in Spain, and certainly the most richly embellished, and tonight, a small part of it was to be León's Moore-ish quarter.

I walked Shinto up to the soaring arched entrance; linen-suited men and their copper-faced, lavishly coiffed consorts strolled ostentatiously out, memorably contorting their nonchalant features when presented by a donkey who'd apparently just run through a dirty campsite covered in glue.

With my animal attached to the nearest available item of street furniture I jogged into the echoingly vast reception hall and up to the desk. The bald incumbent didn't blink at my rather disappointing presentation – it's by no means unusual for pilgrims to spend a night or two here to reacquaint themselves with civilisation – but his rear-facing assistant's shoulders shook with some violence when I mentioned my travelling companion. But when you're paying – oh, filthy nude goblins – *that* for a room, and *that* for the one next door, you don't expect too many questions. Salvador Dalí once took a sheep up to his room in a grand Parisian hotel. And shot it.

Sure enough, when I went back out the bellboys and porters were fighting over Shinto, each of them loudly eager to assume responsibility for valet-parking him round the side. Watching the most senior blue-jacket lead my donkey off along the longest Renaissance façade in Spain and through an arch at its distant conclusion, I understood that despite the umpteen trials of that day and every other, the way of the ass was the right way, the true way, perhaps the only way. Though obviously this was before I'd followed the pair of them into the car park and found the poor, wet-faced porter distantly pursuing Shinto in and out of the Mercs and Audis.

León was the most Roman town on the route, a military stronghold whose name itself is a contraction of 'legion'. For 350 years the city was the capital of this entire quarter of Iberia, and after the last centurion popped his sandals the Dark Ages hardly had a chance to get going. Despite regularly changing hands in the usual manner it remained a city of prosperity and vigour: whilst London remained a benighted outpost of Wessex whose grunting citizenry cowered from Viking raiders in wooden hovels, tenth-century León was a thriving metropolis, the capital of Christian Spain, its grand market squares thronged with international wool dealers and flanked by monasteries and palaces. Its Jewish population was one of the largest in Spain – we have a resident of León to thank for kabbalah, the mystical offshoot of Judaism now so popular with many of our most dreadful celebrities. Madonna based her silly children's book on its central tenets, which I'm afraid means I never want to know what they are.

León got knocked down – all of it – but it got up again. There was so much money in early thirteenth-century León, from both trade tariffs and protection money extorted from the now cowed Moors, that the cathedral still standing was built in less than a century – a blur by the standards of large-scale medieval construction. It was drunk cycling Rob who'd revealed León cathedral as a 2/3 scale model of the one in Reims, which seemed a splendid encapsulation of what the pilgrimage achieved. It was a theme, like so many others, upon which Rob had expanded: as a museum designer with an enhanced appreciation of ecclesiastical architecture he'd described how in any Gothic church along the camino he'd find a ceiling boss or some other modest decorative feature that precisely replicated one in a slightly newer structure back in Britain. In florid terms he imagined the scene, a pilgrim from Leicester staring slack jawed at a cathedral ceiling and returning home with a sheaf of sketches for his local stonemason.

Whilst the mason was drafting up an inflated quote for the bishop, back in León the good times were almost over: like so many along the route, the town was a victim of the pilgrimage's success. Pilgrims brought the wealth and weaponry that by 1350 had driven the Moors almost out of Spain; there was no longer a reason to squash all the markets and monasteries up in the north-west. And they also brought the Black Death.

So at least I learnt, lying there up to my ears in bubbles with a book in one hand, a cold beer in the other and a jar of green olives wedged in the soap dish. Shinto, I'm afraid, was lashed to the air-conditioning plant at the back of the car park, albeit engulfed by bamboo bushes upon whose succulent upper leaves he was noisily feasting when I arrived to fill the bowl at his feet with supermarket porridge oats and French toast.

Many of the San Marcos rooms, I had noted, languished in a contemporary annexe tacked on to the back, but not mine. It wasn't huge, or in fact spectacularly well appointed, but it overlooked the river – a broad stretch of sandbanks and shingle sparsely plaited with streamlets – and was handily proximate to the hotel's most impressive feature: the upper storey of a two-floor cloistered courtyard. I could have propped an elbow on that shady balustrade for hours, a thin-stemmed schooner of amontillado in my rose-watered fingers, gazing across at the scallop-shell medallions on the facing walls. And, most deliciously of all, soaking up the embittered skyward glances of visitors to the adjoining museum of antiquities as they patrolled the formal gardens below. If they could see me now, those pilgrim friends of mine.

My family's route to León required them to fly to Santiago and drive back east, covering in three hours what at current rates of progress would take me nearly three weeks. It was a slightly deflating calculation: I felt as if I'd spent an agonising age acquiring some skill now rendered embarrassingly redundant, like a farm labourer coming back from sickle school to see the bloke in the next field fire up his combine harvester. Everything was about to change, and as I lost myself in a vast towel I realised how far I'd moved away from any sensible definition of domestic normality.

Most of the pilgrims I'd talked to couldn't understand why I was looking forward to my family's arrival. Using language familiar to any woman who's ever proposed attending a poker night, and any man who's offered to carry the bags around Harvey Nichols, they muttered ominously about boredom, filth and danger, when what they actually meant was, This is my outing, and I don't want you spoiling it. Directly or not, partners and children represented what many had come to escape from. 'You are with people on the camino, but you are selfish,' said Jean-Michel. 'I am doing this for myself, and by myself.'

The bedside phone warbled as I was buttoning up the least ravaged of my two remaining shirts. It was Birna. Two minutes later three young faces were carefully surveying me across the threshold of room 454, wondering what this flash-fried, straw-haired castaway had done with their daddy.

Eleven

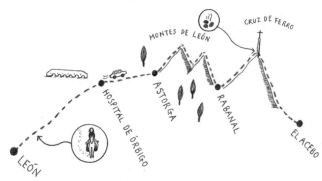

'You are ze man viss ze monkey?'

I looked up from the breakfast table to see the Swiss pilgrims who'd passed me just outside Sahagún. 'No,' I said, extracting a small thumb from my left nostril and elbowing off an incoming salvo from the muffin cannon. 'I am the man with four monkeys.'

Happy as they were to meet their Pilgrim Father, at least once he'd attended to himself with his new birthday razor and tired of affecting solemn conversion to Mormonism, Shinto was the main draw. It was unfortunate in this light that he'd given a very poor account of himself when I'd taken them to meet him the evening before: there was crap in his food bowl, and endeavouring to discard it I was snarled at and butted. If mine was the unacceptable face of family tourism, then here was its unacceptable ass. Nine-year-old Kristjan hardly noticed, but it was clear from the crestfallen alarm on his sisters' faces that their hard-wired affection for the equine race would be tested to its tail-brushing, mane-plaiting limit.

Happily, a new day brought a new donkey, biddable and benign, calmly wrapping his prehensile lips round the bread rolls we'd trousered from the breakfast buffet. The girls were entranced, and launched enthusiastically into the grooming process, but to me there seemed something oddly lobotomised in his demeanour. I found out why as I untied him: beside that

220

restless compressor sat a gigantic floodlight, and the poor sod had spent the hours of darkness in a soul-numbing halogen supernova.

With the children in convalescence from the combined rigours of a long journey and a night largely occupied purée-ing fixtures and fittings into a kind of room soup, Birna and I agreed that it would be best to leave most of the donkey work to me that day. She handed me one of the two mobiles she'd come equipped with, then crammed our offspring into a tiny Toyota amongst all the stuff I'd not be needing during the day. Stripped of everything but his bowl and a pannier half full of food and sun-cream, Shinto was down to his fighting weight, and after I'd waved the family off he set forth across the sun-polished flagstones with spring-heeled gusto.

More wide eyes in rear-view mirrors, more pavement conversations cut off mid-syllable: Shinto chewed up León's guide-book reputation for haughty implacability and left it steaming behind him in a gutter. A filthy face shot through the fly curtains of a sunless bar and smiled in childish wonder; I smiled back. In the end I just smiled all the time, and began firing out a *'buenas dias'* to anyone who passed. I was a better citizen, and the pilgrimage and my donkey had made me so.

The shops gave way to half-built high-rises, a kitchen sink agleam in the rubble, a tiled splashback on an unrendered wall. And so León said its muted farewells, outside a desolate industrial estate whose nocturnal ambience was neatly encapsulated in the generous sprinkling of lipsticked cig butts at the foot of each streetlight.

Next up the road was Virgen del Camino, which sounded beguiling but wasn't, the first of a succession of small towns angrily split in two by the N120, its traffic-soiled pavements stalked by Don Mueble and his warehouse brethren. Here the camino forked, offering pilgrims a choice between cowering all day in a cloud of diesel, noise and mortal danger, or tripping gaily along quiet tracks through an unspoilt rural landscape. The first was 3 clicks shorter; I hung a right and cowered.

In half an hour we were deep in many-laned madness, not

quite as desperate as the approach to León but not far off. It was hot and I was scared, but Shinto was only hungry. The bamboo evidently hadn't sated his need for living matter: even as a sweep of lorries bore down on us up the slip road we were preparing to cross, he was trying to wedge his snout under the guard rail to get at the crisped-up, peed-on, hard-shoulder brownery. A fraught minute later, for the first and only time, I saw him snap the head off a thistle and effect its weary ingestion. Shinto never spat anything out – it was as if doing so would involve an unacceptable loss of face. Once I saw a thick reflective wedge of a shattered CD smuggle itself into his gob with a fat mouthful of roadside barley; he registered its discovery with a look of embarrassment, then defiantly prepared it for his oesophagus with half a dozen ice-cube crunch-squeaks.

The only hill of the day lay just beyond a church crowned with a precarious profusion of haywired stork's nests. If you had a recently fed donkey you pulled, and if you had a bike you pushed. Six Dutchmen doing just that caught me near the top. 'Oh, but he is ill,' said their leader, assessing Shinto's hung head. 'You must let him rest.' I was wondering whether to go for words or upgrade straight to the sticks and stones when a clang followed by three ghastly wet chokes had us looking back down the road, where his most elderly colleague had dropped his bike and was vomiting copiously into the desiccated vegetation.

My phone warbled into life soon afterwards, and within the hour Birna was ferrying children across the siesta-quiet tarmac. With the car empty she U-turned bumpily through the undergrowth and headed back to the hotel she'd booked us into, 5 kilometres up the road, and then walked back to meet us. It was perhaps a little ludicrous, and would be superseded in subsequent days by a marginally more practical but distressingly more expensive taxi-based scheme, but that afternoon I couldn't have cared less.

When the path eased slightly away from the road, seven-year-old Lilja took charge of Shinto's rope; four-year-old Valdis was gently bobbing about up there on his back, hands on the saddle horns, an incredulous beam on the small bit of face visible beneath her sun-hat; Kristjan, being nine, and a boy, was somewhere behind us dribbling Fanta on an ant's nest. I was happy; we were all happy.

Within a click it was apparent that Shinto appreciated the children's presence as much as I did: Valdis weighed rather more than the panniers ever had, but when I briefly removed her he slowed to a sulky shuffle and up she went again. For the first time in days, in fact weeks, his ears stood proudly aloft to reflect eager contentment rather than panic. There was no getting away from the adjectives flat and hot, but nobody seemed to notice. Birna joined us for the last hour, and breezed up to our lonely roadside hotel murmuring that if it was this easy we could try doing 30 kilometres the next day.

The Urbanización Santiago was as beguilingly atmospheric as one might have anticipated, a spanking new but creepily deserted structure with an adjoining restaurant, dropped in the litter-strewn no man's land – sorry, landscaped overnight donkey park – between the N120 and another deserted motorway. The beds in our pitch-roofed attic all incorporated thick rubber under-sheets – I could have depilated a bathed and excitable donkey in there and the mattress at least would have been none the wiser – and were situated tight up against the ceiling's lowest point, guaranteeing nocturnal pain and alarm for any father stupid enough to put his pillow at the wrong end.

Our sole fellow guests were a business traveller I'd seen arranging fabric samples in the boot of his Opel, and a rather furtive couple in the room below who occupied the night with glumly metronomic acts of love. But no other pilgrims. In fact no pilgrims at all, because as far as most of the service-industry personnel we encountered hereon were concerned, I was now just part of a complicated, indulgent and perhaps rather culturally patronising family holiday. As a pilgrim I'd led an almost Amish existence, but here I was, turning up at big hotels with a Nokia pressed to my head and a support vehicle parked round the back. I'd never paid more than €1.50 for a beer; that night they charged me €3.00.

It was swings and roundabouts, though, and the next morning those surcharging waiters were joined in that metaphorical playground by twinkly-eyed old ladies. I'd already been severally impressed with the nostalgic burromania exhibited by Spain's elderly females, but with Valdis in the saddle and Lilja threading a daisy chain through Shinto's tail the overall package proved almost fatally winsome for women of a certain age. As our convoy idled through the first road-dusted strip town of another hot day, its black-clad, waddling citizenry accrued about us, hands clasped to beam-wrinkled cheeks or gladdened hearts.

If Shinto awakened memories of their bucolic, carefree youth, then two young children were a poignant reminder of a time when towns like this resounded not with the dismal roar of heavy traffic but the shrieks and yelps of gambolling playmates. Nationally the Spanish birth rate is amongst Europe's lowest, and in these no-hope, hard-luck nothingsvilles, kids were almost as rare as donkeys. Valdis came out the other side of Villadangos with a Chupa Chup and a balloon; Lilja with an apple, heavily ruffled hair and a furious blush.

An hour along the road we were met by the taxi carrying Birna and Kristjan, and after a brochure-worthy under-tree picnic beside a chuckling irrigation stream, set off *en famille* into an afternoon that was an effective bullet-point summary of my recent experiences. A big horizon bisected by a tapering orange path, a heartless sun, a huge stork homing lazily in on a church tower like a bleached pterodactyl. The sole discrepancy was Shinto's keen zest for the road and faultless behaviour; I was almost relieved when I scooped Valdis off his back as we crossed a small ditch, and looked back a second later to see him galloping tangentially away through the ploughed field we'd just skirted. 'There was a man on a bike with a plastic bag,' shrugged Lilja.

Twelve clicks was barely half a day for Shints, but in this heat I could only admire my children's resilience as we set foot on the Puente del Paso Honroso, at the other end of which lay our hotel. Eight hundred years old, with twenty arches and a total length of over 200 metres, the bridge is astonishing in most ways, not least because eighteen of those arches now span cultivated or developed land, and the town it finally opens into, Hospital de Órbigo, is a bypassed settlement of negligible contemporary scale and importance. As oversized and incongruously sited river crossings go, it's right up there with London Bridge, Arizona. And like that structure, the Puente del Paso Honroso has enjoyed an improbably colourful history, which I related to my dehydrated offspring as we crossed it.

It's 1434, and you're a knight from León who finds himself hopelessly infatuated with an unusually inexcitable damsel. What to do? Well, if your name is Don Suero de Quiñones, every Thursday you wear an iron fetter round your neck. 'This signifies my binding love,' you wheeze painfully, as the fair lady sneers past in the gilded horse-drawn divan of Don Mueble. No matter – it is the age of chivalry, which means you have nothing better to do, and so with the King's permission you organise a jousting tournament with the intention of demonstrating your worth in the grandest manner imaginable: personally offering out every noble horseman in Europe. 'I'll do them all, and I'll do the bastards right here!' you shout, stamping a cleated shoon upon the bridge's central span, before a page whispers in your ear that it's hardly wide enough for one horse to pass, let alone two, so you cough a bit and quietly order the construction of seven jousting arcades in the next-door field. The tents and canopies go up; the word is passed through royal courts across the known world. A life-size mannequin is dressed as a herald and stuck in a hedgerow alongside the nearby camino, and because this is a holy year, no one draws a cock on his tabard.

Noblemen arrive in their hundreds; the stands fill with under-toothed locals and curious pilgrims; feasts are prepared. And then, on 11 July, your first challenger hoists his lance at the distant end of the palisade – a Catalan knight encumbered in a double thickness of steel armour. In a display of quixotic derision you strip off your own light armour and don a flouncy woman's camisole. The crowd cheers drunkenly, and they barely stop for twenty-eight days, at the end of which you hold aloft, in weary triumph, the last splintered stump of 300 rival lances. One knight lies dead, and some leather-aproned inebriate with a rusty saw is looming over a dozen groaning others.

The last true medieval tournament is at an end, and in fitting conclusion you lead a glorious procession to Santiago, hanging a gold band round St James in holy emulation of your own iron fetter, now discarded. 'Pray, good sire, whither the fair lady?' enquires a manservant, and you tell him that was never really the point, and hold forth at great length about the chivalric ethos, and then he asks again and you start crying and tell him to shut up.

Twenty-four years later, an armoured horseman approaches as you're riding across a field. He raises his visor curiously. 'Don't I know you from somewhere?' he asks, and you clear your throat and for the thousandth time begin to tell your tale, except when you get to the bit about the camisole he kills you.

It looks to have been pretty much downhill for Hospital de Órbigo ever since, though the children enjoyed some medieval high jinks in the dangerously ill-maintained municipal playground, and so did I in seeing off a posse of spirited youngsters who clustered aggressively round Shinto after I'd tied him up in a grove of trees by the bridge. Poor Shints. No sooner had his tormentors slunk away than nature turned on him again: a gathering wind loosened a blizzard of seed-fluff from the boughs above and carpeted his dinner in cotton wool.

We could hear his sneezing brays from the tiny room all five of us were wedged in, and so of course could all the other guests from theirs. In contrast with the night before, plenty of pilgrims stayed here – that much was plain from the 'NO HANG OUT THE WASHING IN THE WINDOW' notice Sellotaped to the splashback – and an unfamiliar group of elderly Dutch ones occupied the bar as we walked out to find food. By now I was familiar with the word 'donkey' in most European tongues, and hearing dark mutters about *'de ezel'* I knew they feared for their sleep. And rightly so: the next morning Shinto bugled the whole town out of bed at 5 a.m.

Because we didn't know that then, we lingered over our meal. The restaurant I found down a careworn backstreet offered simple fare, but we had an outside table under a bamboo canopy, a decent bottle of rosé and crayons with which the children were able ruminatively to deface the paper tablecloth. The brandy arrived, and was at length drained; an authentic conclusion to my family's first full day on the way of St James. 'El . . . um . . . bill,' I called across to the *padrone*, autographing air in the universally accepted fashion.

His response was a far more complex gesture, one we were still trying to decode when he appeared beside us bearing a little tumbler of golden liquor. This was laid before me with elaborate ceremony and a hushed flood of reverential words. 'Sorry, but I didn't . . .' I began, but he waved me quiet and backed away pointing at the distant table accommodating our sole fellow diners, an elderly couple. 'Fine,' I muttered, 'go and see to them first, but if this turns up on the bill I'm not paying for it.'

'He says it's fifty years old,' whispered Birna, who'd done Spanish at school. I took a sip. Brandy – very good brandy. I'd downed half when the oldsters stooped towards us. 'Good evening,' said the husband, while his wife gazed at the children in happy reverie. 'Excuse me but it is so that your children are . . . quite angels, as our grandchildren,' he faltered graciously.

'Well . . . that's very kind,' said Birna. 'Thank you.' And in truth they had displayed unusual quiescence, as I believe is common with heatstroke and exhaustion. That said, some of the on-table artwork was a little pungent, and a large text box above my dessert spoon proclaimed in an infant hand that Daddy smelt of donkey bottoms.

We talked for a while: they were pilgrims, and astoundingly had walked all the way from their home in Zurich. 'It's maybe four zouzand kilometres,' said the wife, modestly. I scanned each kind, old face in turn and with all that brandy in me it was impossible not to gawp – neither could possibly have been under seventy.

'So . . . thank you,' said the husband, straightening his back and searching for an appropriate valediction. 'Tonight you are our friends . . . our guests.' I hoisted my ancient cognac. 'And so are you,' I reciprocated chirpily, before brazenly tipping the remainder down my gullet.

When they'd gone I waved an impatient finger-pen at the *padrone*. He glided up with a questioning look. '*La cuenta, por favor*,' said Birna. His brow furrowed further, and with shaking head he held an explanatory hand to the recently vacated table behind us. For a brief but vivid moment everything in my body stopped working. Then I pressed my palms to my face and stared at Birna through two small gaps in my fingers. They had paid it. They had paid our bill, Fanta and food and vintage brandy and all. They'd tried to tell us and we hadn't even thanked them. I threw back my chair and ran out into the street, but it was dark and empty both ways.

When the children were asleep Birna and I stood at our window, and through the neon glare of the hotel sign above noticed activity on the edge of Shinto's forest, right beside the bridge. A recorded fanfare blared out, then gave way to a thumpingly medieval cacophony of pipes and tabors. 'They're dancing,' said Birna. 'Loads of them.' And peering carefully I could see dozens and dozens of extravagantly mobile bodies, cavorting in flailed unison by those hallowed arches.

'There's a festival every July to celebrate that joust,' I mumbled. 'Must be practising.' It was all rather wonderful, possibly even enchanting, yet I couldn't muster any enthusiasm. The more I thought about what had just happened the more it seemed a test of a pilgrim's good grace, a test I had not passed. When I replayed the scene again there was a horrible new detail: after draining that aged liquor I had failed to suppress a belch.

There was a moral, and this was it: Treat all strangers as if they have just paid for your dinner. Actually, there was another. Don't have that second brandy if you're sleeping within half a mile of a donkey.

The new day brought pain and noise, but it also brought hope. Today we would reach Astorga, finish line of the *meseta*, the end of my symbolic death, from whence the camino jumped off its symbolic deathbed and climbed steadily up and over the Montes de León. The only slight worry, having consulted the literature, was that the ensuing spiritual resurrection wasn't slated to kick off until the Cruz de Ferro, highest point of those mountains, leaving me 28 kilometres of soulless limbo after Astorga. But as long as the road went up, or down, or did anything even vaguely three-dimensional, you wouldn't find me complaining.

It would just be Lilja and me with Shinto that morning, and after a slap-up breakfast – or rather the meagre juice-and-croissant pat-up that is the best you'll ever get in Spain – we blinked out into the over-zealous sun. At the end of the road Hospital de Órbigo died around us, and the camino veered back to the N120. Before it got there, however, there was a bridge over an irrigation culvert, a sheet of galvanised metal which sang like a saw when I planted a boot on it. This sensory experience had a predictable effect on Shinto, and with a sag of the shoulders I turned round.

'What are you doing?' asked Lilja.

'We're going back to find another way,' I said, lightly massaging a tender spot on my right temple. My brain seemed suddenly full of curdled brandy, and at this stage of the day I had no wish to expose my daughter to scenes incorporating adult language and strong graphic horror.

As I'd seen so many others do, she grimaced sceptically at first donkey, then bridge. 'But it's *really small*.' I nodded vacantly, then set about wheeling Shinto round. 'Have you tried holding out some of his favourite stuff from the other side?'

'I've tried everything.'

She twisted out a frond of alfalfa from the pathside. 'Can I try again?'

I suppressed a sigh. 'Quickly, then.'

Lilja looked at Shinto in mock reproach, one hand on hip and the other proffering the vegetable lure. Then she leant forward, and whispered, 'Now, Shinty, it's only a little bridge.' His ears shot up and without hesitation or deviation he clanged straight over.

Five clicks up the road we met the back-up crew, clambering out of a taxi on to the hot earth with water, bread and bad news: every hotel in Astorga was full, and Birna had been obliged to book an unseen out-of-town alternative by phone. We'd started late, and now faced an additional 6 kilometres in heat that at 11 a.m. was already almost absurd.

Astorga showed itself as we picnicked atop the most considerable hill in recent memory. It wasn't difficult to see why the Romans had established the town they named Asturica Augusta where they had: a sudden blip in the flat foreground, crying out for a fortress. Beyond, somewhere in that distantly brooding bank of peaks, were some of the empire's richest gold mines, and Asturica stood guard over the road that brought the ingots back to Rome.

When the pilgrims began to arrive, this was an obvious place to recuperate before the vertical rigours ahead; boosted by the additional influx of holy walkers on the Vía de la Plata, the north–south pilgrim route that merged here with mine, Astorga was home to twenty-one hospices – only Burgos boasted more. Where once stood the fort now soared the cathedral tower, still guiding and beckoning pilgrims, still the dominant man-made structure in a generous swathe of landscape. Rewinding through the last month – the last 500 kilometres, thank you very much – I couldn't recall a town, even a city, where any building had stood taller than the tallest church.

The children stopped to roll boulders down a gully, a pastime hypocrisy forbade me to discourage, and filthied themselves further after imaginatively combining a fountain with three sun-hatsful of field. The heat was making everyone clumsy:

Birna tripped up as she returned a farmer's wave, I refreshed myself with a swig of vinaigrette, and every ten minutes a bleat of alarm warned me that Shinto had once again tried to roll in the dust, forgetting Valdis was up on his back. For maybe two hours we weren't on holiday, shuffling silently through the acrid backyard of some sinister industrial complex, watching in drained and lip-blistered impotence as Shinto stooped to sniff the rails whilst we crossed the main line to Madrid.

Between Astorga's peripheral allotments, a splat of tended green in the clods and rubble, and then up the merciless, spiralled ascent to the old town. Birna had parked the car in a torpid, ochre square; there was a ticket on the windscreen but neither of us could summon the energy for an inquest. Lilja had earlier insisted she'd walk on with me, but as Birna soporifically marshalled the others towards the car's smelted interior she shuffled along behind, mumbling incoherently like Little Nell in her final moments. No need now for a saddle; I unstrapped it from Shinto's hot back and somehow wedged it and the fetid blanket on the parcel shelf. A retarded exchange of heavy-lidded farewells, and they were off.

If Shinto looked nude without his saddle, leading him through the streets I looked mad. As Spain's rural populace had discovered in recent decades, deprived of work the donkey has no purpose: with bags and tackle his function was unequivocal, but what was that now at the end of my rope? I caught our reflection in a shoe-shop window and saw what the few locals not dozing behind their shutters saw – some sun-slackened loon taking his daft pet for a walk.

I hadn't seen a familiar pilgrim since León, but there were half a dozen or so on the shadowed benches around the square at the edge of which, soaring improbably above the sunless back ways of the old Jewish quarter, stood the baroque bookend that was the cathedral's façade. A few token hands were raised in greeting: they were too hot to ask where all my stuff had gone, and I was too hot to tell them. ' 'S'closed,' one slurred thickly as I headed to the cathedral gates.

So too was the adjacent bishop's palace, one of Antonio

Gaudí's slightly melted Sleeping Beauty castles. It's hard to look at a Gaudí building with a straight face, but because of the conditions my wry smile somehow came out as an awful, drunken bark. Shinto looked at me sharply: Really, said his eyes, people will start to talk. With his African genes he was never unhinged by the heat.

Dead straight, dead calm, slightly downhill: the road out of Astorga was tailor-made for round-shouldered, jelly-spined stumbling. With the sun sitting on my face I couldn't see or breathe properly, and soon my powers of perception were boiling away. That emerging structure over the road was a new shopping centre, right? A health centre? I stood opposite the entrance sign, wiped a hot, donkeyed hand across my slick face and tried to clear a mind now dangerously befogged by heat and fatigue. *Yabba di flabba da monasterio da flabba di yabba. Monasterio!* I lurched back to the west and started putting my feet in front of each other again. A monastery – a spanking new monastery. Only in Spain, where the churches still looked down on everything and everyone, where boys were called Jesus and girls Camino, where the consecrated host is wheeled through the streets on the Thursday that follows the eighth Sunday after Easter.

That these conditions were punishing even by Spanish standards became clear when we awkwardly skirted a big set of roadworks and had a close call with a Caterpillar driven by a man in his underwear. Up there in that little cab in his sweaty red jockeys, look. And check them out, Shints, those two playing that funny game on that big green roofless squash-court thing. Just over there. Pelota, that's it. Pelota in your big fat pants, Shiz, that's what we're dealing with here. What's that? Oh yeah – you're a donkey. You don't do that mouth stuff with the words. Right, OK, uphill here, look, uphill for 30 clicks now. Come on, mother. David! Da-vid! I never saw that, sir. *Colette choisi le sac. Elle choisi aussi le panier bleu.* Ooop! Here we go, get the old head in that fountain, ready, here we go and a . . . whoooffffthhhh. Pttthhh. Christ al-bloody-Jesus. God. Christ. God.

I slapped my face, filled my hat with more water and put it on. Better. Right – Spain, donkey, walking, family. Good. I'd just walked through a village, but it didn't seem to be the right one. Castrillo, I wanted. 'Castrillo?' Suddenly there was a little old lady with a dog at my side, pointing me back and left. It was very good of her to help, rather than say have me exorcised or burnt. Particularly because if she hadn't been there, as I realised checking the maps that evening, I'd have presently found myself back in Astorga.

Castrillo was only a click and a bit up the road, but it was no place for a man in my condition. Birna had warned me by phone that it was pretty, if a little quiet. Pretty it was. Shinto's hoofs clacked impressively down a cobbled street overseen by slate-built houses with covered balconies: scores of sympathetic restorations and not a stoved-in hovel in sight. In this wall a weathered ceramic medallion, in that some doughty familial crest. The obligatory stork's nest on the church roof. And mercy me: the door beneath was slightly ajar. I stuck my head into the cold dark. Here is the church, here is the steeple, open the door, and here are the people. Except they weren't. There were no people, not here, not elsewhere in this whole town. No cars, even. A little quiet? Those stout and rough-hewn doors had for centuries watched the world go by, but now the world had gone. Walking back round the church I felt like the night-watchman in a model village. The contrived architectural perfection made it all the more creepy: here was a set from *The Prisoner*, only with El Cid instead of Patrick McGoohan. When my phone rang I almost reabsorbed my spleen.

'What are you *doing*?' said Birna. I wheeled about and there they all were, laughing at me from a window set in a battlement of ancient stone.

We were the only guests in our hotel; very probably in town, said the young wife in charge. She spoke some English, and I left her talking to Birna and Kristjan while her husband led the rest of us to Shinto's night field. En route we encountered a bridge fashioned from not quite enough slabs of old stone: I looked at the hoof-wide gaps and shook my head wanly at our leader, then looked round to see Lilja doing her donkey-whisperer thing and coaxing him painlessly across. It was terrible to think she'd be going home in four days.

Birna had found further evidence of life on earth, and when I returned it was sitting around her in our heavily geraniumed guest-house courtyard. As well as the Lancastrian woman I'd met a couple of days earlier outside Mansilla, there was a German woman and an American: all pilgrims, but none staying in Castrillo. 'We're at a *refugio* a mile down the road,' explained my countrywoman. 'They reckoned this place was worth a look, but it's dead creepy, i'n't it?'

'Only twenty year-round residents,' said Birna, primed by the proprietress. 'Five hundred in the summer – most of these places are mothballed holiday homes.' The German smiled wistfully at the first statistic. 'I like this here. The *refugios* are so full and loud and . . . *oweful*.' She bristled in distaste and explained how her mission to 'look deep in the soul' had been wrecked by that all-consuming rush for beds and the inane natter of a thousand sock-washers.

The American, a grey and dapper Steve Martin, nodded. 'I'm just trying to go home.' He sounded weary and defeated.

'Sort of finding yourself, you mean,' offered the Lancastrian, helpfully.

He looked at her askance. 'No. I just want to *get home*, to Boston, to my apartment. This is all just so squalid. You're brushing your teeth and . . .' As he shivered he caught my eye, and I knew what we were both seeing: a pair of gingery Bavarian bollocks in the soap dish.

With the children fed and bathed and nailed to their beds we dined in the empty and extremely wooden guest-house restaurant, our culinary whims catered for by a cook bused in to cater for us and us alone. Birna felt we ought to reward this level of service by ordering almost everything on the menu, but when I peeped through the hatch into the kitchen I saw the cook light up a cig while idly probing her earhole, so instead we shared a single regional speciality. 'Now is your soap,' announced the proprietress a little sourly, banging a huge tureen of lentilled bone-broth down on the table.

As we forked jellied flesh out of sheep knuckles and wished we were drunk, Birna told me what she'd learnt about the region's culture and history, with particular emphasis on the shy and ethnically obscure Maragatos. The racial origins of this mountain people west of Astorga are an utter mystery: possibly Goths who fought with the Moors in the eighth century; possibly Berbers, or Astures, or Visigoths, or Phoenicians. I was pleasantly interested to learn that many had until recently earned their living as muleteers, and soap-chokingly so to hear that the Maragatan male 'invented' sympathetic pregnancy. (He takes to his bed while sending the encumbered wife out to work, thereby nobly drawing the attention of evil spirits away from the woman while she is at her most vulnerable.)

It was difficult to understand then how a tribe of Visigoths could be holed up here, genetically undisturbed, for a millennium, but the next day it was easy. Lilja and I retrieved Shinto and were soon steadily ascending an exposed and spartan scrubland, treeless, thinly heathered and studded with skeletons of dead gorse. It was hot and wiltingly muggy, though the battered and cowering vegetation suggested a default forecast of flaying wind. Nuggets of quartz sparkled under the alien micro-pineapples of a wild lavender bush: it was another world up here. After 200 kilometres I'd finally scrambled up out of Spain's bread basket. The grain was gone, replaced as an agro-commercial staple by the odd flock of penned sheep.

Shinto had suffered a curious and unsightly spiritual collapse just outside Castrillo, bucking and whinnying as if in premonition of imminent seismic activity, and beelined towards the first enclosed bleaters we encountered with ears forward and jaw set: a freshly humiliated bully ready to take it out on a physical inferior. He trotted right up to the fence and brayed viciously at the already panic-stricken inhabitants, dispatching a whimpering, woolly-backed wave right across to the paddock's opposite corner. 'That wasn't very nice, Shinto,' said

Lilja reproachfully as he turned away in grim satisfaction. She waved a finger and he reeled back as if struck. As well as causing me to wonder what I had done wrong and what she was doing right, this reaction also led to Shinto's offside rear hoof being planted heavily on the toes of my right foot. Had my boots not been cured and tempered by four weeks of elemental extremity that would have been my last unaided step for a month. As it was I bellowed things which earned me a finger-wag all of my own.

The humidity was fearsome. As I entered the first bleakly ravaged strip town, my daypack seemed to congeal into the waterlogged flesh below, like a hot and soggy hunchback. We'd drunk all our fluids when the others arrived with supplies an hour later. I'd warned Birna not to expect a taxi rank out here in the Visigoth wastes, so instead she'd recruited a co-driver: English Sara, propped on her stick by the roadside, utterly spent after a night of *lomo*-fuelled nausea. Birna had driven her on to Rabanal, our next stopover town, and once beds had been arranged and our family reunited, Sara was responsible for taking the car back there. 'Poor woman. She's really worried about driving uninsured,' said Birna, as we watched her release the handbrake and crawl off down the road, nose to the windscreen and half a bottom lip between her teeth.

'A minor motoring infraction,' I said, airily. 'But *that* . . .' The Toyota toiled towards a brow in what sounded like ninth gear. 'That's cheating on a pilgrimage. That's straight to purgatory.' And then I shrugged: not my rules.

'Mummy,' announced Lilja, after a carefully timed interval, 'in the morning Daddy said the S word five times in one go.'

The sky lowered and thickened as we walked into El Ganso, a final, lonely outpost of Maragatan culture and construction, an odd thatched roof amidst the formless ruins astride an unpaved street. A shepherd's crook leant against a wall. Two goats tracked us from a yard shared with a pair of rotting four-spoked cartwheels. The air stank of thunder: that humidity pressure-valve was about to burst. 'The porch of the Church of Santiago has sheltered countless pilgrims,' said the red book, and this was a tradition we found ourselves continuing throughout the hours of lunch-time, huddled up on the steps in the gathering gloom with *boccadillos* on our knees. It got darker still, and a fresh wind freshened, yet even as the trees thrashed around us somehow the heavens stayed stubbornly closed. After the fourth round of 'In My Grandfather's Saddlebags' we broke cover.

Ten minutes later the first furious Thor-bolt speared into the black hills up the road, and when the gap between flash and bang was down to three seconds we stoically prepared for a soaking. I pulled my sun-hat down over my ears and handed Birna the poncho: as the first drops hit their mark she stretched it over her head and the children's and together they stumbled on ahead in file, like an over-manned pantomime animal.

But a minute later they emerged – the rain had stopped before it had really started. We peered incredulously about the tilted landscape: streaky dark walls of precipitation to left and right, the cambered road beneath our feet edged by excitable brown torrents, but before and above an airy, white-ceilinged corridor. As we walked into Rabanal an hour later, bedraggled and shell-shocked pilgrims were shuffling out from doorways and porches: Evelyn and Petronella stood drip-drying outside the *refugio*, and palely reported angry bolts slamming into the earth all around them.

'You waited for the rain to stop, yes?' chattered Petronella.

'No,' said Kristjan, solemnly, 'God kept us dry.'

Trooping along the uphill main street past the sodden refugees, even Valdis looked a little guilty and unsettled.

The pilgrimage had made Rabanal, and now it was remaking it. Most of the guidebooks talked of another village in melancholic decline, but the tall and wide-eaved houses stood in proud fettle, and gathered beneath the mighty church like chicks under a hen were a couple of mini-marts and three or four guest houses, all catering for pilgrims. The revival would appear to have been spearheaded by the Confraternity, responsible for the restoration and management of a 900-year-old *refugio*.

In the four days of my domestic exclusion, I can't pretend to have passed too many *refugios* with a thwarted sigh of envy. But I was sorry to miss out on the one in Rabanal, with its library, its British staff, its 10.45 curfew. I was especially sorry when I dragged the luggage up the third flight of stairs and into one of our adjacent windowless garrets: 84 euros the pair, no telly, no windows, a bath the size of a tea chest. And some bloody donkey doing its deafening worst in the yard out back.

Still, our guest house could justly claim an active nightlife, and setting forking into plates of fried stuff we found ourselves involved, often passively, in a dozen competing conversations. The most emphatic of these was maintained by a bibulous party of Irish pilgrims, a score of them walking to Santiago in week-long annual stages. Their leader, a well-fed man with a well-fed voice, recounted with Chaucerian relish his recent encounter outside a church near León. He'd been in conversation with an aged local, and whilst listening to this fellow's sage and mystical ruminations on the pilgrimage noticed a white glow forming around his head. 'I thought, my God, this is it: this is a miracle, a haloed messenger sent to me.' Forkfuls of mashed chips hovered by the children's open mouths. 'Then I put my glasses on and saw it was stork shit.' As the laughter died a steady Gregorian chant moaned out from the church opposite.

'An old witch was supposed to live there, surrounded by no one but dogs.' I'd been intrigued by Foncebadón ever since reading Shirley MacLaine's account of her confrontation with a monstrous pack of wild canines in the camino's most notorious ghost town, an encounter she had only been able to survive 'by being proactive with love imagery'. Once it had become clear that I could defend myself against dog attack just as effectively 'by being next to a donkey', intrigue was upgraded to enthusiasm.

Pilgrims who had read that tale and others – Paulo Coelho's

protagonist was fearfully savaged by Foncebadón's hounds of hell – came tooled up with pepper sprays and ultrasonic 'Dog Dazers', but the hostility was not purely bestial. The shattered remains of this 2,000-year-old village stood just below the highest point along the camino, on a mountainside of such meteorological capriciousness that as late as the eighteenth century the pass would not have opened until 1 June, otherwise known as the day after tomorrow. Even in high summer, the previous generation of Rabanal *hospitaleros* had felt obliged to escort pilgrims up to the village.

No less pertinently, Birna recalled our friend Nicky speak of black-magic rites held amongst the cattle stabled in Foncebadón's crumbling church. As she thumbed through the literature after the children were asleep her misgivings piled up; she recounted the highlights as I squatted in that ludicrous bath. 'In the seventies there were only four people left, and they still had a team of oxen with fox skins over their faces to keep the flies out. And ten years later it was just an old woman with her son, and she had to campaign to stop them taking the church bells away when the tower started to fall down. That was the only way they could raise the alarm.'

'Who would hear them?' I called out. 'We're 6 kilometres away here and this is the nearest town.'

'Just imagine if you did, though,' Birna replied, her voice brittle with foreboding. 'Imagine hearing the bells ring and knowing that something terrible had happened, and that you'd have to . . .'

'What you're saying,' I abridged, accurately, 'is that I'm walking up there alone tomorrow.'

It had rained in the night: the air was fresher, but Shinto was slightly damp and, without the children around, lethargically reluctant. He was giving me the Mad Mr Ed gurn after less than half an hour of uphill hairpins, and when I paused to peer over the guard rail at the indistinct culvert that had once carried gold-panning water to 60,000 slaves working a nearby Roman mine, he spat on my back – a calculated, hawked-up flob.

'Right!' I barked. 'For that you get the cans.'

I'd been hoarding the three empty Fanta tins since a blurt of nocturnal inspiration two nights before. Lashed to a string and trailed across tarmac they would make a potent multi-sensory goad, I was sure, and so indeed it proved. The greater his efforts to distance himself from the harsh grating and sunlit winks of metallic orange, the more frenziedly profound their effect. From 2.5 kilometres per hour we shot up to 4, no mean feat on this gradient: the facing mountainsides, garishly coloured by the yellows and purples of broom and lavender, very nearly flashed by. It was the answer to all my prayers. Assuming, at least, that one of these was a humble request to be propelled to the crumbling brink of dangerous, taut-featured insanity.

After half an hour, and a page full of snapshot memories for my 'Bemused Cyclists' album, with clawed and bleached knuckles I tore the string off at the saddle end and twitchingly crammed the entire apparatus back into a plastic bag. For better or worse, that noise is a part of the man I now am. Sometimes Birna catches me tilting my head and smiling distantly at a tin, or something orange, and when she does I allow myself to be gently eased into the cupboard under the stairs.

This seemed poor preparation for the gaunt rubble and satanic dingoes of Foncebadón, and it was with enhanced disquiet that I slowly rounded a curve and beheld the bent and weathered sign announcing its imminent appearance. Overseeing a panoramic sweep of sloped desolation it was an obvious spot for the Roman fortress that begat the village; equally, one glance at the frost-splintered tarmac and the windswept, uncultivated wildness it traversed was all you needed to understand its contemporary decline.

Speculations in this vein were checked by plentiful human activity about a large building conspicuously lacking the visible signs of dilapidation, and, before that, by a little wooden-roofed roadside information point. 'Experience Foncebadón, where lonely death at the jaws of a hunger-emboldened pack of ghost dogs is never more than a haunted hovel away!' it might have said, but though everything was in Spanish the glossily laminated presentation suggested it probably didn't.

And in fact that building promptly revealed itself as a new hotel, with a dozen cars in the forecourt and a pair of feet sticking out from under a duvet in an upstairs window. What was going on? Some of the houses up the road stood in ruins, but many of them did not. And the church: closed, of course, but completely rebuilt. In place of the dogs were small packs of ambling day-trippers. It was a colossal disappointment, and not just for me. A couple of days later we met the Irish lot again: the year before, their leader – a six-time pilgrim – had arrived with a trowel and a hammer and a determination to fulfil a distant vow that the Lord's word be heard once more at Foncebadón. He'd opened the church door to find a tattooed delinquent on community service up a ladder with a mouthful of nails, putting the finishing touches to the roof.

Half an uphill, crestfallen mile later we were caught, conspicuously, by a middle-aged woman done up like a seventies Barbie: dressed from turbaned head to galoshed feet in white, her features almost totally obscured beneath impenetrable Jackie Onassis shades. She walked unsteadily past, swinging a small plastic bag, then suddenly stopped and turned.

'I know you.' Her accent was almost impenetrably Spanish. 'I see you juan tame.'

'I don't think so,' I said carefully. Surely she couldn't be a pilgrim.

'*Si, si.* I walk camino with . . . like dis, for shopping.' She pulled at a phantom old-lady's trolley.

'I would remember that.'

She angled her black-glazed face at the wild mountains to our left. 'I av problem,' she said at length. 'You elp me?'

'Well, I'll try,' I said, happy to find my voice coloured with rather more enthusiasm than it might have been a month earlier.

She exhaled loudly and let her linen-jacketed shoulders sag.

'In bar in morning, I make friend with men.' It was an arresting opener. 'One men say he av car, an he take to next town my . . . like dis, for shopping.'

'Your trolley.'

A red-nailed hand carelessly swished the clear air: yeah, whatever. 'But other men, he av . . . *big* joy.' Her head lolled about in overawed recollection, but when she held out her hands to indicate the actual dimensions of his joy I felt a lot better about mine. Mainly, though, I felt that the limits of my new-found pilgrim charity had just been spectacularly breached.

Her rouged cheeks puffed out. 'So . . . I smock his big joy, and now I . . . av problem.' She turned now to the uphill horizon ahead, and so did I, picturing myself riding Shinto recklessly over it with a dozen cans tied to my boots and the words of Freddie Mercury tearing from my throat.

'Please,' she said, sounding suddenly frail and lost. 'You walk wid me, please.' Watching me bully compassion into my features she let out a deranged, whooping giggle, and suddenly I understood. The big joy she had smocked was the big joint she had smoked.

Her already secure status as the camino's unlikeliest pilgrim was firmly cemented as we continued onwards and upwards. In a faltering, drug-tinted soliloquy she painted a picture of her improbable lifestyle, colouring small areas in extraordinary detail but leaving great swathes of the canvas utterly blank. Seven months a year in Miami in a villa whose kitchen surfaces were edged with tangerine mosaic tiles, two in Gstaad, with the balance divided between homes in Madrid and Ibiza. Refreshingly, she never once enquired into Shinto; barely acknowledged his presence. She laughed when I asked what she did for a living, and why she was doing this. She laughed loudest of all when I treated her to choice extracts from my donkey phrase book.

'You know wha you say?' she spluttered, subsiding into a huge coughing fit whose convalescence required her to rest both hands and her forehead on Shinto's saddle. *Limpiaré*, not *limpiará*: a tiny error, but a crucial one. Instead of promising the hoteliers and *hospitaleros* that I would clean up Shinto's crap myself, I'd been ordering them to do it.

The angle of ascent declined, the road rounded a curve and there it was: a 50-foot pole topped with a rusted crucifix and bedded in a sizeable hill of pilgrim rubble. The Cruz de Ferro, cross of iron: roof of the camino, birthplace of my spiritual resurrection. No one was sure when the first cross went up there, but travellers had been leaving a stone on that cairn since Celtic times. Those three sin-signifiers had been ready in my pocket since this morning. They'd been waiting 500 kilometres for this moment.

'You juan know why I do the camino?' My drugged companion passed a hand across the gorse-painted geological amphitheatre around us, and up at the cross ahead. 'Is special, is beautiful.'

'Shinto!' There were a few dozen pilgrims taking spiritual stock around the contemporary chapel erected just back from the cross, and one of them was Petronella. I watched her approach, red eyed as ever: she had just left her stone on the summit of shards, and marked it with three heart-shaped tears for her husband and two sons. I turned to do the introductions but Smock Joy had gone, swinging her plastic bag and settling into the descent with small and rapid steps. Someone saw her later, reunited with her trolley and pulling it through a hot forest.

Shinto was happy – rather too happy, in fact – to be left in Petronella's care while I set out to explore this significant site, the closest the camino came to heaven. Every inch of the chapel's outer stonework was etched and even sprayed with names and dates. 'RAMON PEREZ 1996', 'ALBERTO, PALENCIA, 19.7.98': all left by the Spanish students who were the reason I'd been warned off doing this in high summer, all except the one with the really bad ball-point portrait of a man walking a donkey (sixth stone up, seventh from the left if you ever find yourself in the area). But who to blame for the heretical piss puddles up against the back wall, and indeed for the great bollard lugged up to the foot of that giant cairn? That's a Genghis Khan of accumulated wrongness to unburden yourself of.

I'd planted a foot on the narrow, spiralling path that led to the cairn's lofty summit when Petronella called out. 'But you must take him!'

'What?'

'Up there – take Shinto up there!'

I looked up. The indistinct path was no wider than a human foot, and the cairn – composed, of course, of loose stones – was a good 30 foot high. 'Don't be silly,' I said. 'He'll never manage that.'

'It's his pilgrimage too!'

Not since David Leach's sister said she'd leapfrog over me in her knickers if I wrote 'GAYLORD' on Aaron Pumphrey's skateboard has such an unlikely statement persuaded me to attempt something so ridiculous. Already unpacked, Shinto was un-saddled, and without conviction I led him to the foot of the hill.

At the first tight turn he lost his footing and loosened a small avalanche of unburdened sin; I made to turn back, then realised the practical impossibility of doing so. Round and up and round and up: more than once he dug his hoofs in ominously, but each time a gentle tug on the rope somehow got him moving. The turns tightened as we climbed, and then, after a rather technical dressage around two sheep-sized lumps of quartz, we were at the summit.

All around lay the windswept, panoramic proof that here was the stork's nest atop the camino's steeple. To our right, the messy peaks of Galicia; and to our left, down through the heather and then the pines, the misty memories of our symbolic death, the ochred foreshore of that sea of leather, the *meseta alta*. A rain-tossed salad when I'd started out across it, now it lay brown and dry as a day-old burger.

Shinto seemed oddly relaxed, but I was unsettled by the wind and the disorientating vastness of the prospect, and placed a steadying hand on the wooden pole. Its bottom 7 feet or so were fulsomely decorated with a confounding assortment of appar-ently significant objects: a foot-long blonde plait, a cycle clip, an enamel saucepan. Up here the stones had given way to more obscure embodiments of contrition, weathered offerings piled about my feet in ephemeral judgement of the conflicting people who did what I was doing, and the conflicting reasons they did it for. A sock, a bra, a jockstrap. *The Adventures of Sherlock Holmes*. Two postcards of the Virgin; a toy gun and a full pack of Rothmans; boots and shoes and heather. All stacked up around the bottom of the cross's wooden trunk, like someone's crap Christmas.

What was the story behind that bloodstained tea towel? Or that die-cast Peugeot 205? And what of the three humble stones that I now laid carefully to rest at the summit? Trying to think big thoughts I made to round the pole and descend, but Shinto wouldn't budge. There he stood, gazing importantly at the great prairie we had conquered, ears forward, mane aflutter, head held proud, as if imagining himself a stag and this a whisky label. Unsaddled and at one with creation: this was all as Our Mister intended, though what happened next probably wasn't.

I didn't see the tail go up until it was too late. A tactful yard or so away from competing personal offerings, exhibiting a sense of place and history of which I had not been previously aware, Shinto laid down two dozen pebbles of his own. Petronella was so touched when I told her, she cried again, though others she told later were outraged. I didn't care: in my eyes this was as affectingly spiritual an experience as any I had enjoyed to date. No man can ever have felt more proud of a donkey as I did watching Shinto crap atop the Cruz de Ferro. It was, indeed, his pilgrimage too.

Petronella walked with us for the rest of the day. It was by no means all downhill from hereon, but that afternoon it felt like it. Shinto almost leant into the corners as the gradient picked up, and we fairly barrelled into the crippled remains of Manjarin. A grim village with only one occupied house, but an essential stop for a certain type of pilgrim. We saw the queue before we saw the house: eleven sombre walkers seated in auspicious silence beneath an arthritic wooden crucifix.

What is it about the charitable eccentric that compels him to wear a stained beanie hat covered in badges? As soon as I saw Tomas I thought of Mad Eli picking coins off the floor of his headless-teddy grotto in my parents' home town of Bath. Tomas had chosen to pair his own example of the genre with a scrappy white beard and an ostentatiously soiled T-shirt emblazoned with the red cross of Santiago. 'He is a real Templario,' said a Dutch girl I met later, constructing the more mysterious half of a two-part pen portrait, 'but, ah, always with water coming out of his mouth when he talks.'

If Tomas was an endearingly medieval mess then so was his private *refugio*, holes in the roof sheathed with brick-weighted plastic bags, the walls within draped in a wild chaos of old towels and blankets. Templario, I'd vaguely concluded, was probably something to do with pilgrim protectors of yore the Knights Templar, but this edifice seemed less the castle of the self-styled keeper of their flame than a bypass protestors' hut after the first assault by police bulldozers. I left Shinto with Petronella and walked to the darkened threshold: a multi-lingual note under a clock announced that the establishment ran on solar time, alongside a newspaper cutting showing a slightly younger Tomas camped out in front of the electricity company offices in León. My red book had the story – threat-ened with the cut-off for serial non-payment, he'd gone on hunger strike on their doorstep until they'd relented.

Tomas was cavalierly manhandling some sort of pasta salad from a rust-bubbled biscuit tin on to small, scratched plastic dishes; evidently this was intended for the assembled pilgrims, but all things considered – salmonella, botulism, listeria – I didn't think I'd be joining them. As they made their ponder-ous way towards the table I scanned a few faces – a nicotine-bearded Kris Kristofferson, two mouse-haired, mouse-faced women in matching neck-flapped Foreign Legion caps – and found myself strangely irked.

The word passed down the camino had been that Manjarin was in some obscure yet powerful sense different, that its lonely situation engendered a reflective atmosphere which almost guaranteed profundity and inner revelation. Four weeks before I'd have followed all this up with a prolonged rendition of a noise known to aficionados of the whoopee cushion as the Bronx Cheer, but I liked to think my mind had been prised open a little. Either it hadn't or I was right all along: there was something po-faced and horribly pompous about these people, all trying to fashion expressions of zen-flavoured beatitude as they awaited their Special Experience. The ersatz mystical ambience was hardly Tomas's fault – he was just an old chap whose heart was in the right place, even if his head wasn't. In fact I felt genuinely sorry for him, putting up with the humourless likes of this lot day in, day out.

I bought a bottle of water, and as Tomas stickily patted his pockets for change essayed a conversation. '*Tengo un burro,*' I offered proudly, and in response Tomas dropped a mayon-naised 50-cent coin on the plastic tablecloth and shuffled back to his biscuit tin. Probably deaf; certainly bored. Because they're doing a pilgrimage everyone thinks their story is one worth hearing, but Tomas had heard it all before.

With an unreturned farewell I left, and the three of us were soon lengthening our downhill stride towards the valleys, a warm mist settling below the heather line like some kind of semi-tropical Brecon Beacons. Of the next breathless half-dozen clicks, one occupied us for just thirteen minutes – very possibly a 200-kilo class record.

Our entrance to El Acebo was witnessed by a village ancient whittling pan pipes on a rude slate doorstep, an anxious goatherd and his suddenly galvanised flock and the Ray-Banned driver of a low-slung, gleaming convertible. However complex El Acebo's cultural identity, it had evidently proved an economically successful one: the gutter still ran down the middle of a meandering, crudely cobbled street, and passed beneath precarious, stilt-propped balconies, but every old home was well kempt and most were audibly hosting tele-vised football.

I saw the children before they saw me; they were outside a bar being cloyingly fawned over in the usual rural fashion. The bar fronted a restaurant, which in turn fronted the *refugio*. For the first night in a week I'd share a roof with my fellow pilgrims – if not their abysmal conditions, as in cruel emphasis of the ongoing apartheid, Birna had bagged us a family room with an ensuite bathroom, directly above the bunk-house.

The rather dishevelled proprietor relaxed his pinch-grip on Valdis's cheek to assist me with Shinto: the saddle was flung with manly insouciance into an opposite barn, and the donk himself led to a ring-fenced vacant plot on the main street. When I returned the children gave me a quick tour of the village, past the rusted quarrying wagons pressed into service as cattle troughs to the playground where they'd spent most of the afternoon: three swings, a 20-foot crucifix and a dumb-founding highland vista that spanned the compass and did its part to explain El Acebo's adaptable prosperity.

Trooping back, we found the bar filling up with Saturday-nighters, getting the beers in and sparking up cigs as if it wasn't going out of fashion: how they love to smoke, those little men of Spain. The standard soap dispenser in bar toilets comes with an attached ashtray, but it was perennially apparent that no *hombre* worthy of the title would ever consider using this when there was a urinal to block up.

It was an ambience that, with offspring in mind, precluded my brandy ritual. Or should have. The mother of all Veteranos meant the pilgrims beat us to bed; below our family garret, twenty-four of them squeaked and sighed and snuffled them-selves towards evasive slumber. Petronella had sought assur-ances on my children's nocturnal equability, and as a proud father I'd been happy to lie on their behalf; yet even as Valdis belatedly slumped across the fine but well-defended line that separates empurpled, valley-filling hysteria from drained unconsciousness, I knew that was not the end of it.

Shinto's yard was a good quarter-click up the road, but with the last infant shriek still echoing away down the hillsides his first orphaned ululation of the night honked poignantly in through our attic skylight. In the previous week he'd grown far more vocally lonesome, and I thought again how dislocat-ing all this was for a beast whose previous world had been as small and familiar as a medieval peasant's. Then I twisted in my earplugs and slammed the skylight shut.

Twelve

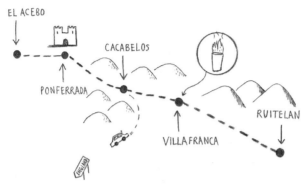

A fter weeks when each kilometre was a fierce and often brutal conquest, thick droves of them were now passing by almost unnoticed. Following an unusually hearty breakfast of deep-fried tuna-filled rolls, Lilja, Shints and I fairly steamed into the long descent, scrabbling down a gully of slated scree with such impulsive glee that we skidded and butted our way past a dozen alarmed walkers.

For the first time I'd begun to believe I would actually make it to Santiago, and I wasn't alone. Regularly now people were leaving little notes for that special pilgrim they'd met and passed along the way, leaving an email address or a phone number in the realisation that this had become a good thing, and so like all such entities would come to an end. You'd find the notes alone, speared through a fence barb, or in a fluttering forest, weighed down under pebbles. Between us, Lilja and I read them all that morning. Bereaved Thomas from weeks back seemed to have found a lady friend, and the jilted exhortations to New Mexico Joe suggested that love will always find a way, even around nasal incontinence and graphically public urination. Most of the many notes addressed for his attention seemed to be missing something, principally the words 'you' and 'bastard': 'I waited in El Burgo Ranero for two days!' 'Return Burgos but no Joe. Soon Hotmail please.' 'Didn't we agree to meet in León?'

Over the next few days I counted messages to him in at least five different hands: he could have walked home across the Atlantic on a crazy-paved pontoon of broken hearts. You could only feel for the man. A certain type of pilgrim does the camino in confident expectation of meeting their mystical soulmate en route, and if they were female and under thirty Joe was the only show in town. All I can say is thank Christ he didn't have a donkey – it would have been like a 774-kilometre Benny Hill title sequence.

Through more resurrected villages almost disconcertingly vibrant with human life and well-tended colour; past the terrible beauty of a broom hare fixing us with a huge, bright eye as it lay crippled and dying at the roadside. We arrived at the familial meet-point well ahead of schedule, but Shinto landed on his hooves, lunching on the very lushest alfalfa in the front garden of a mothballed villa. When the rest turned up we watched him from the restaurant across the road, our *boccadillos* brought over by an apple-cheeked cook done up like Mrs White in Clue.

The road flattened and we distantly circled a nuclear power station, pausing to wonder if Valdis should be plundering the cherry trees whose fruit dangled so temptingly as she sat up there in the saddle. Then paint-sprayed marshalling yards, piss-sprayed back alleys and into the last major town before Santiago. Kristjan had been building up to this moment for days, and burst into song as he saw confirmation on a passing municipal dustcart: 'Hello Mudder, hello Farder, here I am in Ponferrada!'

In pilgrimage terms, Ponferrada is most notable as the home of the Knights Templar, whose enormous castle HQ reared splendidly up before us as we followed the yellow arrows out of a tight and neglected thoroughfare. Some castles have the forbidding look of a building you'd enter and never leave alive, but Ponferrada isn't one of them. It was somehow nostalgic and comforting, like a child's perfect My Big Fortress: plump round towers linked by long, crenellated battlements, fluttering pennants, moat, drawbridge – the works.

I'd felt obliged to read up about the Knights Templar after my brief encounter with Tomas, and over breakfast had dutifully soiled the literature with fish-oiled fingerprints. It's a rattling tale, a saga that, like so many of my favourites, unites chivalry, international finance and necrophilia.

Formed in 1118 by a plucky band of nine knights who had volunteered to stay in Jerusalem and protect pilgrims after most of their fellow crusaders buggered off, the Templars were the first of an unlikely breed: the Warrior Monks. Not for them the traditional monastic life, that shaving of strange parts of the head and shuffling about cellars in a felt dressing gown concocting gaily hued liqueurs – the Knights Templar vowed loudly to slaughter any Saracen who threatened the safe passage of Christian pilgrims (and, less loudly, never to lose a horse, throw a coat to the ground in anger or sodomise one other).

Supported at first by handouts from grateful pilgrims, and then by huge donations from the monarchs of Europe, the Templars were soon active across the Continent: by 1240, the order was 20,000 strong, protecting Christian travellers on a front that stretched from Santiago to the Holy Land. No less valuable to the holy traveller was the Knights' contribution to fiscal convenience and security: such was their reputation for steadfast trustworthiness that a pilgrim could exchange his vulnerable purseful of calling-all-brigands gold coinage for a letter of credit, redeemable at any branch of Templars across the continent. 'In God we trust,' goes that notice by the till. 'Everyone else pays cash.' But in medieval Europe, the Templars achieved the Almighty's credit rating, and in doing so effectively invented banking as we (sort of) know it.

When the Saracens drove the Christians from the Holy Land in 1291, the Templars found their offensive role abruptly reduced, a situation compounded by their own efficiency in helping to drive the Moors from northern Spain. Having largely done their job, the Templars were now a threat – responsible only to the Pope and in charge of a titanic financial empire that was by now lending money to the very kings who'd once sponsored them so generously.

The end was swift and – yes! – brutal. The castle in Ponferrada, a gift from Fernando II of León, was finished in 1282, but the Knights had only been strutting up and down its great halls for twenty-five years when Philip 'the Fair' of France leant on the Pope to authorise the arrest of the Templars, all of them, on grounds of heresy. And, sure enough, with the application of a little medieval persuasion, apprehended warrior monks found themselves reminiscing on long evenings of lavish bum-sex, often whilst flicking the Vs at the Virgin – what with all that and the image of a giant cat to worship, it was no wonder a few horses got lost. One Templar, his memory jogged with particular firmness, recalled having made sweet love to his exhumed girlfriend's corpse; and in fact, now that he thought of it, returning to the grave nine months later to find a chirpy little skeleton son awaiting him like some sort of calcium Pinocchio. The last Grand Master of the order, Jacques de Molay, was burnt at the stake in 1314; before the year was up, both King Phil and the Pope had fulfilled de Molay's fireside curse by dropping dead.

I still don't know where any of this leaves Tomas. Though by the looks of his wardrobe he'd thrown a lot more than his coat to the ground in anger.

The extraordinary rise and fall of the Knights Templar has encouraged all manner of historical speculation, very little of it properly academic, linking the order with the Turin Shroud, Freemasonry and inevitably the Holy Grail. Not surprising, therefore, that Ponferrada, the Templars' camino HQ, exerts a mystical lure that a certain sort of pilgrim is powerless to resist. Paulo Coelho chose the castle as the setting for his pilgrimage's initiatory denouement: 'I took all of my clothes off,' I read, without appropriate fascination, 'and Petrus handed me a perfumed black tunic.' And Shirley lost it big time in Ponferrada, falling over what she calls the edge of reason – a metaphorical precipice, be assured, that is in her case rather more distantly located than might be considered usual. During a sixty-page account of a vision experienced in a Ponferrada hotel room she describes her personal responsibility for founding the human race, budding a male Shirley in that tank of golden liquid whilst alien beings ferry crystal across the skies. Of Atlantis. 'I was completely depleted of potassium,' she explains afterwards.

Drizzled and industrial, Ponferrada was hardly straining to exude a sense of esoteric mystery, but we liked it anyway. As well as the castle there was the bridge, albeit a disappointingly bland contemporary replacement for the one that gave the town its name: a mighty structure reinforced with iron, no inconspicuous achievement in 1082.

We crossed the river en route to the Hotel Madrid, whose dapper, elderly proprietor had, earlier that day, apologetically drawn Birna's attention to the 'COMPLETO' notice on the reception desk. She was preparing to leave when Valdis had abruptly vomited all over his switchboard; because this was Spain he suddenly found two rooms and insisted on personally cutting up the children's veal escalopes at dinner. The largest bath I'd encountered since leaving the realm of normally proportioned Europeans, waitresses in starched and monogrammed tunics serving bread with tongs in a dining room where genteel old dears fanned themselves before a sea of glassware and linen, what may be Spain's only potable white wine, and all this for less than 30 quid a double: anyone curious enough to understand why leaving a tip can be fun should visit the Hotel Madrid. Anyone not in charge of a 200-kilo quadruped.

Whilst Birna and the children were discovering the aforementioned attractions, I was standing between Shinto and a bellboy at the top of fifteen outdoor steps. At their conclusion lay the strip of yard that had been his intended night realm, and though I knew it was pointless, through courtesy and a lack of Spanish I allowed this enthusiastically persistent youth to try his luck. And I'm glad I did, because that first tentative rump-nudge initiated a merry sequence of events that culminated in Shinto being blindfolded by a chef whilst a chambermaid backed down the stairs holding a carrot to those mobile nostrils. Looking at the treasured photograph I don't see a stupid, stubborn jackass; I see a noble martyr proudly eschewing the firing-squad sergeant's offer of a last root vegetable.

With the kitchen staff still filling the Sunday air with loud mirth, the bellboy led Shints and I all the way back up to the castle, down a couple of obscure alleys and at length round the side of a school and into another of those lock-up plots of wasteland. It started raining on the way back, but even though he was only wearing a shirt, and even though the whole operation had detained him for well over an hour, he proudly spurned the note I proffered upon our return. *'Peregrino,'* he said, but these days I wasn't even that.

It was the family's final day together on the road, and walking Shinto through the taunting schoolboy smokers gathered outside his gate I found myself beset by a tangled skein of emotions – impending solitude and rediscovered freedom; economy regained versus luxury lost. From father back to pilgrim. It would certainly be tough for both of us without the family: Shinto would lose his little friends and their daily grooming programme, and regain his full complement of car-borne baggage; I would miss Lilja's quasi-mystical powers of equine persuasion and her mother's and siblings' donk-cheering enthusiasm. Perhaps most tragically, never more would a charmed stranger pick up my dinner tab.

By being ugly and rather dangerous, the route out of Ponferrada helped douse these bitter-sweet ruminations. With Valdis up in the saddle and Lilja clutching the back of my shirt we gingerly traversed huge roundabouts, slip roads and a memorable contraflow assault course, variously harried by impatient motorists and fêted by women of many years, running up their garden paths with bowls of cherries and pre-puckered lips. Only in the afternoon, with the family back up to full strength, did the town begrudgingly peter out into vine-yards and poppies.

As we ambled across a gently undulating landscape I at last realised the sunlit, bucolic reality of the strange but appeal-ing familial interlude I'd had in my mind's eye trooping towards León. In a week we'd gone through the whole Goldilocks routine: the *meseta* had been too flat and hot, the Montes de León generally too extreme, but these, the plump and temperate hills of Bierzo, were just right. Arm in arm with my pilgrim wife, our flaxen-haired youngest riding high and happy at our side, a keenly prick-eared donkey under her rump and somewhere back down the dusty path a couple of somebody else's kids trying to trip each other up: this was as good as it got, and it was ending just as they'd all grown accustomed to fatigue, *chorizo* and the stop-and-drop approach to public urination.

Cacabelos was another are-we-nearly-there-yet extruded strip town, with the pertinent buildings right out the far end. The hotel Birna had found was a new one, run by a family who'd clearly been anticipating Shinto's arrival all day: the eldest daughter spoke French and as Shints and I accompanied her through the streets she explained that her father kept three horses in a farm just outside town. We arrived at a house with a large and messy front yard, and a shrunken figure she identified as her grandmother tottered eagerly out to meet us, gumming her false teeth into place. Everyone smiled and nodded a lot; I did so with such consuming enthusiasm that Shinto was rather negligently attached to a large and oily piece of mechanical jetsam, which left his snout blackened for days afterwards.

Perhaps because my most fearsome donkey-maintenance concern related to the intimate application of unguents, I had successfully forgotten that Shinto's anti-tick treatment had long since passed its expiry date. This took my neglect to a whole new level: the danger wasn't any uncomfortable irritation caused by the ticks themselves, but a reliably fatal blood disease they carried. I remembered as I was getting into bed, and before getting out again I had naturally pre-dreamt the entire procedure. For once fantasy was kinder: instead of having a spike plunged through his ribcage as Hanno had warned me he'd have to, the Shinto of my nocturnal reverie was a huge, prone stallion who obediently rolled over as I anointed each vast, glistening flank in turn with a sort of insecticidal lacquer.

I had Kristjan ball-pen a reminder on my hand – a many-legged blob-monster that was less a tick than one of the Pacman baddies – during our final breakfast together. Looking from face to road-tanned face and suppressing a desire to clasp each to a chest moist with tears of pride and sorrow, I catalogued my children's achievements. Lilja, never previously associated with any act of stamina not involving tiny plastic beads, had defied the critics with an 80-kilometre on-foot total that left her just 20 clicks short of the papal qualification for a certificated pilgrimage. In the pantheon of crowd-pleasing equine/girl combos, Valdis had earned a place on the podium alongside Lady Godiva and the Banbury Cross bint. Cursed with a Y chromosome and bereft of a solar-powered Game Boy Kristjan had found himself frankly bored for long periods, but had tackled this wholly rational condition with doughty endurance. And considered as a three-headed entity, their traditional holiday litany of demands for complicated treats and favours had been eerily muted – evidently some asceticism had rubbed off. They hadn't even been more than briefly insufferable after we'd explained that those people had bought us supper because they liked them. Never walk with children and animals, the maxim nearly went, and I had proven whoever nearly coined it wrong.

Birna bequeathed me a mobile phone and a new shirt as we transferred luggage from foot wells back to saddle. Despite the looming attractions of a daily routine shorn of *lomo*, dung and melted tarmac she was sad to leave: the camino's epic history and all-pervading human warmth had affected her with something approaching profundity. And for my part, a meandering personal pilgrimage had been set back on the straight and narrow: bullfighting, witnessed by the distraught children in a bar a few days back, was to be instinctively reviled rather than studied with growing interest as a fascinating cultural anachronism. By the same token, the girls' instinctive affection for Shinto and its girding influence on him had obliged me to appreciate the value of sweet-natured good humour and encouragement, and indeed its productive efficacy, with donkey as in life. It was the power of love, and my daughters had helped me find the switch. Let's just hope they hadn't taken the batteries with them.

With a child at his side or on his back, Shinto's eager ears had stood like furry exclamation marks; watching the Toyota toot away up the tight street they slowly drooped from rabbit mode to spaniel. The hotelier's daughter, who'd escorted me back to her grandmother's yard to retrieve Shinto, clapped a sympathetic hand on his back, then heaved aloft a welcome gift: a 5-kilo sack of wheat fluff and husks that may easily have been chaff.

Good news for both of us, and just as well, because if any pill needed sugaring it was the one I found myself being prescribed at the vet's ten minutes later. 'No, no!' quailed a horrified white-coat as I pointed first at the Pacman monster, then at the donkey tied up outside to her oversized fibreglass Alsatian, and last, more forcibly, at my own chest in brutal interpretation of hypodermic hara-kiri. 'No, no, no!' she continued, rummaging noisily about in a cabinet before seizing exultantly on a hefty bottle of trigger spray. She held it up to me: the label was dominated by a large blue cat, a small gallery of insect silhouettes with red crosses through them and an absurd price tag. 'Fifty euros?' I yelped, suddenly remembering why I don't have pets any more.

The back end of Cacabelos was well-to-do but rustic: two flour-faced ladies plaiting 3-yard lengths of dough on a bakery trestle, a carpenter knocking up a hefty kitchen dresser in his garage, and yes – a donkey hauling an overloaded hay wain across the bridge heading out of town. '¡Hola!' I called out companionably, then felt my features crumple as the leathery, flat-capped drover curled his lip with almost parodic relish and spat out a furious burst of vitriol. Pilgrim, schmilgrim, appeared to be the crux of his argument: what the fuck did I think I was doing, wasting a perfectly good beast of rural burden on this stupid, bogus promenade?

The road began to roll: the mountains that shored up Galicia, the camino's final province, were massing on a grey horizon. I knew from the electoral prominence of the Galician Nationalist Party to expect a new glut of separatist sloganeering when we got up there, but even down here the independence issue was a live one. The proprietor of the Hotel Madrid had been keen, using the modest overlap in our vocabularies, to highlight the distinction between the pen-pushing leeches of León and the honest-toiling, horny-handed sons of Bierzo. It all seemed rather feudal: his two favourite words were 'land' and 'property', and whenever he said either he pressed a fist to his heart. I blame the language: Birna had explained that there are two Spanish verbs for 'to be', one expressing a state seen as 'temporary or reversible', as might be 'I am lonely', but the second a chest-prodding, emotive iteration of 'a permanent or inherent quality': 'I am Catalan!' And that's it for generations.

As if to highlight the hotelier's sentiments, the road out of Cacabelos seemed to radiate civic pride and stolid rural affluence in a way that I'd forgotten was possible. Window boxes and roses; a slate-roofed dog kennel. The only constant was the penchant for building things in the wrong order: I passed huge new chalets with satellite dishes and carriage lights bolted to bare cinder blocks.

Villafranca del Bierzo was rewardingly like nothing else that had come before, its regal but slightly careworn housing stock scrambling recklessly up the sides of two steep and converging valleys. The stout eminence stacked up behind it made Villafranca the last staging post before the rigours of Galicia, a strategic significance which cemented its role as a bulwark against the Moors during the *reconquista*. Villafranca means 'Foreigners' town', and by 1250 half the residents were expat pilgrims who'd been persuaded to settle there: Dutch, English, German and even the odd Scandinavian. Most, though, were from just north of the Pyrenees – it's said that French was Villafranca's lingua franca until the sixteenth century. Coincidence, perhaps, but following weeks of blithering non-communication with the populace, since Ponferrada it had become weirdly commonplace to find myself exchanging '*bonjour*'s with a local.

We passed the prim and comfy official *refugio* and shortly after arrived beneath the wrought-iron chalices screening the windows of my intended stopover: the famously eccentric *albergue* run by Jesus Jato. A predictably under-groomed old chap with a charismatic twinkle in his smut-rimmed eyes, Jesus was healing a Brazilian woman's foot, rather lasciviously I felt, when we arrived. With cheery nonchalance and a lapful of toes he thumbed us towards a barn lined with old mattresses, and as soon as I led Shinto in the poor animal flung himself at the dusty floor. I jumped swiftly to unburden him – it was wretched when he tried to roll with the saddle on, and not just because of the resultant compression of my belongings: this seemed the closest he'd get to sexual pleasure, or so I hoped, and that was like doing it with a condom. Made out of egg boxes.

The *albergue* shared a familial ambience with Tomas's place up on the mountain, a quirky Scout-hut shambles of plastic sheeting, recycled pallets and eccentric announcements. Two doors off the main dormitory were labelled for the use of the over fifties and 'professional snorers'; plastic flowers coiled up the corners of every treble bunk. 'It was like the Garden of Eden,' said a German girl, reminiscing with Total Shithouse a few days later about their stay the night before mine.

'Yeah,' he retorted, 'if you just trod on the rake.'

It wasn't yet 2.00, and with Shinto sneezing into a basin of chaff I set out to explore Villafranca. That stoutly towered fortress told of an eventful past – I'm ashamed to reveal that the town was most recently despoiled by British troops in pursuit of a retreating Napoleon – and the plunge into a disorientating vortex of narrow alleys certainly made for an exciting present. One was Calle Sucubo: who'd live in a street honouring a female demon who rapes men in their sleep? It was with a heightened sense of relief that I emerged into a broad and beautiful square, its grand ecclesiastical structures arranged around an immaculate rose garden.

On each of the many benches within sat a pair of pensioners, tackling foil-wrapped sandwiches and chugging beer straight from the bottle. I watched them all nodding slowly at the flawless blooms as I worked through a *calamari* roll in a bar opposite, an establishment empty but for the memorable presence of a hairy-legged transvestite. What must life be for an exotic deviant in a small and remote Spanish town with a throughput of earnest pilgrims? No wonder he'd drunk himself to sleep.

The man I would know as Donald was en route to a similar state when I returned to the *albergue*. A second-time pilgrim, Scottish Donald had just finished his two-week tour of duty as a *hospitalero* at the Confraternity's *refugio* at Rabanal. 'Here,' he said, emptying the dregs of a bottle of red into a plastic cup, topping it up with bitter lemon and pressing the luridly mauve consequence at my chest. 'I've just invented a new drink.' His Borders slur was barely intelligible even to a fellow Briton, but retired teacher Donald's most tragic vocal handicap was to sound majestically drunk when he wasn't. Though in fact by the time I turned up at a *refugio* he usually was: his routine was to leave early, arrive early, and spend a long afternoon touring the bars. Four others had helped Donald out with that bottle, but later on a dozen of us had to do our bit to save him from an earthenware vat of fortified monkbrew he'd somehow sourced in town.

Donald was the embodiment of untroubled conviviality: as with many pilgrims a relationship meltdown apparently lay behind his journey to Santiago, but unlike most he kept all the details to himself. Instead he reminisced engagingly of his time as a *hospitalero*, with particular reference to the last-night celebrations that had led to him being locked out of his own *refugio*. Donald had heard all about Shinto and asked for a peek; after we'd both been nipped on the forearms I decided to put the tick-spray business on hold for a day.

We ate with Barbara and Walther in a neat little square just behind the grander one, though I couldn't seem to muster much enthusiasm for either *lomo* or flan. My innards began to percolate ominously as we wound back up the alley-ways, and as darkness filled the valleys I gingerly prepared for an early bed. 'Not yet!' whispered Donald, as I creaked past the over-fifties chamber. 'Jesus is having a *queimada*.'

Obscurely persuaded and hoping this wasn't Bierzan for wet dream, I shortly found myself stooping beneath a line of damp socks in the gathered gloom, cornered by wide-eyed, flame-lit faces. Before us, on a trestled altar rigged up in front of the toilets, Jesus was throwing handfuls of sugar into a burning crucible of alcohol, mumbling significantly as he did so; periodically, his mutters swelled into a moaning chant, and when it did he drew a ladle of blue fire, raised it above his head and dramatically returned the contents to the mother bowl from on high. Beginning to understand why the two previous *refugios* erected by Jesus on this spot had been burnt to the ground, I also marvelled at this national fascination with pouring intoxicants from a great height: as well as all that flourish with the glass spouts at Santo Domingo, the cider I'd ordered in Cacabelos had been delivered from bottle to glass by a hotel barman with his stiff arms at five to eight.

'*Peregrino . . . mystico . . . Maria, Dio, universo . . .*'

To the many Brazilians in attendance it must have seemed like the collected works of Paulo Coelho made flesh – ethereal, flame-lit flesh. Everyone suddenly produced cameras, and so I did too: the legacy of my diplomatic eschewal of flash was an indistinct portrayal of tramps arguing round a brazier. The incantations rose to an ominous climax, and in an atmosphere of palpable expectation Jesus poured a cupful which was passed from hand to hand with whispered instructions. 'We're not even to *sniff* it yet,' translated Donald, his frustration apparent even at minimal volume. I was glad he was here at least – the rest were all cyclists, and it seemed a shame to develop a supernatural rapport with people I'd never see again.

Jesus made an announcement which included the word '*alfabético*', and followed this up with a questioning look around the flicker-lit faces. '*Australiano*?' Silence. '*Brasiliano*?' A dark forest of hands, a massed, rapt babble and a thwarted yelp of protest from a bloke who'd ridden by that morning with a Belgian flag on each pannier. I wasn't surprised to see Jesus's finger alight on the same pneumatic silhouette he'd been massaging earlier; with an expression of sanctified gratitude she stepped out of the shadows and as instructed decanted the mystic brew into shot glasses. Rather anticlimactically Jesus quietly refused to partake, his wistful sigh suggesting a recent day of medical judgement.

My little beaker was still fiercely aflame when it was passed over, and with a shrug and the realisation that this was the finale, I downed it unextinguished. Campari bitter, Cointreau sweet and somehow, despite Donald's distress at that wasteful incineration, still alarmingly potent. So potent that when I stumbled urgently to the loo in the night it didn't even hurt when I smacked my temple against the frame of the bunk opposite. Well, not the first three times.

Barbara and Walther had stayed in a hotel, and walked up as I prepared Shinto for departure, crouched biliously at his rear end with an upturned hoof in my lap and a vacuumed cramp in my guts. They were sweet people, and had taken to initiating every fresh encounter with a summary of their latest reflections on Shinto's bridgeophobia. 'In Turkey one time we see men pulling some animals across a bridge wiss the tail, the back way.' I glanced frailly up at Walther's kind and open face. 'Tim, have you tried the back way wiss your monkey?'

They helped me with the straps, then insisted on a gentle guided tour of the church just behind Jesus's gaff, another low-key Romanesque hall. 'Saint Agatha,' breathed Barbara, nodding at a figure regretfully proffering her own severed, lumpy tits on a tray, like a bad school dinner. Back outside, a quietly enthused Walther decoded the carved mysteries of the arch above what is known as the Puerta del Perdón, a doorway through which dying or severely enfeebled pilgrims could pass to receive a papally authenticated sick note granting them full sin-remission. Walther's hands and words described the doleful procession of hunched pilgrims shambling up to God, ready with the Book of Truth open on his knee, then skipping weightlessly down the other side, redeemed and ready for paradise. If I'd felt able I might have reciprocated with an overview of the Puerta del Salmonella, with the facial expressions reversed and the Book of Truth replaced by a squid sandwich.

Under thickening skies I took my leave, leading Shinto uphill through outskirts whose tentative construction exuded an air of frontier finality, the last staging post before the untamed highlands. Drizzle brought out the snails, and Shinto's hoofs noisily dispatched them. The quiet N6 looped steadily upwards; the rain abated; the birds twittered their relief; the clouds darkened anew and quickly shut them up. Shinto seemed strangely eager, too eager, fired with a sort of vindictive determination, as if startled and angry to find himself on some stupid wet road in Spain. 'Right, you bastard, let's get this over with,' said his quarter-to-three ears and brusquely striding gait; after five weeks of trying to tap into his reserves, I'd somehow struck the mother lode. I was always astonished by the power and heat Shinto managed to synthesise from raw grass, but the human body is a less efficient machine; fuelled by a pair of unenthusiastically ingested Marie biscuits I struggled to keep up.

About 3 clicks up the hill a tiny old woman motored past, elbows working furiously either side of a colossal pack. As I watched she slowed, then stopped, clasping and unclasping her left hand around something that wasn't there. She turned and walked back towards me, dead eyed and robotic. '*Ma canne*,' she muttered blankly as our paths crossed. Her stick was back in Villafranca, and she was going to get it. I thought about the 6-kilometre round trip that lay ahead and felt my pre-knotted innards contract in nauseous empathy. Painfully accustomed as we now were to the medieval concept of speed, the unclaimed clothes and even cameras at almost every *refugio* reception emphasised that this pain was only bearable if every step was a step in the right direction.

The N6 passed beneath the motorway that had sucked away all its traffic, and slalomed us up to a village where barrels the size of covered wagons rotted under thunderstruck oaks.

Something wretched happened to me at a Super Spar in the next settlement along: driven in by an enfeebled lust for Coca-Cola, I watched in frail disbelief as the girl at the till emptied her cash register in laborious demonstration of an inability to give precise change for a €20 note. 'That's fine, really,' I pleaded, pressing the money at her and demanding to be over-charged, a display my family and friends would certainly have found interesting. At first she didn't understand, but when she did I found myself fixed with the sort of bewildered distress you might expect after shaking an infant niece awake to tell her Father Christmas was a drunk.

Running on pure pilgrim power I stumbled on after my bloody-minded donkey, pausing now and then to do something brief but terrible behind a tree, supplementing the arc of tissued awfulness that backed every convenient trunk and bush along the camino. It was flat now, but soon the dense rain that had been screening the worst of the forthcoming peaks came down to remind us that this was very nearly Galicia, the urinal of Spain. Cyclists sluiced by, supplementing the poncho-fed canal running down into the top of my boots. The drumming on my plastic head-cowl built to a spastic crescendo, and when it got there Shinto abruptly slammed in the anchors. He just stopped dead at the side of the road, Mohican mane flattened, an unbroken stream trickling from each horizontal ear. I looked at him: all he needed was a Hamlet smoking soggily in the corner of that flabby, wet gob.

Lacking the wherewithal for a showdown I leant back against the hard-shoulder crash barrier, blowing drips off my nose for perhaps ten minutes; then, as suddenly as he'd stopped Shinto started again, covering a brisk half-click before coming to a jarring halt once more. It was as if he'd been switched off, as if water had got in his electrics. During the fourth cycle we approached a large petrol station, and noting the generous canopy over its attached car wash I pulled off the road. Passing the pay booth I exchanged glances with a pump attendant through the glass. It's a tough job, said his. And nobody has to do it, mine replied.

No one was claiming this as a high point: not me as I disconsolately fumbled biscuit parts into my damp and trembling maw, not Shinto as he browsed the dieselly weeds poking up behind the jet-spray lance. There was evidently some sort of quarry hereabouts, and every two minutes or so a gigantic truck full of boulders would pull up with an explosive pneumatic hiss, sending Shinto off in panicky, taut-roped semicircles around the compressor I'd lashed him to. Shuffling over to tighten the knot I caught sight of my reflection in the spattered Plexiglas: tanned but consumptive, a wasted, refugee vacancy in that hollow face.

After an hour the rain abated, and after another we packed up and tentatively set forth. The hills, now that we could see them, were stacking up dramatically around us, the occasional rugged precipice topped with the ruin of a castle erected to protect pilgrims from bandits perennially attracted to lonely uplands. A bickering party of French couples fussed wetly past, oblivious to our conspicuous presence, and were followed soon after by a fresh-faced girl in tentative control of a small, plump and ostentatiously excitable mongrel. 'Sativa!' she called, as Shinto found the small gaps between his hoofs threaded with a loud, brown blur.

'Isn't that something to do with cannabis?' I whispered, as her charge yapped about in Shinto's measured, even gaze.

A slow, freckled smile tightened the wet bandanna across her forehead. 'Excellent power of dedudication.' She was Dutch, of course. And so the four of us walked on together up the puddled tarmac, tousled and steaming like rejects from the Ark.

The Dutchwoman was not like other pilgrims I had met. She conspicuously spurned all conversational banality, withholding her name and any detail of her domestic life, refusing even to comment on the weather on a day when there'd been little else. When I asked how she found places for Sativa to sleep, knowing that dogs were banned from *refugios*, she gave me a curious, disappointed look and said, 'Well, that is where the real magic begins.'

'It is?' I said, looking up ahead, where my target village of Ruitelan was taking form beneath two distantly vertiginous spans of a gorge-vaulting motorway viaduct.

'I have slept in a cave,' she said. And after a long, pregnant minute the wet hillsides were suddenly shaken with manic, motiveless laughter.

'The Mary Poppins of *refugios*,' someone had written in the Ruitelan *refugio* guest book, 'practically perfect in every way'. It shouldn't have been, with the nagging, worrisome drone of airborne motorway traffic and an outdoor ambience still reflecting the long, cowering decades when all those flying lorries had been down here, barrelling fearsomely between these grimy, shell-shocked homes. That it was is the legacy of the splendid but tiny *hospitaleros*, Luis and Carlos, who when our tri-species party arrived were respectively signing in pilgrims with faultless serenity and belting out show tunes over a hot stove.

At wee Luis's bidding I led Shinto back down the road, tethering him in the tossed-salad undergrowth behind an election-postered substation, then returned to be shown up to the attic dorm. Raw concrete underfoot, and overhead a roof polka-dotted with pinholes of light, but with a bunk-bed to myself and the dim air faintly coloured with rising incense and music, I felt slumber's caress pulling me under. Later I'd go down to enjoy a jovial and toothsome four-course dinner, served up by the rheumy, theatrical Carlos as eighteen of us sat pinioned, ear to shoulder, elbow to throat, in the tiny dining room. Later still I'd join Donald in the rather spartan bar over the road, watching reporters clamber about a train wreck as we tackled our huge Veteranos. But that afternoon, after 18 wet clicks on half a dozen wet biscuits, I would be one of those God-awful, tutting 5 p.m. dozers.

Thirteen

Planting his filthy, calloused feet atop the blasted brow of O Cebreiro, the pilgrim of yore might for the first time have pondered what the professor who translated the *Liber Sancti Jacobi* called 'the ultimate reality of belonging to the great nation of marchers to Santiago'. He stood in the last province, on the last mountain: the end was nigh, or nearly nigh.

This was an epic day, and the Ruitelan boys knew how to set the tone. At 6.30 a.m. a ratcheting orchestral cataclysm filled the house, the *2001* theme turned up to distortion level. As the kettledrums tom-tommed up the stairwell in mighty exultation, I looked around the attic: it wouldn't have been funny had that rustling, ponchoed pilgrimator not stomped over to turn the lights on half an hour earlier, but because he had, and we were all therefore awake, it was.

Stoked by a Carlos breakfast spectacular I hit the road with sturdy enthusiasm. A hawser-limbed Belgian woman in the neighbouring bunk had carelessly mentioned covering 51 kilometres by nightfall: fuelled with a brimming reserve of hatred she was hoping to beat her ex-husband's record of fifteen days, St Jean to St Jim. ('Maybe next year I go for the world best,' she smiled, scarily. 'In 1981 a Frenchman of forty makes Santiago in eight days.') Something about the morning made me want to match her, click for click, and had that something included an audibly approaching search-and-destroy party of Alsatian-led storm troopers I might have. For it was a splendid day to be a pilgrim abroad: after long weeks of thick, unventilated heat and a short day of savage precipitation, the laundered air was sweet and bracing, the prospects verdant and rollingly fecund. Dewdrops winked in the sun, sleek livestock graciously browsed lustrous pastures. I felt like a happy hobbit coming home.

We passed through a couple of scrubbed and healthy villages, all as conspicuously alive with productive morning activity as so many of their camino predecessors had been dead and decrepit. Even the pets were glossed and sturdy: this was a realm of fat cats and early birds. A farmer's wife with a basket of eggs strode past us and into the last house of the last hamlet, and thereafter, first with gentle stealth and then callous indifference, the path began to climb.

Round a shaded curve we found ourselves faced by a steepling rise of wet slabs, stacked up like a natural staircase, and as Shinto faltered out came what I now thought of as the choral prod. Chivvied stridently along by Level 42 – what was even that name doing in my head, never mind four choruses? – he slipped and stumbled upwards through a tunnel of boughs still heavy with yesterday's rain. I wondered at the merry larks they must have had climbing this in that scalp-flaying downpour, and queuing breathlessly behind three Frenchmen at one of the world's more incongruously sited Coke machines I found out.

'It's Tim and Shinto, right?'

My jaunty, packless interrogator was coming the wrong way, heading down the mountain. He knew me, but despite an unforgettable pupil-juggling squint I didn't know him. The price of conspicuous celebrity: it happened at least twice a day. Alan was a Canadian pastor, I learnt in his introductory sentence, and he'd come up to O Cebreiro the day before. 'Just came back to find out what it was like down here,' he said, addressing himself simultaneously to Santiago and Roncesvalles. 'Didn't see much in the rain.' A tight little smile – at the storm's ferocious apogee he'd been forced to wedge himself in a sheltered tree stump, watching as the path became a shin-deep torrent. The Frenchmen departed in a chorus of carbonated clicks and hisses; I flicked in my euro and a can dropped with a muffled, dungeon thump.

'Everyone asks why I'm doing this,' Alan suddenly proclaimed, even though to my certain knowledge I at least had not. His tone suggested a rather jarring upgrade from banter to sermon; in preference to the awkward lottery of eye contact I fussed minutely with the opening tab. 'And you know what, Tim?' I hazarded a quick glance at the bridge of his nose. 'I have no idea any more.'

'Not a . . . a Catholic, then.'

He took a deep, stagey breath of mountain air and angled his head back towards the unseen summit, like a television historian preparing to announce, 'And it was here, on a crisp June morning not unlike this . . .' There was certainly nothing in his demeanour to suggest that he was about to say what he did, which, in tones of breezy liberation, was this: 'I don't believe in heaven or hell, Tim, or that Jesus died for our sins. Boy, did Christianity fuck up 2,000 years back.'

Perhaps I coaxed out a laugh, but if I did it was as small and timid as an orphaned vole. What demonic work was this that sledgehammered the cornerstones of a curate's faith, that placed such vile heresies on holy lips, and that did all this on the sacred Way of St James? Before I could crystallise a coherent inquest into this evangelical meltdown, he clapped his hands on his haunches in rousing reassurance and made to continue downwards. 'Hey,' he said, checking himself and holding aloft a self-interrogative finger. 'I'm walking backwards, right?' A wet-lipped, leering smile made the bottom half of his face as alarming as the top. 'Maybe that means I can do a little more sin, huh?' He essayed a curious little half-jig and those Picasso eyes danced with asymmetric mischief. 'Maybe I could . . . *push over that Coke machine!*'

'Maybe you could,' I agreed in measured tones, taking a

small step into the muddy space that separated pastor from appliance, 'but please don't actually do that.' For a vivid moment that strange face was alive with unhinged brinkmanship; then with a superfluous roll of the eyes and a get-outta-here hand-swish, he walked off in search of his lost faith.

We passed a couple of *pallozas*, circular, shaggily thatched Asterix homes of Celtic design, and continued up the margin of a glorious overview of blue-misted, fat-treed valleyhood. Then the farm-fresh Alpine air carried across a thin suggestion of bagpipes and in a moment there we were by O Cebreiro's church, looking across at 'a tiny village of nine houses and another step back in time' or 'a camera-necked mass of coach-bound Austrian rent-a-pilgrims', depending whether you trusted the Confraternity guide or your own eyes.

It was a surprise more than a pity to find this fabled, almost mystical hamlet host to at least half a dozen inns and lodges of over-elaborately authentic construction. An eccentric priest had once serenaded his cattle with Bach blasting out of a huge PA speaker secreted in the church tower, but now the piped music of O Cebreiro is of the fluting, droning variety, and its audience the tourists wooed by taverners and the vendors of ethnic ceramics. Like the *pallozas*, Galicia's music – they call bagpipes *gaita* – is another link with the Celts who settled here in the fifth and sixth centuries after being harried from Britain by the Picts and Saxons. As indeed was Donald, waving happily through the window of what didn't look like his first bar of the day.

I left Shinto to his publicity commitments in the churchyard and wandered in through the porch, happy at least that a village that had prospered from the old pilgrimage was doing so once again. And happy, like my medieval forebears, to have made it to this auspicious beginning-of-the-end, to an eminence imbued with such symbolism that it has attracted legends like Brits to brandy.

None more so than those witnessed in this church, for the chalice that lay somewhere at its dim, grey-washed fundament has been touted as the Holy Grail from which Jesus drank at the Last Supper. During a communion at some inevitably unknown date in the fourteenth century, the fêted receptacle cemented its claim with some hard-core transubstantiation: as the priest made with the wine and wafers they morphed into real blood and hunks of raw flesh. Even the statue of the Virgin leant over for a better look: 'What you done to my boy?' she should by rights have shrieked hysterically, but because this was medieval Spain she didn't. (Later, King Ferdinand and his Queen Isabella demanded to have the relics removed to a more impressive location, but – splendidly – the mule hired to handle the transport refused to budge, and they stayed put.)

I was shuffling along up the aisle towards these enchanted icons behind a hushed and dutiful tourist procession when a considerable commotion broke out to our rear. Shouts, laughs, and a stroboscopic frenzy of camera flash; I pushed through a few shell-suited bodies and outflanked a few more, and then, peering over the heads of the most diligent paparazzi, found my eyes blankly met by Shinto's. He had walked straight in through the tall, green church doors and now stood by the rearmost pew in mild perplexity, blinking as another delighted compact-zoomer snapped an album highlight. Inveigling myself to his side, I caught the rope and led Shinto outside through a corridor of Germanic enchantment, as proud and embarrassed as a father helping his infant tap-dancing prodigy down from a restaurant table. It was a moment of mane-ruffling incorrigibility, as oddly stirring in its way as that excretory trespass atop the Cruz de Ferro.

A delighted codger trotted forth from his grocery with an armful of old bread and a bulging carrier bag of grain; as Shinto ate from his hand and posed fetchingly for the redoubtable Austrians, the Dutch girl wandered ethereally up the roughly paved street behind a restless, zigzagging Sativa. In passing she whispered the conclusion that the portentous climb to O Cebreiro had offered her: 'The camino is about temptation and sadness.' I nodded as sagely as I felt able, then, watching the grocer ease another baton into Shinto's crumb-haired food-hole, felt myself succumb to O Cebreiro's mood of contemplative stocktaking.

Probing the dynamics of our relationship, I arrived at an arresting conclusion: Shinto's ingrained sloth was nothing more than the by-product of genius. Laziness is a luxury few animals have known and fewer still learnt to enjoy. That dog for one certainly hadn't – all that wasted energy, all that blind obedience. In the wild, of course, sloth usually meant death; for a domesticated animal the trade-off was a little more complicated. A beast of burden had to do his job or face being that dog's dinner, but there was nothing in the small print that said he had to do it with a smile or turn up for unpaid overtime.

I looked again at Sativa, scampering but ultimately subservient, and realised how much happier I felt with Shinto's free-spirited work-to-rule. His only duty was to himself, to do just enough to stop me throwing good barley after bad and abandoning him by the road. My gnawing fears that one day he would simply refuse to walk were misplaced: he knew exactly where that line was, and had been walking along it now for – ooooh – 620 kilometres.

On we went, out past the *refugio*, following a line of huge pylons up and over a forested escarpment. Everyone, it seemed, had encountered a camino *Doppelgänger*: only the day before Petronella and her dog-following compatriot had both unsettled locals with ashen double takes, and a week earlier Birna palely recounted exchanging mute waves with a good friend of ours as she drove past a bus; a phone call which can only have compromised this friendship confirmed that he had not left Ireland in months. It seemed appropriate that I had my close encounter with this phenomenon near O Cebreiro: topping a gentle false summit and glancing into a pine copse I found myself face to haunted face with the living image, the very spit of Kurt, who had died ten years before almost to the day, and was a cat.

After all that two-dimensional trudge, there was now much too much landscape. Epic prospects opened up on all sides, undulating, rain-fed fertility receding into a distant distance. It was like Wales with lizards; *How Green Was My Valley* isn't a question, but if it had been, then the answer here was Really Very. A monumental contemporary bronze of Santiago stood guard over a swooping descent through pimpernels and hazelnut trees: a gleeful swish of metal and Lycra on the neighbouring tarmac reminded me that it was here my friend Nicky's cycling companion had vaulted the handlebars and wound up in a ward. And because this was A Significant Place, she'd blamed divine retribution for their skimping at a *refugio* honesty box.

Gravity placed its firm hand on the Shinto arse, but though from hereon in the camino was helpfully marked with count-down-to-Santiago posts every half-click, he seemed to have an uncanny awareness of when I was trying for an official speed record. 'I don't know what to say, coach, it was all coming together, I felt good, I'm coming into the last 50 and then there's like this big load of dried cow shit at the side . . .' At the next village, another Hospital, the road bounced back upwards, and with unexpected violence: after 3 unholy kilo-metres we stood on frail and shaking legs at Alto de Poio, almost 100 metres above O Cebreiro.

This wasn't a town so much as a couple of head-of-the-pass bars either side of another quiet strip of the N6, but one of them had rooms and Petronella was sitting outside it in a receding triangle of late-afternoon sun. 'Looking good, Shinto,' she said, rising to manipulate the more tactile parts of his face. 'That spray for the little bugs must have helped.'

Cock, piss and tits. How had I forgotten? And so, watched by Petronella, another of her many middle-aged pilgrim compa-triots and, less intently, a trio of professionally bored Frenchmen, I lashed the unburdened Shinto to an adjacent garage door and swaddled his eyes with the strip of tablecloth that chef had used on him at Ponferrada. It was sad before I'd even started: hearing me prime and agitate that big blue bottle of badness, he flinched and ducked like a hapless POW at a mock execution.

Here was a scenario beyond any bestial rationalisation: Shinto might feasibly have been equipped to connect most of my previous maltreatments with his own cowardice or reluctance, but what had any donkey ever done to deserve this cold-hearted, systematic torture? I swallowed hard, shook again, and holding the trigger at arm's length let him have it square on the forelock. Shinto backed blindly away and flailed so violently that he head-butted the up-and-over garage door, a great basso profundo gonging that boomed out sickeningly and raised faces from many a beer at the windows of the bar opposite. All that to treat an area equivalent to half a cat's nose. By the time I'd finished, a huge toxic cloud hung over our corner of Galicia and Shinto, poor Shinto, was leaking mucus from all the many holes in his poison-plastered head.

The great thing about animals, though, other than the shortfall in intelligence and dexterity that enables us to rule the world, is their capacity to forgive and forget. (Realistically, it's probably just forget.) Less than half a minute later he was browsing blithely through the weeds, with only that discharge to remind me and the harrowed Dutchwomen of his recent passage through a blinded, nightmare realm of choking awfulness.

I checked in and hauled my stuff up another three flights of unlit stairs, then returned to ask the rather surly girl at the desk, or rather bar, if she could suggest a suitable overnight grazing area. '*Tengo un burro,*' I heard myself say once more, 'I have a donkey.' Her expression clouded, and after repetition did not clear. Following my third attempt she nodded, though with a lack of conviction that was justified when her hand stretched under the counter and emerged with a box of huge cigars. This was Galicia, I reminded myself, where they had their own language, and so it was mime time again, a small treat for the three aged locals hunched over small glasses of luminous alcohol at a table behind. '*Ah, un burro!*' she said, before immediately morphing her happy enlightenment into a giant, sulky so-what.

Her face was promptly replaced by her back, and as she

sauntered away down the bar I felt my pilgrim soul sullied by a grim lust for immediate revenge. But discretion proved the better part of valour, and it was only once she'd slopped us out a four-course pilgrim menu in a record thirty-five minutes – gruesome in most ways though at least devoid of tit-for-tat scabs and phlegm – that I crept outside and tied Shinto up at the distant end of her back yard. Just by the vegetable patch.

I'd been looking forward to the next day since the first big climb out of Villafranca. From Alto de Poio to Triacastela the camino dropped 700 metres in 12 kilometres: during that debilitating scramble at the end of the previous afternoon I had pictured Shinto trotting gleefully downhill at mane-fluttering velocity, building up an easy momentum that by rational calculation would set us up for the easiest 24-click day to date.

Conditions looked good, too, with our long, hard shadows spanning the quiet 8 a.m. tarmac and just a bracing hint of Alpine dew in the delicately herbal air. I walked briefly alongside a tiny Englishwoman on her second pilgrimage: 'As a C of E heathen I wasn't having their blasted compostela,' she announced scathingly, the first time in an age that I'd heard organised religion mentioned with any sense of pertinence.

It was as she walked off ahead down the open road, apologising at her need to press on, that I first accepted we weren't quite hitting our targets. My legs ached to bound down that invitingly sinuous descent with elastic, whistle-accompanied strides, but instead we were steadily slipping to a stiff-limbed, cortège shuffle. All that painfully acquired altitude was proving just as painful to offload. And the choral prod didn't work, not even when wielded with iron-throated abandon, not even when sharpened with the lyrical adulteration of Madonna's 'Like A Brayer', or 'Burn Donkey Burn' ('Shinto Inferno'), or 'Just Get A Sodding Move On' ('You Shiftless Wazzock') (*trad*). Shinto didn't even bother counterfeiting hunger or the usual crap-sniffing displacements: this was pure, stubborn inertia, and all those ruminations in praise of his finely calculated indolence were slowly returning to taunt me.

By the time the path left the road at Biduedo, I was hauling him along with glowering, manic resolve, the rope over my shoulder for extra leverage. Pilgrims squeezed past in pairs and trios, their bright and voluble expressions withering into baffled concern as they took in my toiling, hunchbacked stance. Sweat embittered with the essence of pure frustration sequinned my brow and coursed into the eyeholes below, smearing out a gorse-thicketed hillscape: I'd hoped to be in Triacastela for lunch, and at 12.00 we weren't yet halfway.

When the descent tilted recklessly into a dappled corridor of ash and holly I went round the back and pushed, a hot hand on each recalcitrant, grizzled buttock. The path re-crossed the N6, and as I laboured him over the dotted white line Shinto dug in for a last stand. A rare vehicle was gunning down towards us in low gear, maybe three bends up; that nearest corner was blind, and as I'd been severally reminded nothing dispatched more pilgrims to premature paradise than road traffic. I leant and shoved and bellowed, but the considerable pride he had invested in this show of resistance proved greater than my diminished physical reserves. With the still unseen motorist almost upon us I turned uphill, preparing to halt him with a frail and desperate *Railway Children* entreaty; as I did so, a hefty brown hand appeared on my shoulder.

'*Tranquilo, tranquilo,*' breathed its large, vested owner; I surrendered, silently anticipating a demonstration of donk-lore distilled through many rural generations, and being therefore rather taken aback when my Samaritan snatched up the rope in both hands and yanked with such explosive, roaring gusto that I cringed my eyes shut, expecting when I opened them again to see Shinto's tattily severed head flying over the tree-tops, trailing its rope like a field event at the Mafia Olympics. Instead, just as the car shot past in a cloud of horn noise, I beheld those huge yellow eyes, suddenly limpid and conciliatory, looking back at me across the tarmac.

The outskirt villas of Triacastela were now watching us through the hefty oaks, but it was clear that we'd not be going much further that day. I could usually depend on a road gang for some spirited taunting, but when the four blokes peering out of a pathside trench took in Shinto's laboured stumbling they issued only a muted round of sombre applause, as if watching the last finisher in a marathon stagger drunkenly up to the line. A concentration of sun-hatted loungers by a whitewashed building in a field up ahead alerted me to the *refugio*'s proximity, and we were perhaps 15 yards from the indicated turn-off when the camino was traversed by a grate-covered drain. I planted a foot on it and Shinto froze at my side, like a cartoon pointer dog. Only once, on the first day, had he expressed serious concern at such an entity; and this, with a span of perhaps 6 inches, was handsomely the poxiest non-obstacle he had yet refused.

After all the day's travails we'd both had enough of physical force. I sat down against a dusty, lizarded wall on the other side of the grate, pulled my hat down over my face, and waited. And ate, and waited, and slept.

'Perhaps it looks like a cattle-grid to him,' said the voice that roused me. I jerked my head straight, stoutly smiting the wall behind, and found myself blearily contemplating the Englishwoman, heading a small crowd that had apparently wandered up from the *refugio* and now formed a semicircle around Shinto. Heavy lids, lowered head – he seemed to have downshifted into stand-by mode, like an unattended laptop. Arching my back and smothering an epic yawn, I critically surveyed those modest galvanised louvres at his feet. 'Perhaps,' I conceded at length, 'but what we've got here is more of a gerbil-grid.'

I creaked upright and took stock of what, before a North European audience, had just become a rather diminished pool of options. The Lilja Method was by far the most humane, but when my proffered handful of wild barley earned only blank rejection and the bursting snort of poorly stifled sniggers, I strode purposefully through the pilgrims – largely French, as that sibilant muttering made plain – and bid them stand aside. Once Shinto's stolid hindquarters lay at the end of a cleared corridor I inhaled prodigiously, and before I could change my mind charged through the sunburn and sandals, shrieking and clapping like an ergot-addled peasant. The corridor widened dramatically, a flock of birds took panicked flight, and, waiting until I was almost upon him, Shinto took the solitary lethargic step that was all I required.

'Blimey,' breathed the Englishwoman as I picked up the rope and prepared to lead Shinto away with what little dignity could be rationally justified.

'*Mais . . . ça va pas!*' came a shriller voice, a voice which swiftly rose in timbre and volume to a piping blast of accusatory outrage. *Affreux . . . anglais . . . agressif:* I didn't catch much, but what I did was more than enough. The phrase 'living-room tou-tou' marched impressively into my hot head, and I swiftly formulated a furious bilingual riposte about this theme with which to wheel round and counter-attack my accuser. I never did, though. Partly because nobody would have understood, not even me, and partly because I had suddenly and alarmingly pictured Shinto as my child, and considered in this light what I had just done represented an act of cruel and certainly unusual punishment. That was rubbish too, of course – what was I going to do, shoulder all his bags and give him a piggyback? – but it still seemed a tough brief, defending myself against a charge of screaming at a laden animal.

Clearly the *refugio* was no longer an option, and tying a slouched Shinto to a tree on the verge by a town-centre supermarket I cobbled together an alternative: stock up here with overnight supplies, and strike camp in that field over the road. That would do. Or rather it wouldn't, because when I came out with my arms stretched taut by carrier bags of tinned fish and ale, he was down. On his side, not this time in luxuriating repose but enfeebled collapse, one set of panniers pinned beneath him and the other rising and falling to quick and shallow breaths. Dragging my provisions I rushed over like Groucho Marx, yanked out the underside saddlebags and managed, with some effort, to heave that huge head off the grass and into my lap. He wheezed out a soul-rending gurgle, an awful, obstructed sniff through some matter-clotted life-pipe, and as I looked into his glassy, dimming eyes I felt my own sting and leak. Oh, Shinto, not like this, not here, half on the pavement outside a Super Spar.

And what could I do? I had a phone, but taking my previous donkey-related exchanges with the people of Galicia as a guide, any SOS call would result in a visit from a twenty-four-hour mobile tobacconist. Two elderly ladies walked up, arm in arm, but allowed us a generous berth, flicking a rather-you-than-me look as if I was helping a stricken tramp to vomit. A bus driver slowed to allow his fare-paying vultures an enthralled gloat, and the supermarket manager stood in his threshold wearing an expression of commercial concern. '*Burro* doctor?' I called out pleadingly, causing Shinto to lever himself effortfully erect. The manager's eyes dilated, and looking up I saw why: Shinto's entire flank was afoam with bubbling death-sweat, a thick, slick slather of heavy froth. '*Burro* doctor!' A more urgent yelp, but the glass door was already swinging closed behind him. With a geriatric, grunting huff Shinto laid himself down beside me once more; my lap hurt, and so I inveigled his granite skull on to my shins. And as I did a burst of familiar yapping broke out, and there was Sativa, and her owner, and a lanky fellow of Mediterranean appearance.

'My friend Ramon has a telephone,' said the woman I now knew to be Letje, appraising the situation succinctly. Ten minutes later a chubby, smoking vet pulled his Citroën up on to the grass, and by the time he'd trotted over, additional vehicles were disgorging supplementary vets on both sides of the street. The final tally was four.

Like a child at the doctor's Shinto perked up immediately, jumping to his feet and rediscovering an interest in the newly turfed grass around. The terminal froth-bubbles were the only obvious symptom of his malaise; a svelte young lady vet palmed off a sample and rubbed it dubiously between her thumb and forefingers. A sniff, and a smile: it was my multi-purpose washing-up liquid, fractured in Shinto's collapse. Her colleagues fussed about his head, and the one who spoke

English asked a few questions before delivering a prognosis I had myself begun to suspect: that tick spray was completely inappropriate for equine use, and Shinto had in consequence suffered an asthmatic reaction.

That beastly, chiding Frenchwoman had been more right than I'd wanted to think: like a cold-souled guard on the Burma railway, I had force-marched the sick to work. 'Just some little rest, maybe he is OK tomorrow,' he reassured me as his co-vets began to depart the scene with good-luck waves and toots. I held my money belt out helplessly, and he waved a mockingly reproachful finger at it. 'No, no. You come . . . I show you place to rest.' Ramon had gone, and as I led Shinto into line behind the Citroën pootling back up the hill I thanked Letje and asked her to thank him. 'He is on the path to wisdom,' she called out over her shoulder, ideally meaning 'Righty-ho', before ineffectively calling Sativa to heel.

Fifteen minutes later we followed my lovely vet up a brief drive, and promptly found ourselves in the grassy forecourt of a modest but attractive detached home. He swung open the car door and slipped chirpily out. 'Here?' I said, uncertainly contemplating the fruit trees and garden furniture and imagining them respectively stripped bare and hosed in allergenic slurry. 'Sure, of course,' he said, stroking that shirt-stretching stomach with proprietorial satisfaction. '*Burro* here, you there.' He inclined his head at the front door. 'Is my house.'

Mario was his name, and no sooner had he deposited my stuff in the guest room than the phone rang, heralding much manipulation of that iron-filing stubble, his fifth cig of the hour and, with the receiver down, a faltering explanation of pressing cow matters. 'My girlfriend Maria here soon,' he fumbled, scribbling something on a drug-company note pad and instructing me to pass it on to her. And with a wink, a toothy Latin smile and a genial slap on the back he was off, leaving me alone with his Led Zep and 'Legalise Pot' posters, an enormous library of DVDs and a menagerie whose Ark-like abundance would become shortly apparent.

Mario and Maria? It all seemed a little unlikely. Such

trusting good nature was so alien to a suspicious urbanite that I felt almost bemused: if not a miracle, this was at least a bona fide parable. I'd read some Englishman's contention that 'luck on the camino is 2 to 3 per cent greater than it should be', and here was the tangible evidence to verify that apparently ridiculous statistic. From the kitchen I watched Mario drive back out and off up the road, then looked down at Shinto, now happily embarked once more on his mission in life, the processing of lawn into crap.

Imagine for a moment that your partner is a veterinarian of unusual enthusiasm, and that you are not. Your homes are separated by a three-hour drive, and conflicting patterns of work restrict your time together to a single weekend a month. After two years you have perhaps become accustomed to the reality that this weekend will be regularly interrupted by bovine miscarriage and bastard strangles, and that when it is you will be left alone in a small house with six relentlessly voluble canaries, a tiny dog of similar persuasion, two tanks of fish, four mewling newborn kittens and a shelf replete with jars containing the pickled embryos of memorably deformed cattle. But now imagine that you arrive at the Friday afternoon commencement of one of these rare weekends to find your partner absent, that offbeat petting zoo supplemented by a foaming donkey and his master, and the unkempt, foreign latter bearing a foolish smile and a note ordering you to feed and entertain him.

And yet having read this, Maria – auburn and petite with a smile as ready as her cheerful beau's – elected not to slop me out a bucket of twin-headed-calf tripe on the doorstep, but instead sat me down at a little round table which she began to fill with the fruit of Galicia's arable cornucopia. Dark, cured *chorizo* that cast my daily sarnie-filler in the most unflattering epicurean light, a decayed pastille of greying dairy matter that offended every sense but taste, a winning marriage of rich cream cheese and honey, and all this washed down with crisp local beer that demanded the back of a hand to be drawn across a grateful mouth.

281

We talked as we ate. I learnt of Galicia's difficult history, a poverty so endemic that – another link with the Scots and Irish – economic migration has been a way of life for 500 years. I learnt that jobs are still hard to come by in Galicia, explaining that ludicrous monthly commute from her IT post in the coastal city of Ferrol, and I learnt that ten in the native dialect was pronounced 'death'. 'Mario, his shoes are always with the shit of the cows,' said Maria in a mock moan, and yet her man plainly adored the animals in whose company he spent the vast bulk of his professional hours. As well as that distressing homage to foetal mutation, there were cow posters on the walls, cow milk jugs in the kitchen, and even, on a shelf by the huge flat-screen telly that was his extracurricular existence in the pre-Maria period, the scale representation of a Friesian pelvis.

Overwhelmed with calories and kindness, I dearly hoped Maria would now allow me to wash up, or perhaps even deworm a couple of budgies. Instead I was led outside. 'We go to Samos,' she said, opening the passenger door of her Renault Clio and ushering me in. 'Is old *monasterio* of six century.' But I wasn't listening. Gingerly lowering myself to the velour I felt a rush of primal vitality spark through every neurone in my body, a rush that came out of my mouth as an ineffectively smothered whoop of exultation when she fired up the engine and reversed slowly away from a suddenly curious Shinto. I was in a car, and it was moving.

We rolled on to the tarmac, she engaged first and soon we were travelling at a velocity that was literally superhuman, and for the first time in my life actually felt like it. If speed was indeed a drug then I'd been cold turkey for five weeks, surely the longest since my father had driven his wife and last-born child away from the maternity hospital in a Ford Zephyr. I gathered from Maria's commentary that we were passing through a valley of big beauty and histories, but all I cared about was sensing it swish by. I felt my scalp shrink as the kilometre posts thwicked past, my brain unwilling to accept what my eyes were telling it, that what had been taking twenty weary minutes or more was now, as we hit mean Spanish cruising speed, a matter of thirty carefree seconds. It was too fast, but then it wasn't fast enough, and as we pulled up outside a large institution of ecclesiastical aspect I was rocking forward and back in my seat, a child coaxing the last vestiges of momentum from his go-kart.

Maria did her best to enthuse me at Samos, pointing out the monks tending its garden, the scallop shells on its railings, its general ancient vastness. I tried, I really did: slowly pacing the perimeter with my hands linked behind my back in academic rumination, gamely nodding – the works. 'Is one of most old and most big in Spain,' she said, and I raised a dutiful eyebrow. Samos was off the route but a popular option with the sort of pilgrim who didn't mind an additional 9 clicks; why, look – there's Donald, hoisting a beer at us from that bar. Regrettably, though, the monastery's sombre façade arrestingly incorporated a petrol station: one look at the pumps and I felt an itching desire to reprise my performance as an unsophisticated Victorian ruralite on his first train ride. 'Listen, this is all great, Maria,' I said as we walked past the forecourt, 'but I feel we ought to be heading back.' At immense and glorious speed.

Mario was slumped in front of that huge telly when we got back, showered and happily knackered, another notch on his calving forearm. We shared more beers, and talked merry garbage to the accompaniment of flamenco and progressive rock, and posed for a self-timer shot I have before me now: the three of us huddled together, four tanned hands on neighbouring shoulders and a small pet in the spare two, fag smoke rising from a table full of bovine-themed crockery and empty bottles. The frame before depicts Shinto's dead-eyed head on my lap, taken for the reference of veterinarian or coroner, and as I rapped my donkey goodnight on the window and drooped towards that lovely guest bed, what had seemed the worst day of my pilgrimage was ending as one of its very best.

*　　*　　*

I was up with the lark, or rather the skull-shuddering bray, and leaving a fond note of thanks against a ceramic udder by the phone dragged my bags out into the chilled half-light. And there was Shinto, contemptuously staring out a plump brown dog as its owner slowly brushed his mane. 'It's quarter to seven,' I said, in a tone better suited to a slightly smaller hour. Letje looked up with a distant, *Mona Lisa* smile. 'Ramon found this address for me. I have met so many people who live in a completely different dimension.'

As Mario had predicted, Shinto was a different animal after his lay-up. And just as well, as the camino's last great climb began just outside Triacastela, a sunless slog up through chestnuts and crippled hamlets that Sativa's darting, barking underfoot presence and Letje's gnomic pronouncements didn't make any easier. 'I feel a strong light in my heart,' she panted dramatically as the track tilted upwards, 'and the light is blue.' Then the chestnuts eased back and we were up on the brow, stout, fat-headed oaks straight from Hampshire theatrically sidelit by a low sun that cast long shadows across copper-misted pastures.

The camino broadened into a fat swathe of fire-break, and as the Triacastela overnighters caught us we gradually found ourselves part of a pilgrim army, three or four abreast, marching to folk songs bellowed magnificently by a pair of hugely gay Italians. 'A true spirit sings in their sleep,' opined Letje, moving ever closer to a conversation composed entirely of slogans culled from Japanese sportswear.

A scowl, a tut and a Shinto-directed 'Oh, *mon brave*' heralded the passing of that Frenchwoman, and then there was Ramon, balefully hungover. His presence procured a brief respite from the one-sided exchange of obscurely epic platitudes and those manic convulsions of baseless laughter. 'Ramon's aura was not so good last night,' Letje murmured after he'd stumbled fiercely by, 'and I think he is now a little angry that I don't walk with him.'

'He is?' Ramon was young, wiry and by Spanish standards a freakish giant.

'Yes, and when he is angry . . .' She shook her head in harrowed recollection of some Ramonian act of malevolence.

'Ramon is your . . . boyfriend, then,' I said, my voice tinged with concern.

Letje emitted a grandiose snort of derision. 'This is maybe *his* belief.'

Now near the back of the column we began to descend through a landscape of lurid, rustic abundance, the greenometer turned up to eleven. Fields divided not with fences but palae-olithic slabs of slate, a woman chasing a horse round her farm-yard, an old Escort with a hay-bale wedged in its boot, a proud family in their Saturday best off to market in the back of a tractor trailer. This land was rich but its people clearly were not: the camino pulled a little train of foreign wealth through the poorest parts of a poor region, and in contrast to their neighbours the Galicians were keen to nurture and harvest this in a regulated manner.

The pilgrimage infrastructure had been lavishly overhauled for the 1993 Holy Year – fountains like the splendid scallop-shell grotto we passed that morning, all those marker posts and a network of staffed *refugios* constructed to a standard design. And the locals had warmed to the task, sticking Coke machines in their farmyards and opening up craftily sited cafés at likely break stops, such as the place everybody piled dustily into for elevenses. 'She didn't spill that on you,' intoned Letje as an errant French elbow knocked steaming chocolate into my lap, 'but on the world that she hated.'

The heat that Mario had declared almost unheard of for this time of year got going as we emerged. Farmyard filth should have held no olfactory terrors for me by now, but the sun-ripened slurry and silage were so cloyingly over-fermented that I began to dry retch. And retch and retch and retch, as Shinto pressed his snout to the pat-splattered path and progressed with savouring sloth.

During that coffee break I'd mentioned to Letje that I still had no idea what to do with Shinto when we reached Santiago, and she'd instantly thrown her hat into the empty ring. 'As a little girl I had a pony,' she blurted, in her excitement absent-mindedly casting a small shaft of light into the otherwise pitch-black cupboard of her life history, 'and I am walking back to Holland.' Her eyes began to shine. 'Now I could be the girl with the dog *and* the donkey.' She had expanded on this theme over lunch, and after it I could see her casting covetous, dreamy glances at Shinto, already imagining the airy romance of a Vaseline-lensed return journey as she led her winsome menagerie through the wild-flowered meadows with an enigmatic half-smile. It would be like a three-month shampoo advert.

This should have been a special moment for me, too: I'd proved extremely adept at blanking out Shinto's post-pilgrim-age fate, even as the issue grew into a colossal, long-eared silhouette on a steadily advancing horizon, and now a solution had dropped into my chocolate-stained lap. Yet all I felt was an odd but powerful resistance. Though it apparently hadn't troubled me as I'd barged him wheezing into Triacastela, the concern was Shinto's welfare. With an equine heritage Letje would be kind and probably responsible, but it didn't take an animal psychologist – though by Christ what I'd have done for one – to deduce that Shinto really, really hated that hyper-active, barrel-bellied yapper.

What made this especially entertaining was Letje's convic-tion that the two of them had struck up a quirky inter-species friendship, like one of those 'Just Fancy That' pictures of a fox touching noses with a rabbit or something. 'See this – they are playing!' she'd exclaim, and I'd turn to see Sativa barking frenziedly up at Shinto from close range, while he gazed down his long nose with a look that neatly blended scorn with pity. At lunch Sativa had leapt up and nipped Shinto on the back of the knee as he grazed; with faultless technique he'd cast a lazy glance at Letje, and satisfied to see her scanning the rear-ward heavens with an air of poetic auspice had flicked out a robust rear-hoofed punt that filled the hot afternoon with whining yelps. 'Oh, you missed it,' I sighed, as Letje swivelled about in concern. 'They just did this really sweet thing with their . . . their legs.'

In a very real way, it had brought my donkey and me closer: we had this thing together, that we both despised that dog. The two of us had been bound by a common love for my family, but the emotional adhesive here was somehow stronger. I'm sorry, modern Christianity, but nothing unites like a hatred shared.

'You have some water for me,' ordered Letje when we shuffled into Sarria, up a pavement laid from the dismantled ruins of its castle. It was perhaps the fifteenth time I'd thus supplied her that day, and the lunch she'd eaten had also come straight from the canteen on Shinto's back. Exploiting his capacity to provide for others always gave me a small thrill of logistical fulfilment, the same thrill that I feel when the rear-facing seats in my Volvo estate are pressed into service, but after the next cadged swig I felt obliged to enquire as to the contents of her own modest pack. 'Just some clothes and toothbrush,' she said, unhappy to find herself in a conversation debased by such trivial drudgeries. 'Ramon had many bottles. I don't find it important to carry food and water.'

'No, you don't,' I said with perfect neutrality.

Were Shinto and I merely the latest stooges to accept gullibly a baton most recently dropped by Ramon? Or – dread alternative – one he believed I had snatched from his angry Latin hands? Either way I was eyeing Letje rather more carefully. And for her part, she had grown palpably disillusioned with my cosmic inadequacy: in essence, I was just far too silly an arse.

Digital photography has much to commend it, but in puerile hands that profligate immediacy can become a curse. Panic fluttered my innards as I returned from a behind-bush comfort stop to see Letje idly beeping through the day's images.

'What is this?'

I looked over her shoulder: it was a snap I'd taken in the bar where we'd had our morning coffee. 'Um . . . well, that's a bottle of gin, I believe.'

'Yes – this we have at home. Fockink Dry Gin.'

I didn't quite know what to do with my face, though when

she repeated the phrase with quizzical deliberation it began to crease and pucker compromisingly. 'Ah, yes,' she said, nodding scientifically. 'You laugh because the sound is a little like another word.' I shrugged feebly. 'The word of fucking.'

That night I checked through the shots she'd have scrolled through to reach that one. There were three, and two depicted Shinto's anus at full and monstrous dilation during an epic act of voidance. The third was of a poster advertising some forth-coming night of modest parochial revelry, or at least a close-up of the incorporated legend 'Océano e Cunters'.

Sarria was built up a hill, and with the shadows at their short-est Shinto downshifted in treacled reluctance. We lurched unsteadily up the precipitous main street, beneath pilgrim washing lines strung from the *refugio*'s upper windows, and though her rhapsodic camino persona proscribed displays of frustration, I could see a little enthusiasm trickle from Letje's open features. This trickle became an unstaunchable flood when, having very nearly failed to cross a railway line half an hour outside town, Shinto eased to a halt, with an air of up-to-the-buffers finality, before a broad and lazy stream traversed by a rude wooden bridge.

'He will not cross this?' she asked, frankly incredulous, as I paid out the long rope and walked across to the opposite bank. There was a sudden aquatic commotion, and we looked back to see Sativa hanging by her jaws from the rope, hind legs thrashing the water in search of purchase. Shinto surveyed the scene with an air of disappointment, flinching in distaste more than fear as the dog relinquished its quarry and churned hysterically across to us. 'Certainly not now,' I said.

To her credit Letje refused to accept this verdict. Determined not to give up that Timotei dream without a fight she beck-oned Shinto with encouraging clucks, then tugged tentatively on the rope, and finally let the mask slip with a red-faced, double-fisted yank that left her panting, furious and prostrate. 'Your animal has a personality defect,' she rasped, spanking dust off her canvas pedal pushers and glowering over at Shinto, his eyes half-closed like a contented cat by the fire. 'He is . . . *autistic!*' I knew exactly what Letje was going through, but having gone through it so many times now found myself infused with an almost saintly calm.

With tree-filtered sun speckled across the path and bejewelling the gentle water that traversed it this was a capital spot; I went over to extract a carton of rosé acquired during that ill-fated dash round the Spar in Triacastela. Settling myself down on a smooth rock I tore the carton open and offered it to Letje, who with brittle thanks declined. After an extended, throat-bobbing swig I wiped my mouth and announced I didn't really care what happened, that I'd camp here if it came to that. 'Sitting on the Dock of the Bay' came to my lips and stayed there in a nonchalant and, in hindsight, infuriating hum, and presently Letje blurted a curt farewell and marched off up the stream's impressively severe valley with Sativa in noisy tow.

For a peaceful hour we rested, the two of us flat-lining either side of the bridge. At 6.00 the mosquitoes started to bite, and feeling that perhaps I ought to do something I sluiced the remaining wine into the stream, ambled over the bridge and led Shinto back up across the train tracks. There was an alternative path of sorts, running parallel to the railway's lofty embankment in vaguely the right direction, but it proved no beaten track. Within 50 yards the undergrowth was overgrowth: I looked behind and only Shinto's ears were visible. Wrestling through the shrubs and saplings we presently arrived at the same stream, here swollen to twice its previous girth. It was a merrily hopeless scenario.

'OK, Shints, we're just going to walk across this now,' I announced, in a voice stoutly purged of defeat or desperation. As the water topped my right boot, some gifted clairvoyant behind the controls of a distant locomotive applied his shrillest klaxon, and a busy moment later I was on the other side, drenched and laughing and leading a newly alert Shinto towards an arch cut through the embankment.

I met Donald a click and a bit up the road: roused by Letje's desperate prognosis he'd been dispatched from the *refugio* on a salvage mission. He placed a beer in my hand and a hand on my shoulder – tea and sympathy à la Scotsman. 'Post-traumatic distress counselling,' he smiled, and though by standards of certain early evenings I in fact felt jauntily chipper, this was another humbling moment. Twice in two days the milkman of human kindness had left me an extra pint.

Donald led us up to Barbadelo, a trim but ancient hilltop hamlet now dominated by one of those nineties *refugios*, its whitewashed concrete already mossed by the Galician elements to a simulacrum of some wartime military installation. Both floors were loudly replete with the energetic young Spaniards whose presence would from hereon be a bracing ubiquity, but somehow Petronella had fended them off to save me a bunk by the window. I went to hug her and . . . there they went, a tear down each crimson cheek.

Letje was laying her stuff out under a lean-to by the municipal football pitch that fronted the *refugio*: as so often, Sativa's presence excluded her from an indoor berth. We exchanged conciliatory smiles as I led Shinto to the distant tangle of wild peas and clover that would be his campsite, but this was to be our final encounter.

Sucking up peasant broth with Donald and Petronella at the village's solitary commercial establishment I began to curse myself for the gratuitous folly that had effectively spurned the first and only offer to address the post-Santiagan Shinto situation. Why had I done this? In terms of that awful dog Shinto could have looked after himself: one well-timed kick and she'd be canine history. Perhaps, after all, it was envy – if Letje had welcomed the camino into her soul, then I remained a spiritual pygmy, scrabbling foolishly through the transcendental low-ground as all the Big Answers passed overhead.

We were halfway through our digestifs, this time, at Donald's insistence, a fearsome local distillation known as *aruxo*, when Ramon strode sternly in. I gulped reflexively, never a good idea with a throatful of over-proof lava, and expectorating alcohol into my cupped hands wondered if this would end in awkwardness, humiliation or both and a good shoeing. Ramon stopped at the head of our table and closed his eyes. 'De beauty is seemple of trust and pain,' he intoned, palms held up as if weighing each word individually. And when he opened his eyes again with a smile of apologetic glee, I wasn't the only one choking.

Fourteen

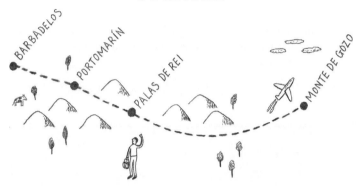

It had been a moist night, and as I re-pegged my still-damp laundry to Shinto's saddle an ancient rustic ambled by with a scythe over his shoulder; another in a wide-brimmed felt hat sat against the base of a garlanded stone crucifix up the road. The yellow arrows around here were occasionally supplanted by a red cross of Santiago, but daubed on boarded-up hovels these succeeded only in casting a bring-out-your-dead contagion on the more conspicuously abandoned hamlets.

This was perhaps the most impoverished area we'd yet traversed, and it was ever thus. The ground floors of most of the older farmhouses were illuminated feebly by slitted openings in the stonework – not, as I'd first thought, for shooting arrows through but keeping burglars out. Even the little corn cribs outside every farm, so like oriental shrines with their stilts and narrow pitched roofs, were treble padlocked.

Yet this was already becoming one of my favourite days. I'd long since given up trying to walk behind Shinto, like a true drover, and so was astounded when I went back to retrieve a wet sock that had snagged in a pathside vegetative tangle and saw that for once he hadn't stopped to wait. I retrieved the rope and held my station at his rump; he ambled forth. After more than a month of palm-flaying yanks and hauls, this was very heaven, this donk-cam view of bucolic vitality, the Thomas Hardy meadows bordered with dry-stone walls and foxgloves, the sturdy trees bursting into the flawless sky like mushroom clouds. The fat of the land had never been more chubbily larded.

Another smart local entrepreneur had opened up a little bar just past the 100-kilometres-to-go post – its digits almost illegible beneath marker-penned autographs – and there were two separate parties in permanent, rolling progress. One for the *arriviste* young Spaniards, and the other for the weathered long-haulers, respectively commiserating over their huge outstanding task or toasting each other in mute, rapt disbelief that so little remained. A hundred clicks was the papally authenticated minimum tariff to procure a compostela; from hereon in the camino could seem a parade more than a pilgrimage, with a knock-on effect upon room-at-the-inn ratios.

Counting down into double figures also had the effect of concentrating my attention on the pressing issue of Shinto's fate: I could be in Santiago in five days. Tragedy in the form of disease, theft or accident had for weeks seemed the likeliest settler of his destiny; in recent days, as our safe arrival became a realistic possibility, I'd been hitherto reluctant to tempt fate via any contemplations that would constitute taking it for granted. Only now that I'd palmed away a solution did I find myself considering the problem in sobering earnest. Throughout my rural peregrinations I had encountered fewer than half a dozen rival donks; the probability of finding Shinto a home in Santiago or indeed anywhere in Spain had never seemed more hopelessly remote.

On I strode, back-seat droving up gentle hill and down modest dale, viewing a happy world past a chaos of straps and panniers and laundry, that half-baguette sticking out of a plastic bag and neatly bisecting the gap between Shinto's pricked ears. Life at the back end had its downside: now handed executive control for route planning, Shinto displayed an infallible sense for the absurdly wrong-headed. Follow that army of walkers up the straight, broad path ahead or veer purposefully into a foot-wide gap in the hedgerow? Left fork, or right fork, or – hang on – how about between those two tractors, round the corn crib and into that tiny dark barn? For Shinto there was only ever one option. Once he even tried to climb in through the open rear doors of a Transit van.

If that was a blow to this bold new initiative, then the death knell was struck in a cloud of dust and hoofs as the path narrowed into an oak-shadowed corridor between pastures. A leathery cowman was ululating his herd from field to camino just ahead, and clapping Shinto into a burst of speed I just managed to get past the gate before the lead cow blocked our way. Or so I thought until we meandered round the next dappled bend, and there, spanning the camino broadside on and scrutinising us with clueless intensity, was the true front runner: a bull-horned, tan-hided colossus, half a ton of milk monster.

Neck bells and the cowman's guttural encouragement were gaining from behind; stuck fast at a cock-eyed twenty to two, Shinto's ears elucidated his mounting concern. I would be a liar if I said I wasn't a little worried myself. In fact, I would be a liar if I said I wasn't very close to tears. The cow ahead turned to face us head on and rasped out a noise that explored the overlap between moo and roar, a noise whose galvanising effect was instantly translated into the more urgent hammering of rearward hoofs. With the beef sandwich about to spread itself in pilgrim chutney, Shinto abruptly charged forwards into a gap that wasn't there. But somehow he made one, and with my left-hand daypack strap swishing against a horn tip and the right snagging a tangle of hedgerow, somehow I followed him through. I re-established contact with Shinto half a breathless click up the road, and once I had it was clear that from now on I'd be back up the front.

The first of the day's two auspicious phone calls was taken in our lunch-time field, as I crouched camera-faced by Shinto's raised tail, poised to capture the anus-domed breaking of wind that would complete my excretory trilogy. It was from my brother Simon, at a loose end and a low ebb after a brutal cull at his place of employment, stating that he fancied popping out for a bit of a walk; quite soon, perhaps; in fact why not tomorrow. That was good news, and the second brought more of the same, received just after a rather stilted wave at the straight-faced farmer who had clearly been contemplating my photographic performance over the gate for some time.

'Tim? It is Hanno.'

He was answering a text message I'd sent him the night before, desperate for guidance with my impending donkey surplus. But there was a lot more to say; too much, indeed, particularly at £900 a syllable. Hanno was reasonably dumbfounded to hear that my partnership with Shinto had somehow survived nearly six weeks of cack-handed, cack-hoofed fear and ineptitude, and having heard coughed out a query.

'Uh, *alors*, you have ideas how to do with Shinto in Santiago?'

This was the very question I had texted him, but having fielded it myself at least five times a day I allowed the default response to trip thoughtlessly off my tongue. 'I'm going to beat him to death with a chair on the cathedral steps.'

'*Comment?*'

'No, well, there was some Dutch girl with a fat dog, but she had a blue light in her heart.'

'Ah . . . Tim?'

'I've really no idea, Hanno. Sorry. I was hoping you might have some suggestions.' I remembered him mentioning a live-stock market in Santiago, but now a familiar image crystallised in my head, of Shinto gambolling in slow motion through a Pyrenean pasture towards a whinnying throng of eager donkeys. Hanno butted in before I got to the bit where they shoved him up against the caravan.

'It has been sad for my family without Shinto,' he began, causing me to recall those farewell tears, 'and for the other donkays also.' I heard him suck in and exhale. 'Tim.' A new and forthright tone. 'I ask to take Shinto back.'

Never have six words that didn't include 'explicit', 'chilli' or 'free' made me so happy. So happy, indeed, that after a rather one-sided bout of donk-trading I found I had agreed to compensate Hanno fully for the 2,300-kilometre, five-day round trip required. Instead of trading Shinto in for a profit, I'd just committed myself to the lavish funding of his joyous return from Santiago. And I had done so because he had earned a reward, and not one that saw him ending his days in seedy-toed solitude, lashed to the shafts of a Galician scrap merchant's wagon with a nosebag full of slops and sawdust. I had done so because I wanted to see him happy. Because . . . because, heck, I loved that great big fool.

I was gaining a brother, and losing a donkey. It was big news, which I vainly endeavoured to process as the camino plunged down to the banks of a mighty, dammed river. The town at the distant end of an interminable bridge handled by Shinto with brittle composure was Portomarín, built in 1962 to replace its ancient forebear, lost beneath the waters when the valley was flooded for hydroelectric purposes. That four-square Romanesque fortress of a church was moved up the gorge to the site of the new town block by shed-sized block; in 1998, when the reservoir was briefly drained, the church peeked down at the slathered ruins of its former home, Roman bridge, water mills and all.

For a town forty years old Portomarín had not aged well, cement barns shoulder to shoulder with homes and knackered warehouses up the main street. The whitewash was flaking and lichened, gutters ran up the middle of the road and the municipal pool was streaked and empty; Franco's civic ambience has much in common with Castro's. The generalísimo was a Galician. So was Fidel's granddad.

A round of sardonic British laughter diverted me towards a party of part-time pilgrims, halfway through an attractive two-week programme of guided rambling and bacchanalian indulgence, the fun run to our marathon. They offered me a glass from the one full bottle of white on a parasoled table of empties, and in return I offered them exclusive, first-rights news on Shinto's fate. Then Donald, Petronella and Evelyn wandered across from the adjacent *refugio* – walk a donkey into town and you might just as well have been preceded by trumpeting heralds – and I told them too. 'Well, you've got to get the animal there first,' said Donald, though I barely heard him above Petronella's sobbing. All three had scouted out a spot for Shinto round the back of a school, and as we led him there Evelyn removed her sunglasses to reveal a colossal aubergined bruise. 'Face down on the road to Samos,' she explained with a crooked smile.

The Portomarín *refugio* wasn't quite to the standard Galician design, but had certainly captured the spirit. Central to this was an enthusiastic embrace of the diminished expectations of personal privacy that had been part of pilgrim life since around the halfway stage. For weeks now we had lived with the lockless toilet and shower cubicle: some saw this as part of the shedding of physical insecurities in preparation for the looming spiritual rebirth, others as the gradual erosion of the norms of civilised human behaviour, depending on which side of the North Sea they lived. But in Galicia it all went a little fundamentalist. The curtainless, unisex showers of Barbadelo were perhaps the apotheosis of this trend, but it was at Portomarín, buttock to lathered buttock with Donald and a hairless Dane in the open bathing trough, sudded clothes underfoot, that I experienced its repulsive nadir. The loo door opposite us eased ajar, and there, huge pants billowed round swollen hairy ankles, sat the camino's fattest man; a young Spaniard who after the blind Japanese was only the second pilgrim I had beaten for pace over the course of a day. 'Please,' he quailed, his bristled moon of a face generously puckered in desperation, 'you find paper please?'

The curfew was half an hour later than usual, which at least afforded us a rare opportunity to experience dining amidst the crockeried babel of locals. We were joined by a French Canadian woman with her son, who had only started in Astorga and so found themselves vulnerable to our wined-up, road-weary condescension. Raising glass and voice above the clamour I held forth with alcoholic obstinacy on Flans I Have Known; Donald delivered a more thoughtful but no more concise address on the epic landscapes of the *meseta*.

It was only as we were into the brandies that the mother

quietly revealed her walk as a spiritual gesture for a dying friend. That was sobering, and it needed to be. Once we'd bid them farewell with muted contrition it all went rather maudlin. Bracing himself with the dregs of his snifter, Donald told us of the Spanish pilgrim who had arrived at Rabanal one evening during his tenure as *hospitalero*. 'I can keep that in the office if you like,' he'd offered, spotting a torch-sized silver phial in the man's hand as he filled in the register. Translations from a bilingual pilgrim in the queue and a quietly polite refusal; the man's ten-day-old son had died after a sudden seizure three weeks previously, and the phial contained his ashes.

Walking up the valley bank away from Portomarín, a medieval pilgrim must have believed he'd make it to Santiago now. This was the home straight, and he set off up it with a spring in his step and another down his pants: the stretch from here to Palas de Rei was a 24-kilometre al-fresco knocking shop, patrolled by prostitutes who would lure single males into the woods. 'These whores are not only to be excommunicated,' fulminates the *Liber Sancti Jacobi*, 'but also are to be held in shame by all and have their noses cut off.' Hardly the kind of morally edifying company you'd expect a pilgrim to keep, but by the cold logic of Catholic repentance, what did they have to lose? It would all come out in the Santiagan sin-wash.

Evelyn, Petronella and I set out into a heavy morning mist and up the wooded valley it filled: there were plenty of bare bottoms on show in the bushes, but only doing what I'd seen them do a hundred times before. For the contemporary pilgrim the sight of the finish line inspired not a frenzied venting of pent-up licentiousness but brooding introspection: our road-hardened bodies had now acquired resistance to pain and fatigue, and emotional strains came to the fore.

Many had come here to be left alone with their thoughts, but some looked as though they'd been locked up with them in a wardrobe for a month. Those who'd come to get away from something would soon have to go back and face it. For anyone expecting cosmic insights, or miracles, or spontaneous orgasms, impatience had been upgraded from disappointment to spirit-wringing anguish – particularly as it seemed the mystical rewards had been granted only to those who'd come with no such expectation. There were few pilgrims more doughtily sensible than Evelyn, but here she was cheerfully discussing her conversations with St James, typically held in the aftermath of those testing nose-to-the-tarmac moments, and asking if anyone else had found themselves walking with dead friends and relatives.

And yet the enforced meditation had unravelled lives more tangled and complex than the preposterous night knot that now attached Shinto. Souls had been searched for six weeks, and the figurative fugitives brought to book. A marriage would be ended, another salvaged. A new career, a new child, a new therapist. That afternoon I stopped stock-still: I hadn't given my father a birthday present for three years. Well, it was something.

Almost 150 pilgrims left Portomarín by Donald's reckoning, and by mine a good two-thirds of those were Spanish Jaime-come-latelies in jeans and fancy trainers. '*Buen camino!*' trilled each one in passing; perhaps the old me would have cracked a vainglorious sneer at this belated embrace of camino etiquette. (Though the old me came to the fore when a party of parvenu pilgrims buzzed by on matching mopeds. See you on Judgement Day, iron donkeys.) They passed as we wound through villages, where the dark faces now tracking us belonged to cows in barns rather than men in bars. They passed as a headscarfed young Bo Peep led a panicked bleater across the path, as a cow-dog rounded up an errant Friesian with an udder bag like a tandem Hippity Hop, as his master unleashed a rolling, resonant exhortation that precisely echoed the Hanno-noise I had so conspicuously failed to reproduce.

But pass they all did, and having rejoiced that I'd never again find myself hung out to dry and broil alone in a torpid afternoon, once Evelyn and Petronella succumbed to the need for speed and pressed on ahead, there I was doing just that. I sloped past the 77-kilometre-to-go post and suddenly it didn't seem that near: that was still 10 per cent, still the distance from Valcarlos, where I'd started, to Windmill Hill, where I'd almost finished.

I lunched late, watching Shinto graze and doze and then roll with bareback, lascivious abandon in the sunny grass: my Braymate of the Month. Yes, I had kissed him now, and inveigled a probing digit deep into those ears, and begun to savour the almost sensual suedeness of that soft area around his nostrils. It seemed so wrong, and yet it felt so right.

'Does he like that?' called out one of the fun-run Brits when she'd seen me dreamily tracing a knuckle through Shinto's erogenous head zones.

'Dunno,' I drawled back, thickly, 'but I do.'

When I saw them all later outside a bar their greetings seemed oddly muted.

If last week had been Wales with lizards and yesterday England with hard cows, then today, into the pines and with bald-topped moorland hillocks backed by mist-wreathed peaks, was Scotland with cabbage trees. That's right: along with a corn crib, a small allotment of spindle-trunked, 10-foot *berza* was a Galician farmyard staple. The prized foliage is harvested for the much vaunted regional broth I had sampled in Barbadelo, and which I can commend as a heady tribute to the culinary possibilities presented by hot water and leaves.

Simon had tentatively arranged to meet me at Palas de Rei, but as I sidestepped the rat-playground wheelie bins that announced the town's imminence there'd been no call and his phone wasn't ringing. It was a stubbornly dreary town, cleaved in two by the N547, a road whose auspicious terminus screamed momentously from every signpost. The grubby hotels fostered an air of downbeat transience, and the church was pebble-dashed. If there was no sign, even the most archaeologically tenuous, of the King's Palace that gave the town its name, then I was accustomed to that. So it had been with the phantom three castles of Triacastela, and the many unhospitalled Hospitals I'd passed through.

A couple of staircase-circumnavigating detours led to an encounter with Evelyn and Petronella, turned away at the seam-bursting *refugio* and now in search of alternative accommodation. 'Could you save a twin room for me and my brother?' I asked as they prepared to walk off. Then I looked round and he was sauntering up the alley towards us.

Group hug-ins had become second nature for most at this stage of the pilgrim game, though for an Englishman they were at best fourth. Extricating Simon from an entwinement of hot female arms I introduced him first to Shinto, and then, after a brotherly parade about the more obscure backways of Palas de Rei, to the art of lashing a donkey to an old bulldozer in a small area of urban undergrowth. 'Is that a bowline knot?' Simon asked, nobly excising the words 'supposed to be' as I bent the last snake double and forced him gut first down the well.

Simon is a bit taller than me, and as is often the way with big brothers, a bit older. You won't be familiar with an early seventies ad campaign for Ideal evaporated milk, and if I am it's because of a chord deeply struck by its concise analysis of the fraternal dynamic. 'My Ideal day is a day by the river, both of us fishing, big brother and me. He shows me how, and I catch the big one . . .' I can't remember the last line, but at the end they both go home to enjoy some apposite comestible reward, perhaps condensed flan scooped snarlingly from a rusty bucket with clawed hands.

As boys we never actually went fishing, but there were plastic Spitfires to be camouflaged, and seaside dams to be constructed, and improvised explosive devices to be detonated. Simon showed me how; yet, however frailly metaphorical, I never caught the big one, unless it was a chest infection or a telling-off. So here we were, three decades on, both of us pilgrims, big brother and me. This time, I figured, I'd at last be able to show him how, but passing that tangle of rope meekly into his hands it was clear that if the tables had turned, then they'd turned full circle.

Our wasteland was handily overlooked by the rooms Evelyn

and Petronella had located, above a bar and with here-be-pilgrims clothes-pegged washing lines strung beneath each window. We swished and bundled saddlebags up the stairs and into our tiny, spartan room: nothing electrical beyond a bare bulb, and furniture fashioned from varnished pallets. 'Is it always like this?' asked Simon, gingerly propping his enormous rucksack against a wall of uncertain geometry. 'This? This is great,' I called out, flumping down on my institutional bedstead with a smile, a rusted twang and the English-language copy of *El Pais* Simon had been given on the plane – the first newspaper I'd been able to make proper sense of for more than forty days. If he appeared slightly taken aback then at my delight in such modest facilities, you should have seen his face when I filled the bath with Fairy Liquid and soiled clothes before jumping in.

With crude oil still coating much of the Galician seabed a year after the *Prestige* tragedy, I'd been told not to expect oral contact with the region's most noted marine delicacy. But I'd seen a *pulperia* during my trans-Palas wanderings, and when Donald popped his head into our bar and said it was active, we necked our chilled ales and went straight down there. *Pulpo* is octopus, and you don't leave Galicia without trying it.

'It's like pregnancy, this,' said Donald as our jolly, hair-tossing waitress found a place between the many jugs of rosé for a wooden plate piled with pepperoni-sized discs of chilli-slathered sea-flesh. One of Donald's daughters was imminently expecting, and when he wasn't phoning home for an update he was constructing complex analogies. 'You know, at this stage of the walk you just want it to be over with.'

Indeed so, I thought, laboriously masticating a mouthful of Creole washers, but how awful to fuck up at this stage, like the woman I'd seen wincing hopelessly along backwards to try and spare her tendons, like one of the gay singing Italians who we saw being hobbled by his boyfriend towards a bus-stop the next morning, like the sixty-nine-year-old whose 1993 memorial, dolefully incorporating a bronzed cast of his walking boots, stands by the 26-kilometre marker. Or in fact like the thousands of medieval pilgrims pushing up the alfalfa in crypts and church-yards right up to Santiago, some even within sight of its cathedral. Every time the cartilage in my right knee gave me some gyp, which it had done to embarrassingly vocal effect in many a crowded nocturnal dormitory, or I felt a twinge in an ankle, or Shinto stumbled over a rock, I'd think, No, please, not now. Just as I thought seven hours later, in fact, when our recovery from the brandy club's initiation of its newest member was rudely foreshortened by a town-quaking asinine cacophony.

Shinto maintained his alarm in snooze mode, six brays every fifteen minutes. More emphatic, these: in place of the little-donk-lost bleats of yore here was a bugled, galvanising call-to-legs. At 7.00 we succumbed, and leaving Evelyn and Petronella to a more benign convalescence hit the funereal streets of Palas de Rei. For us a bakery breakfast of pizza – not sure how that happened – a bowl of chaff by a lamp-post for Shints, and off under a low and heavy sky.

The meteorology wasn't representative and nor were our surroundings. Just as I settled into a drawling, cocksure commentary on corn cribs and cabbage trees, we found our-selves deep in a Vick-scented grove of flagpole-trunked eucalyp-tuses. And as the digits clicked down on the marker posts, so the increasingly well-developed pilgrim infrastructure began to suggest an almost processed experience that seemed a debas-ing affront to those weeks of lonely, biblical toil. Every time the camino crossed a road, it did so between red-triangle warning signs alerting drivers to the presence of blob-headed gourd-toters. There were taxi phone numbers daubed on walls to tempt any hellbound idlers; we passed a *refugio* and noted condoms festooned horridly in the adjacent undergrowth. 'It hasn't always been like this,' I insisted stoutly as we clopped over a Roman bridge towards the pilgrim crowd gathered round a humble church. Inside a priest was signing photographs of himself.

Most pilgrims were overnighting in Melide, and because we

weren't it quietened down after lunch. Indeed, the weirdly eucalyptine forests notwithstanding, it was very much business as usual. A mouthy little donk in a neglected paddock spotted Shinto and charged over to bray and bellow and hoof his fence in frustration; Shinto skulked away, then shat himself foully round the corner. In a shaded dell we came up to a wooden bridge, and watching my dear, daft donkey settle into that familiar melancholy stupor before it I felt an odd surge of pride. 'Aren't we even going to try to . . .' mumbled Simon, and leading Shinto gently about I smiled in happy resignation.

The detour meant, as ever, the road, and that at least meant a turn of speed. For an hour we mixed it with the truckers and sales reps; then one of those pilgrim-crossing signs appeared out of the clearing murk and eight legs padded back on to the dust. Simon's brought up the rear: it was good to have someone to share the droving with, and it had long been apparent that Shinto prospered in a triangular relationship.

The night before I had delivered a keynote tutorial on donkey propulsion, heckled throughout by table mates who had witnessed nothing but farce and mutiny. 'Eeeeeuuuwwww!' we'd all ended up grunting at each other, like constipated weightlifters: I've rarely known a bill to arrive so promptly. And yet when Simon first essayed this discredited ululation under camino conditions, ostensibly in jest, something in his tone and meter imbued it with such gruff potency that Shinto leapt into a luggage-bouncing, click-devouring trotlet. What did he and Hanno have that I so patently didn't? Imposing physical stature and a generally more resolute bearing were answers I'd rather not have found myself contemplating, preferable as they were to the prognosis suggested a few months later when medical analysis discovered an accumulation of environmental oestrogen in my body.

Thus it was that with the sun finally bullying its way through the cloud, we marched up, down and through a fitful parade of fly-blown hamlets before descending the breakneck valley into Ribadiso with almost triumphant panache. The medieval pilgrims had nicknamed this site Puente Paradiso, and it wasn't hard to understand why both they and my friend Nicky had found the *refugio* here so delightful: a comely scattering of rustic structures, now sturdily restored, set in sheep-nibbled lawns that sloped down to a chuckling stream. The French *hospitalero* was almost overwhelmed by Shinto's presence, patting and petting and posing with an effusiveness that had the happy benefit of distraction – Simon was now travelling under a *credencial* I'd picked up for a laugh in Sahagún, and which identified the bearer as a nine-year-old donkey.

We made the *hospitalero* happy, but he sadly wasn't able to reciprocate. It was the busiest night of the year to date, apparently, and having installed Shinto in a field across the way we swiftly accepted that with every bunk taken it was going to be the flagstoned refectory floor for us. And yet I watched Simon unpack and unwind with an air of fond nostalgia, recalling my own debut travails on the nursery slopes of Mount Pilgrim: the speculative prodding of nascent blisters, that first harrowing encounter with the oppressive nudity of bulbous strangers, the gradual discovery that happiness was a prize simply won out here on the Way of St James – a hot shower, a green field, and a monstrous vat of wine. And, that night at Bar Mañuel back up the hill, a sassily bucolic waitress, a real innkeeper's daughter, who kept the vat brimming and called us both Chico.

Flanned and brandied we decamped to the outside tables, largely replete with weary young Spaniards watching the dying sun cast an Antipodean burnish across the euc-topped ridge ahead. Out came all my maps and books, and for once I surveyed them not with awe at what lay ahead but at what lay behind. Every four days or so I'd crossed a fold in my Michelin map of northern Spain, and now we were on the last, the one with the sea at the end, the one that told us we'd entered the camino's seventh and final province: A Coruña, La Coruña, depending on who you were trying to offend. For so long appended on road signs by the kind of comically hypothetical distance seen after Sydney or Osaka on a novelty tourist finger-post, Santiago was now a local destination on local roads, the town where that waitress probably went to get a haircut or a CD.

'He's saying goodnight,' said Simon as a stentorian blare rose up out of the day's fading crimson conclusion, permitting himself a paternal smile. Though actually he was saying, as the unusually muffled denouement should have suggested, 'I've improbably found my way out of the field and on to the bridge, and now find myself lodged neck-first in a noose of my own making.' When we went back down an elderly Scottish couple were effecting his complex release. 'It's the second time he's done it in an hour,' said the wife, that smile wavering as our effusive thanks clouded her in vaporised intoxicants.

As relief stoked a sense of melodramatic fuddlement, the dining hall seemed rather a grand dormitory, with its high-beamed, rough-hewn, open-fired Tolkienesquery. I can say that a little of this mead-bearded mystique was eroded when the rude reveille I'd warned Simon was inevitable announced itself in a ringing, rustling lights-on stomp at – squint, groan, xeno-phobically blaspheme – 4.30 a.m.

What breakfasteering agents of Satan were these who clanged cup to oak and spoon to bowl with such clumsy relish at such a monstrous hour? Four sodding thirty – and here we were, less than 2 score clicks from the end. One of them began to hum, and when some of his many table mates put that hum to words, I found myself pondering just how tragic it would be if, so close to their goal, even one of these people – heaven forbid every last man jack of them – should find their love parts nail-gunned to the fireplace. A heavy boot compressed my sleeping-bagged ankle, and suddenly these ponderings were given pungent vocal life. 'You swear and he doesn't,' had been Petronella's preliminary verdict after the Moore Bros Spanish première. Glancing over to see Simon sigh benignly at the dark and distant rafters, the mild offence with which I'd greeted this assessment had never seemed more starkly misplaced.

'*Wankers*,' I spat, not for the first time, as the last of them coughed and banged out the door. I creaked myself aloft and scanned the table. 'And look how they've left the place!'

Oranges, bread, yogurt, cheese . . . I saw waste and chaos, but then I saw lunch. 'Right.'

I'd filled half a plastic bag with rolls when the door opened again and there stood the last man out, returning with a large plastic box in his arms. This he placed on the table, and eyeing me levelly began to fill with what lay upon it. If I'd been wearing more than pants he might have said something. And if there hadn't been an orange wedged in my gob I might have said something back.

It was an almost Himalayan morning, all spindly trees on misted ridges, and we were out in it before the sun was born. Another scabby, vacant town, another inadequate bar breakfast, and thence off into the corn cribs and dung, the curled cinnamon strips of eucalyptus leaves and bark still jarringly weird under our feet. (We'd read the night before that the fast-growing and ruthlessly invasive trees had been brought in from Australia in the 1860s for construction purposes, and having proved utterly useless for these were now fitfully culled for garden furniture. I expect the whole thing was an Antipodean plot to pay Europe back for the rabbits. If not for the donkeys – introduced in the nineteenth century, the common ass found outback conditions so much to his liking that the Western Australian authorities felt obliged to shoot 1,000,000 wild donkeys in the 1980s alone. 'Hee-haw, hee-haw BANG!' laughed a spokesman I just made up.)

With Simon at the rear we were really laying down some fat camino: everyone we knew had stayed in Melide and they hadn't passed us yet. We were overtaking as often as overtaken, and a man of apparent youth and vigour was visibly extended during a drawn-out pursuit from the rear. '*Vive Quebec!*' he panted over his shoulder when at breathless length he breasted past me. At the top of the next hill something seemed to occur to him, and after a pause he turned about with his arms spread wide and an exultant bellow already half out of his throat: 'The queen is a beeetch!'

But I did find a familiar face soon after, and it was looking out of the window of a Bedford camper parked up in the shade. John, St John, in his St John's Ambulance. Astonished handshakes, a résumé of the 620 kilometres that had elapsed since our previous encounter, coffee for the brothers and a biscuit for their donk. It struck me that here was a true keeper of the Santiagan flame, a spiritual descendant of those bridge builders and leper lovers who had made the medieval pilgrimage what it was. Men have been canonised for less. If it was down to me John would be a saint by now, but then again so would Eddy Merckx and the bloke who invented crisps.

So how much sadder it was to discover that we now lived in an age when even a pilgrim cannot quite summon unquestioning trust in his fellow man. As I kept John up to speed with Shinto's faltering progress, every other passing walker spurned his charitable entreaties with a nervously polite shimmy of the hand.

My new esteem for camper-van owner-drivers received a further boost a couple of villages down, when we found ourselves invited to dine in the mobile headquarters of a Swiss–Australian family. She walked, he drove and they met up via walkie-talkie every four hours to enable her to breastfeed the younger of their two young sons: a logistical undertaking far more imaginatively ludicrous than anything experienced in the multi-vehicular donk-o-kids phase of my pilgrimage. While their three-year-old rode Shinto round a solar-seared car park we filthied the van's climate-controlled interior with our dusted buttocks, feasting on chilled dairy products and tales of their pioneering determination. Nine months they'd been on the road; the baby's first words had been in Spanish. 'But I mean, you've had it *really* tough,' said the bearded father, tilting his head in the vicinity of my unseen donkey.

Had I? The clicks were falling away with such bewildering haste – 28 to go, then 24.5, then 19 – that my camino now seemed to be coasting towards the line rather than grinding to an exhausted conclusion. An hour before we'd even managed to get Shinto through a ford with only a little light brutality.

When I contemplated the friction scars on my palms these days, it was with something approaching scepticism.

Heat was the only enemy, and it stealthily engaged us as we pressed on through the airless balsam of the eucalyptus groves. When he wasn't plunging it under fountains, Simon was swaddling his head in a turban of damp fabric. After eschewing a *refugio* blighted by its proximity to the uncomfortably popular N547, we dragged our gluey limbs back into the woods, then back out, and presently found ourselves gawping soporifically over a fence at the first water-filled swimming pool I had so far encountered. Two fat men were lazily disturbing its shallow end, and I was about to mumble some envious incivility when Simon said, 'I saw them pass us earlier. They're pilgrims.' And with that in mind we appraised the chalets bordering the pool, and having noted their appropriately commercial aspect shortly found ourselves at the reception desk, saddlebags round feet, donkey in car park, twitching in anticipation of the delicious baptism that awaited.

Our welcome was disappointingly equivocal. The receptionist's bright countenance clouded as she plucked the last key from the rack, before beckoning us unenthusiastically across the rearward lawns to the door it opened. A handsomely appointed living area appeared, low-slung furniture arranged artfully on the cool terracotta tiles, but before we could even think about soiling it all she was coughing us apologetically towards the room's dim fundament. Another door; a double bed. I looked at Simon and we exchanged shrugs: a bit of inadvertent nocturnal footsie was a small price to pay for the aquatic facilities on offer.

'*Hermanos?*' she enquired, expectantly.

I looked at him again. Did that mean what I think it meant? Simon's mild alarm told me it did. 'No!' I protested stoutly. 'No, just, you know . . .' And all I could think to do was place a fraternal arm around Simon's shoulder and pull him heartily towards me.

Well, that was silly. After she'd left us the key with a look of perfect blankness, I got the dictionary out: *Hermano, a*

309

[er'mano, a] nm/f brother/sister. He'd show me how, and I'd catch the big one.

Two beers and an immersion later we didn't care. Our medieval forebears prepared for arrival in Santiago with a ritual cleansing at the springs of Lavacolla, 8 clicks up the road, and we were just a little early. And a little more chaste, despite what they might be muttering about us in the bar: Lavacolla meant 'wash bollocks' in the Romance argot of the day. Christians routinely ridiculed Muslims and Jews for their hygienic fastidiousness, and this rare act of personal propriety was only warranted to sluice away the ripe and heady love-smells still clinging from those encounters in the woods after Portomarín.

Replete with a shared bottle of red and a great bucket of stew, I felt as good as I had for some time. Shinto was happily installed in a dark corner of the garden, the last flakings of chaff at his feet, and through the trees above him, veined by branches, a heavy full moon, the moon I had seen wax and wane and wax again in that big Spanish sky. 'This is just too, too perfect,' sighed Simon, placing his hand on mine for the benefit of the waitress arriving with our brandies.

Every one of our fellow guests had been a Spanish pilgrim, but the happy glow of confraternity we felt seeing their rucksacks lined up by our breakfast table was upgraded to fierce, rod-backed righteousness when Simon noted (a) that their owners had all already left, and (b) that each rucksack bore an adhesive label specifying a hotel address in Santiago. A pair of taxis arrived to collect the luggage as we walked out to meet Shinto. If you were being charitable you could have claimed that this was no different from the nobles who paid an underling to walk to Santiago and received their indulgence by proxy. If you weren't you could have switched all the labels round. But I didn't do that, because as Simon so rightly pointed out with a significant glance at Shinto, at least they had carried some of their own stuff some of the way.

Not for the first time, my donkey had wound the night rope

round and round a tree, thereby reeling in his nocturnal grazing diameter from amphitheatre to paddling pool. Immobility had also obliged Shinto to cast a fearful symmetry over his camino by despoiling the children's play area, and we were dispersing the grim evidence from the sandpit with boot and stick when an aged woman squeaked up pushing a wheelbarrow piled high with freshly cut grass. '*Por burro,*' she croaked jovially, upending it effortlessly before his eagerly probing snout. Another act of kindness to reward with garbled Spanglish and gestures of gratitude, rendered more inadequate even than usual when we saw her stoop into a barn over the road: these weren't just lawn clippings, but half a winter week for some poor cow.

With Shinto the fat filling in a Moore sandwich we were soon back in the VapoRub forests, wondering at the origins of a slightly cloying overtone to the usual smell and finding out when Simon read from the guidebook. No matter how accustomed I might be by now to my surroundings, you couldn't say I ever felt completely at home: 'an unfortunate local custom' where I come from usually means solvent abuse or Morris dancing, but the reference here was to animal carcasses hurled into the woods.

The trees let us out, and there – *sweet Jim almighty* – there was a DHL cargo jet, ripping upwards into the blue heavens right before us. 'Santiago airport,' announced Simon automatically when the world came back into focus. It happened again as we walked under the red-and-white landing-light gantry by the end of the perimeter fence, and even as that great, kerosene-streaked belly blotted out the sun above us like the opening credits of a sixties thriller, Shinto barely checked his languid stride.

He was a donk of the world now, I thought with pride, a member of that long-eared elite who knew what went down not just on the other side of the fence, but on the other side of the border and a hundred leagues beyond. This plucky steed had experienced more in six weeks than had his forebears in six generations.

Simon needed to confirm his return flight, and eschewing

a wait back at the perimeter fence, I plumped for the more entertaining option of accompanying him up to the terminal building. Walking to an airport, as I've discovered whilst mixing it with taxi and minibus in many an underpass, is rarely a straightforward procedure; throw in the donk factor and you've got yourself a tragicomic 'And finally . . .' news story waiting to happen. Such at least was the theory, but aside from a little excitement at the barrier to the short-term car park and a couple of giggling stewardesses we made it without confronting mishap or bewildered outrage. The city was still 12 clicks off and out of sight, but we were clearly now within the civic radius of seen-it-all pilgrim fatigue. Still, it floated my boat (all aboard the *HMS Duncechortle*): the *burro*-to-go snap Simon took of Shints tied up between Fiestas in the Hertz lot remains a cherished favourite.

Back across the dual carriageway we rejoined the parched camino, a meandering conveyor belt through the final examples of what had seemed an endless production line: the last hot and shuttered hamlet, the last chain-straining barker cowed to silence, the last sundried scattering of nasally seductive horse crap. We weren't sure where Lavacolla was, but Simon found a likely spring and filled our hot hats in it; Shinto sucked up a bowl and a half and I sluiced the remainder over his neck. As we were being watched by an elderly local this wasn't the moment for a bollock-wash, but I had at least found time to hose down my ass.

Past two TV stations and a big campsite, the odd house with Gaelic fifes and drums filtering out from behind windows curtained with banners decrying the *Prestige* oil disaster: '*Nunca Mais*' – Never Again. A large German saloon cruised past, and the ageing hoodlum at the wheel buzzed down his window, showing a hand with rings under every knuckle and emitting a rasp that I could only hope was one of gruff congratulation. Then up a broiled eminence so considerable that I was left without the wherewithal to take in the significance of the single digit on the marker post at its brow.

The road flattened, then gently rose again. We could be in

Santiago in three hours, be there tonight. But that wouldn't happen. That would be like opening my presents on Christmas Eve. A titanic 3,000-bed hillside *refugio* lay just outside the city limits, and to observe the proper rituals you stayed there, gathered your wits, and set off in the morning unsullied by heat and fatigue, in an attitude of appropriate reflection. Pursued by TV crews, Shirley MacLaine ran the last 15 clicks in darkness, an unhappy, unseemly conclusion that no pilgrim deserved.

There's one just outside Jerusalem, and seven girdling Rome. Every pilgrimage has its nearly-there-now Mount of Joy, the hill from whose summit the final destination is at last revealed, and Santiago's is Monte de Gozo. By tradition, pilgrims race each other to the top, with the first to lay eyes on the twin Compostela towers granted the honorary title of king. '*Le roi*' to the French pilgrim majority, the origin of the name Leroy. If you were on horseback you walked from Monte de Gozo; if you weren't you took off your ravaged shoes and did the last stretch barefoot, bellowing hymns as the cathedral fuzzed out of focus through a veil of overwhelmed tears. Pilgrims fell to their knees on the hilltop; an eighteenth-century Italian reported those around him kissing the earth a thousand times.

Today Santiago is a city of 95,000, and the literature warned that urban sprawl and an ill-sited copse had combined to obscure the bell towers and so denude Monte de Gozo of its visually dramatic symbolism. By now a link in a strung-out chain of toiling walkers, we topped the hill and found ourselves on the lip of a huge and hazy hollow, filled with rush-hour traffic and vertically conspicuous commercial structures. 'Well, there it is,' said Simon, and I sucked in a long, steadying draught of hot air. Then a taxi rounded us with a derisive toot, lurched to a halt by a gate down the road and deposited a fat hot man and his rucksack.

The last time I'd seen those buttocks, they'd sat untrousered upon a tissue-less latrine, and if this had the effect of portent-management, then so did the complex that opened up beyond that gate. Bungalow bunkers as long as streets, dozens and dozens striped up a hefty swathe of hillside, the empty concrete boulevards between them pierced by the vegetation of neglect. At the conclusion of every forlorn vista, lichen-streaked statuary corroded into the undergrowth.

We clopped between two of these pilgrim prison blocks, both clearly empty, and presently found ourselves in a desolate plaza bordered by facing parades of self-service canteens and largely moribund retail units. Unsychronised wisps of Celtic pipery echoed from Tannoy stalks. Here was the dominant legacy of Galicia's efforts to commemorate and facilitate the 1993 Holy Year, when the Pope visited Santiago, yet it had all the soulful ambience of a holiday camp for low-ranking party officials in the Chernobyl exclusion zone. 'This is *awful*,' I said, hands on hips in front of a whitewash-windowed ex-launderette.

My two companions were wanly scanning the urban horizon in underwhelmed concurrence when the biped froze. 'There,' said Simon, simply, quietly, half-raising a finger to a gap in the trees atop a block-studded middle-distance hillock. I narrowed my eyes, scanned the relevant area of smogged horizon, and saw it. Them. Rising gingerly through the sunlit urban fuzz, the tapering baroque rockets of the cathedral of Santiago de Compostela.

Well, I can't tell you how that helped. One of the few active enterprises around us was a souvenir shop, and suddenly its glib offerings seemed not an insult to our achievement but a celebration. For days now the images of Santiago Peregrino, St James as a pilgrim to his own tomb, had been gathering in profusion: a statue in a church, a sticker on a bumper, and now in this window a keyring, a corkscrew, an ashtray. Scrutinising them I felt a pulse of fraternal affection for this mild apostle of gourd and staff, a perfect study in mournful, pious sincerity: 'It's just so tragic,' he always seemed to sigh. 'If only I could even begin to find the words to explain what a great, great guy I am.'

And those blue tiles glazed with yellow arrows or stylised scallop shells: we'd been following those for forty days, and I wanted people to know that we had. I'd have one each of those for my garden wall, though not yet. Not just yet. The converging lines on the scallop shell were said to represent the converging pilgrim routes to Santiago, and we weren't quite at that auspicious confluence. I didn't get one for the same reason that I hadn't yet worn my scallop shell, the one Nicky had given me before I'd left. You acquired your shell in Santiago as an indication to medieval contemporaries that you'd been and gone and done it, a medal of achievement, not intent.

Reanimated we went down to check in at hut twenty-one, my fêted jackass entered beneath us in the register by a happy young *hospitalero* as Shinto Moore, travelling on foot, aged eleven ('Is *minimo* here for *peregrino* ten years old,' he explained with a tickled wink.) Shinto was led as instructed into an adjacent strip of meadow by the laundry lines, and watching him settle down to his Last Supper we went off for ours. There was only the one option, and this involved celebrating the imminent remission of my sins by pushing a tray along a stainless-steel counter, watching as a succession of blank-faced women filled it with small plates of shrink-wrapped food. It was abysmal, so abysmal as to be excellent. Sucking on Capri-Suns we scanned this strip-lit environment and its scattering of smartly cardiganed Spanish *peregrinos*, the handbag-carrying hundred-clickers sharing our hallowed penultimate ponderings. And we laughed, and were still laughing when we slid our trays into the rack of empties and retired to our room.

This was an airless, fetid eight-bunker, one of fifteen such in each barrack block, and our six fellow last-nighters were already locked into the gentle, automatic snoring of the hot and weary. Simon tutted quietly, but I felt oddly comforted, almost nostalgic: it had been four days since last I'd shared my sleep with pilgrims. And, I thought, as the mattress planks took my weight with a splintered sigh, at least an earthly lifetime before I ever would again.

Fifteen

MONTE DE GOZO

SANTIAGO DE COMPOSTELA

W aking in a cell crowded with grubby, mumbling strangers, pulling on underwear foot-laundered in last night's shower and still perhaps four hours from comfortable dryness, shampooing with household detergent: it seemed that almost everything I was doing I'd never do again, unless I took my trousers down at a North Korean border post.

Or unless this whole business had indeed left me strangely changed beyond repair. Maybe I'd return and decree bedlinen a satanic extravagance. And hot water. Certainly there was a worrying moment when Simon dropped his old socks and pants in the bin – his wife Catherine had dispatched him with a disposable wardrobe – and I restrained only with difficulty an urge to retrieve them.

Bright eyed and, yes, bushy tailed, there was the large grey animal who had earlier conducted another of these last rites, for the final time drawing his master from unconsciousness with that klaxon reveille.

Shinto fixed me with a look hungry for adventure, eager, almost intelligent. Bareback in the hock-high meadow grass, he called to mind a gold-rimmed, hand-retouched collector's plate in a colour-supplement advert: 'Alert to the Call: a fresh spring morn, and this lively little Pyrenean jack has been exploring. (Penis not to scale.)' Scrutinising him with a sense of potent déjà vu I suddenly recalled the dream his braying had cut short: Shinto had been awarded a prize for special achievement at some sort of pet pageant, but as I led him through the crowd with applause in my ears and a Tobleroned lump of pride in my throat, there between us and the podium stood a taunting trio of stairs . . .

For the last time I squatted down by his side, upturned hoof in lap and scraper in hand, the submerged percolations of that huge, warm stomach bubbling in through my ear. I might not quite have fulfilled Hanno's prediction by eating from the same bowl as my donkey, but for a week now his chaff and my crusts had shared the same sack. Sighing and puffing I packed and repacked the bags, and brushed and rebrushed Shinto, trying not to think that this was The End, the final instalment of a forty-one-day life within my life, but at the same time unavoidably aware that it was and willing myself into a suitable climactic frame of mind.

At the mouth of every hut behind us were groups of pilgrims facing the same inner turmoil, grooming themselves for an appointment with eternity like corpses in a coffin. An ironed shirt kept flat-packed at a rucksack's fundament now retrieved for the benefit of St Jim, a comb pulled through sun-mangled hair. Simon nudged me and inclined his head, and through a bathroom window I saw two faces pressed close to a mirror: an elderly man shaving his middle-aged Down's Syndrome son.

It wasn't until 9.00 that we left, exchanging knowing, bracing nods and half-smiles with those around us, like students massing outside the hall of their final examination. It was a steep descent round the perimeter of the Monte de Gozo complex, and as our strides lengthened with the gradient so the skies above suddenly darkened. No sooner had we broached the outskirts of Santiago proper than those guiding towers were smeared out by a flash downpour, one so violent that by the time I'd extracted and unfurled my poncho Shinto had slammed in the anchors. 'Um,' I said, through a curtain of hood drips; then there was a creak and a crank and a big up-and-over garage door beside us pivoted aloft.

Inside the dim void thus revealed stood a blasé, full-faced

mechanic, who thumbed us in whilst critically assessing the tiny cigarette stub pinched between his thumb and forefinger. In a minute there were half a dozen of us in there, and in another the one with four legs had somehow sniffed out a sack of grain. Still addressing himself to his dwindling fag end the mechanic palmed out a scoop and let Shinto snuffle it up from his hand. Then a young chap in a red cagoule held a tentative hand out into the open, morphed it into a thumbs-up and in a moment we were all waving our gruff protector farewell.

The pocket storm was merely the first of a sequence that in three swift stages formed a perfect microcosm of every alarum of the previous six weeks, every phobia nurtured by Shinto in those 770 clicks gone slowly by. We'd been on the wet pavement less than a minute when it fell away down a hefty flight of stairs. The backtracking detour was moderate by the standards of many endured, but at its conclusion lay a busy, narrow road bridge whose bolt-on pedestrian portion was assembled from wooden planks. For the last time I saw Shinto assess the middle distance with that look of mildly perplexed helplessness, as if a direct causal link existed between this obstacle and the sudden inactivity of his limbs, as if it wasn't a bridge but a force field. Look, said his eyes, I can assure you that this is just as frustrating for me as it is for you.

These days I almost agreed. As our marriage had matured so those stand-up rows had mellowed into gentle bickering, and I squeezed the three of us on to the tarmac, between guard rail and elbow-flicking wing mirrors, with an air of fond indulgence. My affection for Shinto had now reached a level where it seemed a poignant tragedy that those splendid genes lay nowhere but his own ageing body (though given a good innings, that body had every chance of outlasting mine). He was Shinto the First, and Shinto the Last. My passage through the pilgrimage literature had been regularly enlivened by the descriptive appellations of medieval monarchs: Sancho the Fat, 'the hunchbacked Orduno IV the Evil'. It was all a question of spin: with bad PR you were Henry the Impotent, with good PR Alfonso the Chaste. So here, before me, was King Shinto the . . . Beige.

The bridge proved the last of the morning's To-be-a-Pilgrim trinity of trials, and our approach thereafter was not one designed to nurture tearful portent. A construction site half-staffed with idle donk-baiters, receding batteries of slightly scabby housing estates, waiting for the little green man with my little grey donkey: had it not been for the tiny and diminishing digits on those camino marker posts and an unusually jaded citizenry, this could just have been another of those surreal and stressful trans-metropolitan experiences.

We drew breath for the final assault with just one more of those inadequate bar breakfasts of cake and *café con leche*, then headed across our last dual carriageway and into the cloistered alleys of the old town. Walls narrowed and houses rose, shielding the cathedral towers from view and making every rounded corner a mouth-drying, spine-fizzing anticlimax: this was surely it, and if not then this, and if not then this. The last yellow arrow led us down a flagstoned hill, and sensing that this really was it Simon respectfully melted forward into the morning shoppers. I contemplated the rope in my calloused hands and what it led to, and in doing so felt pride abruptly tempered by a gauche self-consciousness, like a boy wearing school uniform for the first time, a reprise of the sensation that had for so long dominated my every moment at Shinto's side.

Tightening my grip on the rope and breathing hard I felt rather than saw a moss-stoned ecclesiastical structure looming up to our left; but as the street ahead passed down towards it and beneath a grand archway so it devolved into a stairway. A final, numb-limbed diversion round a circling, anti-clockwise road to the right, a road which a minute later ejected me into the bottom right-hand corner of a belittling cobbled sea, a great, broad square sparsely populated by tiny mortals and imperiously dominated by the lichened, mildewed, florid might of my destination.

With my overborne faculties condensed into a reedy, whistling tinnitus and the sensation of wet heat on my cheeks I apparently continued walking, distantly aware of the swelling crowd

I was dragging across the grey stones. At any rate there I soon found myself, in the shadow of that swoon-inducing façade, at the foot of the weighty double staircase that accessed its lofty entrance. 'Photo, photo!' piped a shrill voice in my ear, not caring that the head to which it belonged now lay buried in a warm, soft neck, not knowing that through that head spooled a messily spliced loop tape of mud and sun and barley, of treble bunks and double brandies, of flan and friend and midnight bray, of trial and tribulation. 'Photo, photo, photo!'

My brother was watching from the Plaza del Obradoiro's distant opposite bank, and later reported that my tourist entourage had all exchanged shrugs – and, in one case, swivelled-fingers-in-temples – before clicking away regardless. When I raised my head and blinked out the last tear one snapper came up and pressed a euro in my hand; I contemplated it blankly, too fraught and drained to protest. I'd had this down as a humble alms offering until an unkempt man in a brown felt cape and scallop-brimmed hat shuffled into shot for a piece of the action – his outfit was set off with a staff and gourd in one hand and a cig and a multilingual note in the other: 'Foto with me €2'. Simon had crept up unseen with my camera and captured the scene as my rent-a-pilgrim struck a photogenic pose with his head arched down to Shinto's, and looking at the result now I'm rewarded to note those long ears flattened back in sour hostility.

I walked on before I began to feel like the false medieval-ist, or that caped and gourded dog with the same notice over there, or those Pentax-toters sticking their head through the comedy pilgrim cut-outs over there. Still the crowd surged and eddied around, shouting out all the old questions in French, in English, in Spanish, but always now in retrospect: what did he eat, where did he sleep. I again had the certain feeling that Shinto knew this was an important, defining moment in his life both as ass and pilgrim, and again I was right. The oohs and aahs morphed into ohs and urghs, and sure enough when I looked back he'd laid down a dozen hot markers on those holy cobbles.

Simon jogged up just before a pair of finger-raised police-men, and together we crinklingly dispatched the unwanted souvenirs with plastic-bag mittens. Returned to earth more literally than ever before we stood, sagging crap bags in hands, and embraced carefully. 'I'll stay with him,' said Simon when we'd finished, 'and you go off for your certificate.' The compostela – my Get Out of Hell Free card, and I'd forgotten all about it.

Obtaining this might have held more significance had the process felt a little less like renewing a TV licence during a water shortage. Queuing in the strip-lit Pilgrim Office at the end of a long line of unwashed, unfamiliar arrivals – snorers to a fat-bellied, big-nosed man – I felt a suggestion of the anti-climax that many pilgrims had written about. Half an hour later I was dictating my name to a bored official, who after a little scribbling handed me a small scroll. Topped by a sepia depiction of Santiago Peregrino and fulsomely bordered with scallop shells, in a Latin rubric unchanged from the fourteenth century this detailed the devoted ambulatory achievements of Dnum Timoteum Moore. '*Compostela por mi burro?*' I asked, in an unexpectant tone that perhaps made the ensuing refusal too easy.

Jubilation was what I'd wanted, and happily it had taken hold in the streets by the time I bounded outside. Simon and Shinto were already beleaguered by familiar and now ecstatic faces: English Sara, Jean-Michel, the Scottish couple who had rescued my donkey from suicidal garrotting at Ribadiso. Our hugs were cut short by the dull gonging of huge bells; midday, and the daily Pilgrims' Mass. Leaving Shinto in Simon's care once more, outside a bar with the singing gay Italians, I trotted up the double staircase and into the cathedral's dim but thronged interior, a majestic Romanesque cavern encased beneath that baroque icing.

In that buffeting crush of rucksacks and day-trippers, it was never going to be easy to work myself up to the spiritual orgasm this moment seemed to demand. Too restless and hassled for insight or manifestation; no statues here you could imagine sweating blood. Perhaps the closest I came was while pressing my hand into the column supporting the welcoming image of Santiago, into five finger holes worn deep in the marble by the grateful, weary touch of pilgrim digits over 900 years. Yes, that was a moment.

More of a moment, certainly, than my contact with the brashly gilded representation of St James that loomed up behind the altar. Only after twenty minutes in a significance-sapping queue, jostled throughout by nattering, nonchalant tourists, was I granted my swift embrace, clasping those giant golden shoulders from behind as if trying to blag a saintly piggyback. Two impatient schoolkids nudged me onwards, down through the crypt for a quickstep shuffle past the silver casket, inside it the bones that had brought so many millions all this way.

But then they hadn't really brought me, or in fact more than a handful of us. In the literature, medieval relic worship was consistently paralleled with today's veneration of celebrity memorabilia, and if so then St James wasn't shifting many albums. Shuffling back down the teeming aisle in search of an empty pew I saw occasional religiously overwhelmed pilgrims genuflecting or crossing their chests: they were Jim fans, and in the final analysis, we weren't. All this was certainly spectacular, but wedging myself between two gossiping Hispanics near the back I felt slightly removed, as if watching a grand sporting finale in whose outcome I had no particular interest.

A squad of sombrely resplendent clerics took their positions in front of the apostle, and when the first took his place at the mike and spoke it all got better immediately. In a Eurovision-judge drone he began to recite the nationalities and their point of pilgrim departure, and when the words '*Valcarlos, Inglaterra*' echoed out of the Tannoy I felt my features tighten. At length a tiny nun took his place, and when she unexpectedly filled the world with soaring, mellifluous hosannas I couldn't restrain a wet blink. Looking ahead I noted the backs of two familiar heads three rows up: Evelyn and Petronella, the latter once more twitching with fluid-faced emotion, but this time by no means alone.

Incoming tourists squeezed into my pew as the mass trundled on, as we stood, and sat, and kneeled, and stood and sat. The collection plate came round and I clanged down the euro I'd been given in the square outside; a queue began to form for the bread and wine. A sudden exhaustion had pinned me to my seat, and I'm glad it did because as I belatedly sidled towards the exit my attention was drawn to a conspicuous phalanx of robed curates. They staggered to the altar bearing upon their shoulders an arresting burden: an enormous and elaborate silver receptacle, an FA Cup the size of a dustbin. Everyone rushed to the front: this was the *botafumeiro*, Catholicism's largest dispenser of holy incense, only brought out on days of especial religious import.

Its contents ignited, this glinting quarter-tonner was laboriously lashed to a rope and hoisted high into the vaulted darkness; then, yanking the cord like tattooed bosuns, the clergymen began a process originally intended to neutralise the stench of a thousand filthy, footsore walkers. Twenty fat-armed heave-hos had the smoke-belching colossus swinging from one side of the distant, vaulted roof to the other, whooshing between the aisles with dreadful momentum: one degree either side and we'd have had a messy strike of pilgrim ninepins. It later transpired that the bishop had authorised this astounding spectacle at the financial behest of a party of visiting Germans; some were outraged, but I figured that the hard-nosed mercenaries who ran the medieval Church could only have approved.

I emerged overwhelmed and smelling of holy mothballs, exhausted at this unseemly rush of events and experience after all those long weeks of measured toil. It was worse for my poor donkey: back at our table outside the bar I found him enduring the worst excesses of Shintomania, patted and petted by a three-deep throng. Evelyn and Petronella arrived, then Sara, and Barbara and Walther, and Janina and Anna, then Donald, who'd somehow got lost on the run-in and spent half a day circumnavigating the ring road. Simon shooed away the more persistent paparazzi, and as the fearsome clamour subsided we all slumped wordlessly round a big tin table.

Beers arrived and our weathered, rural faces crumpled in silent joy and wet-faced disbelief: we had made it. We had all done what at various times we all thought we never would. In the eyes of pilgrim history, we had lived through what so many did not. Glasses were raised in triumphant toast, but before mine reached my mouth I rushed inside the bar with Shinto's bowl. '*Tengo un burro,*' I rasped emotionally at the barman, wondering if I'd ever hear these words pass my lips again. I realised I would, and quite soon, when the barman pushed the bowl slightly further down his counter and carefully placed a large cigar beside it.

Simon was gathering up his belongings when I at last emerged with Shinto's aquatic reward. I looked at my watch: he had less than an hour to get to the airport.

'A million steps,' he said, shouldering that vast rucksack.

'Sorry?'

'I worked it out last night. That's what you've done. A man's pace is around 75 centimetres, and you've done just over 750 kilometres.' I tried to look intelligent. 'So that's a million.'

'If they told you that at the start,' piped up Donald, already on beer two, 'you'd turn round and go straight home.' I just nodded blankly, then looked down at Shinto, hosing up the last dregs by my feet. A million for me, and double for him. One small step for a man was two for his donkey. In fact more like eight, the way mine had been going.

I found a room for myself, overlooking an alley filled by day with the entreating cries of souvenir hawkers and by night with the unhinged revelry of exam-ending students. With rather more difficulty I found a field for Shinto, up in a covert corner of the Monte de Gozo grounds. Back over that bridge, back round those stairs.

If the sun was up I was generally to be found walking from my place to his, or vice versa, a two-hour round trip I did twice a day. When the moon took its place I met my pilgrim friends and we ate octopus and drank brandy and blurted the odd belated confession: you might as well know now that my wife's left me; I probably never mentioned before that I was a Buddhist; did anyone see me catching that bus from Ponferrada? Then I went back to my bed, kept awake not by phlegm-throated bed noises but book-hurling bacchanalia. And when that finally subsided, by the hollowing contemplation that for the first time since we'd met, I was out of audible reach of even his most desperately plaintive bray.

On the third morning, along with nine fellow compostela-brandishers, I went for my free meal, ushered briskly through the quadrangled magnificence of the Hostal de Los Reyes Católicos and into the staff canteen. Sitting there in a prim whitewashed cell, trays of breakfast leftovers on our knees and a mighty magnum of local red passing from hand to hand, we seemed appropriate keepers of the pilgrim flame. Two hours and nine farewells later, on schedule with the last of many telephonic arrangements, I was hugging a bearded Belgian on a hot hillside.

'Ah, Tim?' began Hanno, extricating himself from my embrace. 'I cannot find him. Shinto.'

A slight hesitancy in his manner echoed the poorly veiled astonishment with which Hanno, three days earlier, had greeted news of my safe arrival. Don't tell me, said those furrows on that great long face, please don't tell me that this Anglo-buffoon is mad as well as silly, that he's mislaid a large animal weeks ago and can't admit it even to himself.

'He's right down in the corner, under those trees,' I said, raising a finger and bullying forth a smile. I could understand his suspicions. Everyone who knew me had predicted this whole thing ending in tears, but certainly not the sort it was about to. 'I thought I should kind of hide him.'

Hanno set off across the heat-hazed meadow with loose-limbed bounds, and I scuttled behind in his wake. In my hand was a plastic bag that had accompanied me throughout, orig-inally containing my blister kit, but home since day three to Shinto's brushes, rock-salt and cock cream. 'Boots' it read; then, only faintly legible now, 'Ideas for Life'.

So, here we were, back where it had all begun. Was my life different now, or did I at least have any new ideas? Well, I had learnt to be more patient and less fastidious, to cope when many of the basic decencies of modern life were absent, to relish them when they weren't. I had made sense of a complex world by appreciating the humble solidarities of the past; learnt the true value of water; acquired a Dark Ages lexicon of livestock feed and disease. I had learnt to accept, even befriend people I'd have previously dismissed with a cheap and ugly laugh: brittle-spirited mystics, policewomen, Austrians.

An Englishman following a Belgian across Spanish fields towards their French donkey, I could hardly avoid contemplating our collective past as Europeans, the past of that multinational medieval parade into Santiago, the past that some of us at least seem to have subsequently forgotten. I was more of a world citizen, and somehow more of a human. Two evenings before Evelyn had recited the dedication to her family, inscribed on page one of her pilgrim journal, and I'd joined my table mates weeping freely into their flans.

Time would be the judge of any lasting legacy, whether I'd be one of those who came home inspired to teach Galician, or play the bagpipes, or who embarked upon any of the slightly off-kilter life redefinitions I'd read about in that Californian anthropologist's book. 'In Santiago I said goodbye to engineering,' I remembered a German telling her. 'In the meantime I volunteer at a windmill.' Perhaps it was because of this sort of business that I'd never been able to take a full and active role in the many earnest group prognostications along these lines. I was just happy, more accurately dumbfounded, to have made it here. 'Santiago is just the beginning of the pilgrimage,' I had been severally informed, and I'd nod importantly, thinking, The fuck it is.

'Eh, Shinto!'

Those exclamation-mark ears sprang to attention above the tall grass, and I half-stifled a dry gulp. Over the last seven weeks the pair of us had evolved into a single, man–donk entity; I had set off, we had arrived. With those ears at my shoulder we had spread a little happiness along the streets of five cities, and, more thinly, across the epic plains and peaks that separated them. If I had a euro for every photograph, and even just a Santiago-backed cent for every smile elicited from brown-eyed, gap-toothed bairn to red-eyed, gold-toothed barfly, the 800 euros I'd paid Hanno would have been recouped long ago. Give me another couple of months with Shinto and I might even have clawed back the additional 1,000 I'd just handed over. They say you can't put a price on happiness, but perhaps I now had.

If I had started off on my pilgrimage sharing many of Shinto's more negative traits, most notably stubbornness and sloth, then now, at its end, I had discovered and become imbued with his redeeming qualities: sociability, hardiness, and a schlong down to my knees. Defying his breed's definitive quality, Shinto had learnt something too: he'd lost that fear of water, or at least puddles, and expanded his epicurean horizons to include clover, plantain and certain varieties of giant dandelion. The animal I had once dismissed as a sub-standard jackass, a donkey reject, now stood proudly atop the burrocracy, the paragon of his breed. Hearing of his achievements, Shinto's fellow jacks would shake their long heads in mute awe; the most radiant jennies of his age would be biting their saggy lips bloody at mere mention of his name. And if to love a donkey was a crime, then yes – I too was guilty. It is? Well, maybe in some countries.

He could see us now, and as we approached the circumference of his night rope Shinto gambolled eagerly forth through the flattened grass. Then, angling his head curiously at a distantly familiar face, then at mine, then back again, he stopped. He made a little dart towards Hanno, checked his stride, then trotted purposefully up to meet me. A journey of perhaps 3 yards, yet I was emotionally unravelled before its end.

I led Shinto back up the hill, Hanno nodding silently at my side, then together, with something approaching grace, we eased him into that old horse trailer. 'There you go, Shints,' I said, or rather tried to. A final farewell, a slammed door, the roar of an ancient engine. My shaggy-donk story had reached its punchline.

I watched the trailer bounce softly away down the hill, those ears swivelling about above its side walls. The brake lights distantly winked, a right-hand indicator flashed; after all those westward weeks, it was back to the east. Then I put one foot in front of the other, and again, and again, still with my hands behind my back, still with my body slightly bent forward, urging on 200 kilos of warm reluctance that was no longer there.

263 MOO

Moore, Tim

Travels with my donkey : one
man and his ass on a